YORK HAND

GENERAL EDITOR:
Professor A.N. Jeffares
(*University of Stirling*)

# A DICTIONARY
# OF BRITISH AND
# IRISH AUTHORS

## Antony Kamm
MA (OXON.)

LONGMAN
YORK PRESS

YORK PRESS
Immeuble Esseily, Place Riad Solh, Beirut.

LONGMAN GROUP UK LIMITED
Longman House,
Burnt Mill,
Harlow,
Essex

First published 1990

ISBN 0-582-03590 2

Typeset by Pastiche, London
Produced by Longman Group (FE) Ltd
Printed in Hong Kong

# Contents

# Preface

THIS IS A biographical dictionary of 246 authors who were born in England, Ireland, Scotland, or Wales, or of British parentage, with the addition of three who became British subjects and one who became an Irish subject. All of them wrote or have written in English or in Scots, and some of them in both. Each one has made a significant contribution to English literature or to that of their country of birth or adoption. The 250 is not a mystical figure: it is the number of entries of a suitable length to do some justice to each author which could be fitted in to the extent specified by the publisher.

An asterisk before a name indicates that there is a separate entry for that person. A definition of the term 'sizar', which recurs throughout the book, is given in the entry for George Farquhar, where it first appears. Further useful information will be found in Martin Gray's *A Dictionary of Literary Terms* (new edn 1989) and *A Chronology of English Literature* (1989), as well as in the books listed at the end of each entry.

I am grateful to the Chairman and editorial staff of Balberry Publishing for the initial research into potential inclusions and for helpful suggestions at manuscript stage. I am especially indebted to two people, without whose efforts this book would not have been begun, let alone finished: Derry Jeffares, for his encouragement, advice, and editorial flair; and Eileen, my wife, for her continuous support and her encyclopaedic memory not only of the contents of each book in the house, but also its whereabouts.

Antony Kamm
Dollar, November 1989

# THE DICTIONARY

**Addison, Joseph** (1672–1719), essayist, critic, poet, dramatist, and statesman, was born in Milston, Wiltshire, son of Rev. Lancelot Addison (Dean of Lichfield 1683–1703), and educated at Charterhouse (where he first met and became a close friend of *Steele) and The Queen's College, Oxford. His precociousness at Latin verse led to his transfer to Magdalen College, where he was a Fellow 1698–1711 — 'Addison's Walk' along the River Cherwell still bears his name. His interest in politics brought him a Treasury grant to travel in Europe for five years and the commission to write a celebratory poem on Marlborough's victory at Blenheim, published to great acclaim in 1704 as *The Campaign*. With a succession of government posts in prospect, he was able to lend Steele money for his theatrical ventures. In 1708 he was elected a Member of Parliament, which he remained for the rest of his life. While Chief Secretary in Ireland, he contributed essays anonymously to Steele's *Tatler*, and when the Whigs fell in 1710, leaving him out of office, he and Steele became founder editors of and chief contributors to the daily periodical the *Spectator*, which like the *Tatler* consisted of a single sheet printed on both sides. In two bursts (March 1711 to December 1712 and June to December 1714) it had great success, and was also published in book form (1712–15). Addison's verse tragedy *Cato* was performed in 1713, its popularity being due partly to its political implications and partly to the fact that it is a good play of its kind. A comedy, *The Drummer*, flopped in 1715, but in that year, with the return of the Whigs after the accession of George I, he was reappointed to the Government and to his former Irish post, and published his own political journal, *Freeholder*, which ran for 55 issues. In 1716 he married the Dowager Countess of Warwick, and in the next year he was appointed one of the two Secretaries of State under the Crown. His health was failing, though, and he retired in 1718, to die of 'asthma and dropsy'. He was just 46.

The periodical essay, which particularly flourished in the eighteenth century, reached its acme as a vehicle of critical, philosophical, and political opinion and of cultured amusement in the hands of Addison and Steele. The aim of the *Spectator*, propounded by Addison in issue 10, was 'to enliven morality with wit, and to temper wit with morality'. The wit was enhanced by the introduction of experiences of members of the fictitious Spectator Club, notably Sir Roger de Coverley. Addison's series of essays on the 'Pleasures of the Imagination' (issues 411–21) and his 18 weekly essays on Milton beginning in issue 267 — also published in book form as *Notes Upon the Twelve Books of Paradise Lost* (1719) — are admirable in the context of the attitudes of the times, and stand among the most elegant examples of early eighteenth-century literary criticism. See *The Spectator*, ed. Donald F. Bond, 5 vols new edn 1987; Peter Smithers, *The Life of Joseph Addison*, 1954.

**Amis, Kingsley** (*b.* 1922), novelist, critic, and poet, was born in London and educated at City of London School and St John's College, Oxford. He was a lecturer in English at University College, Swansea 1949–61, and a Fellow of Peterhouse, Cambridge 1961–3. Two volumes of poetry — see *Collected Poems* (1979) — were followed by his novel *Lucky Jim* (1954), which describes the tribulations of Jim Dixon, lecturer in history at a new university. Though not the first of the wave of novels which gave their authors (and the dramatist *Osborne) the sobriquet 'Angry Young Men', it was the one which did most to suggest the existence of such a movement. Amis's fiction is comic in that, especially in the earlier novels, heroes tend to be accident-prone and set-pieces are farcical, but in the later, more socially-aware novels — notably *The Anti-Death League* (1966), *Ending Up* (1974), *Jake's Thing* (1978), and *The Old Devils* (1986) — comedy gives way to satire of a fiercer kind. He has, however, used a variety of forms to express what he wants to say — *The Green Man* (1969) is a ghost story based on local folklore; *The Riverside Villas Murder* (1973) is in the form of a detective mystery. *What Became of Jane Austen* (1970) contains a revealing and readable selection of personal and critical essays on literary and other topics. Among other anthologies, Amis has compiled *The New Oxford Book of Light Verse* (1979). See John McDermott, *Kingsley Amis: an English Novelist*, 1988.

**Arnold, Matthew** (1822–88), poet, educationist, and critic, was born in Laleham, Middlesex, and educated at Rugby School (where his father Dr Thomas Arnold, the celebrated educational reformer and religious leader, was Headmaster) and Balliol College, Oxford, where he won the Newdigate Prize for poetry with a poem about Cromwell (1843). Otherwise his academic studies took second place to his social life, but a disastrous final result was partly compensated for by an appointment as a Fellow of Oriel College. Here he joined his close friend and literary 'mate' *Clough, in commemoration of whose death he later wrote 'Thyrsis' (1866), one of the best of his shorter poems and a neat blend of the classical and the colloquial. In 1847 he became secretary to Lord Lansdowne, Lord President of the Council, and in 1851, the year of his marriage, he was appointed an inspector of schools. He retired in 1883 on a civil list pension, which gave him time to indulge in lecture tours, including two to America. He was Professor of Poetry at Oxford 1857–67.

Most of his poetry was written in the 1850s. *The Strayed Reveller and Other Poems* (1849) and *Empedocles on Etna and Other Poems* (1852) were both written under the pseudonym 'A'. They were followed in 1853 by *Poems*, including the famous 'The Scholar Gipsy', which reflects his unease with contemporary society, and his narrative poem 'Sohrab and Rustum', whose lush style and a sometimes jerky rhythm are redeemed by splendid touches of detail and an ending whose image of still night and a gently flowing stream recurs often in his verse. *Poems, Second Series* (1855) contained 'Balder Dead', based on Norse mythology. The meditative 'Dover Beach', though it was first published in *New Poems* (1867), was written much earlier, along with other poems expressing despair, and it was the feeling that poetry can only record experiences, not effect reforms, that led him then to concentrate on prose.

Arnold's literary criticism influenced his attitude to the state of society, for which he saw a remedy in culture (including religion), with literature as the key. This and his natural bent towards the classics led him to favour literature which had 'high seriousness', a quality which he found lacking in *Chaucer, but for all that he was a sound, innovative, and eloquent critic. In *Essays in Criticism, First Series* (1865) and *Second Series* (1888) he drew together recently published studies on the nature of criticism and religion, and on *Milton and the Romantic poets. *Culture and Anarchy* (1869) is his central statement on bringing the forces of culture in its widest sense to bear on the ills of society, represented by the Barbarians (the aristocracy), Philistines (the middle classes), and Populace (the working classes). See *Matthew Arnold: a Selection*, ed. Miriam Allott and Robert H. Super, 1986; Park Honan, *Matthew Arnold: a Life*, 1981; Lionel Trilling, *Matthew Arnold*, rev. edn 1949 (critical biography).

**Aubrey, John** (1626–97), folklorist and antiquary, was born at Easton Piers near Malmesbury, Wiltshire. At Trinity College, Oxford, his studies were interrupted first by the Civil War and then by smallpox. His father died in 1652, leaving Aubrey (by his own account) £2800 of debts. A series of lawsuits led to his bankruptcy in 1670, after which, largely to avoid his creditors, he did the rounds of his friends in London and the country. In 1649 he had discovered the significant megalithic archaeological site at Avebury, and in 1663 his literary and scientific interests won him election to the Royal Society. His itinerant existence was good for research but bad for collating and writing up the results. The only work published in his lifetime was *Miscellanies* (1696), a compendium of superstitions and supernatural experiences. His literary fame, however, rests on the mass of notes which he offered to his cantankerous friend, Anthony Wood (also à Wood) for a dictionary of lives of Oxford writers and bishops, *Athenae Oxonienses* (1691–2), and which, having quarrelled with Wood, he deposited in the Ashmolean Museum in 1693. The edited versions of *Brief Lives* reveal an eye for descriptive detail, a nose for gossip, a lively wit, and an appreciation of the biographer's art — much of the information he assiduously collected was from first-hand accounts. See *Brief Lives*, ed. Richard W. Barber, new edn 1982; Anthony Powell, *Aubrey and His Friends*, new rev. edn 1988.

**Auden, W(ystan) H(ugh)** (1907–73), poet, dramatist, and critic, was born in York, son of a doctor, and educated at Gresham's School, Holt, and Christ Church, Oxford, where he was unofficial literary leader of a number of young poets such as *Betjeman, Day *Lewis, *MacNeice, and *Spender. He was a schoolmaster for several years, then travelled in Europe and China. With other like-minded intellectuals he served in the Spanish Civil War, as an ambulance driver. He emigrated to the USA in 1939 and became an American citizen in 1946. He was Professor of Poetry at Oxford 1956–61.

While Auden acknowledged the influence of such diverse poets as *Wyatt, *Hardy, and *Eliot, and the inspiration of *Tolkien's lectures on Anglo-Saxon and Middle English poetry, he says in 'Dichtung und Wahreit' (1959), '... of any poem written by myself, my first demand is that it be genuine, recognizable, like my handwriting, as having been written, for better or worse, by me'. The energy and objectivity of his verse, combined with a sharp sense of humour, a delight in pastiche, a penchant for popular speech and everyday images, and a sympathy with the feelings of ordinary people, distinguish his work throughout the two main phases of his life and poetic progress, variously called 'the English Auden' and 'the later Auden', or 'the Marxist Auden' and 'the Christian Auden'. His first book, *Poems* (1930, rev. edn 1933), contained an extraordinary variety of moods and verse forms, and included 'On Sunday Walks' and 'This Lunar Beauty'. With other contemporaries, he was concerned in the 1930s with the need for social, political, and spiritual reform, which he expressed with growing bitterness and anger, though to this period also belong 'In This Island', 'Lullaby', 'Night Mail', and the tripartite 'In Memory of W. B. Yeats', as well as 'Spain 1937' and several sardonic cautionary-ballads, including 'James Honeyman'. His re-conversion to Christianity in the 1940s introduced a religious tone and religious themes to his canon, notably with 'Horae Canonicae' — in the collection *The Shield of Achilles* (1955) — and the Christmas oratorio, *For the Time Being* (1945). His increasing fear of loneliness is reflected in *The Age of Anxiety: a Baroque Eclogue* (1948). *Homage to Clio* (1960) contains a greater proportion of lighter verse.

As adapter or librettist Auden was associated with many stage performances. He also wrote the verse play, *The Dance of Death* (1933), his most extreme statement of Marxism, and, with Christopher Isherwood (1904–86), *The Ascent of F6* (1937) and two other plays. Some of his criticism is collected in *The Dyer's Hand and Other Essays* (new edn 1975) and *Selected Essays* (1964). See *Collected Poems*, ed. Edward Mendelson,

1976 (incorporates his final revisions and omits poems he had discarded); *The English Auden: Poems, Essays, and Dramatic Writings 1927–1939*, ed. Edward Mendelson, new edn 1986 (includes all the poems he wrote in the 1930s); Humphrey Carpenter, *W. H. Auden*, new edn 1983 (biography); Stan Smith, *W. H. Auden*, 1985 (critical study).

**Austen, Jane** (1775–1817), novelist, was born in the rectory of Steventon, Hampshire, seventh of eight children, and apart from being at boarding school in Oxford, Southampton, and Reading between the ages of seven and nine, was educated by her father and elder brothers. The family home, in which she lived all her life, moved to Bath (1801), to Southampton (1806), and to the Hampshire village of Chawton (1809), her father having died in 1805. She was the first of six brothers and two sisters to die, which she did from a form of anaemia at 42, tragically young for a novelist. Two of her brothers rose to the rank of admiral in the Navy. Though she never travelled outside the south of England, and never married, her family and social life was not uneventful, and she had the right environment and upbringing to write, which she did from childhood. All the novels published during her lifetime appeared anonymously, though her brother Henry, who acted as her literary agent, disclosed the authorship of *Pride and Prejudice* from what she calls in a letter 'the warmth of his Brotherly vanity & Love'. The six novels, in the order in which they were first published, are:

*Sense and Sensibility*: published 1811 by Thomas Egerton (of the Military Library, Whitehall) with a revised edition in 1813. It was rewritten in 1797 from an earlier story in epistolary form called *Elinor and Marianne*, and further revised in 1809.

*Pride and Prejudice*: published January 1813 by Egerton, with a second edition in November 1813. As *First Impressions*, it had originally been offered in 1797 to Thomas Cadell, who turned it down.

*Mansfield Park*: published May 1814 by Egerton at the author's expense, a second edition being published in 1816 by John Murray. It was written between February 1811 and June 1813.

*Emma*: published by Murray in December 1815, and written between January 1814 and March 1815.

*Northanger Abbey* and *Persuasion*: published together in four volumes by Murray in December 1817, after the author's death. *Northanger Abbey* had originally been written between 1798 and 1799 as *Susan*, and was accepted in a revised form in 1803 by Crosby and Co. of Bath, who paid £10 for the copyright, but never published the book. The author wrote to them in 1809 under an assumed name, demanding action and offering to supply a copy if the original manuscript was lost. Crosby said that they were under no obligation to publish, but offered to return the manuscript if they could have their money back. Nothing was done until 1816, when Henry Austen retrieved the copyright from the unsuspecting publisher, who was unaware of the author's identity. It was now revised for publication as *Catherine*. *Persuasion* was written under the title of *The Elliots* between the summer of 1815 and August 1816. The final titles of both books were chosen by Henry.

Other significant contributions to the canon are: *Love and Freindship*, a short burlesque in letters, written when she was 16; *Lady Susan*, a longer epistolary novel, and the beginning of *The Watsons*, written in about 1806, which Q. D. Leavis (1906–81) argues in *Scrutiny* Vol. X (1941–2) were subsequently reworked into *Mansfield Park* and *Emma* respectively (if this theory is correct, it would account for the years during which the author appears to have written virtually nothing); and *Sanditon*, twelve chapters of which were written between 27 January and 18 March 1817.

Jane Austen can claim to be the most frequently re-read of all novelists in English literature, a distinction which calls for qualities far beyond those required merely to delineate characters, depict settings, and devise plots. In a letter to her nephew (16 December 1816) she described her medium as 'the little bit (two inches wide) of Ivory on which I work with so fine a Brush, as produces little effect after much labour'. It is the depth, drama, and selection of detail with which she invests her society and its manners, the acuteness and deadly precision of her observation, the deftness with which she develops a situation and displays her characters and their changing relationships with each other, and her devastating wit, whether she is writing in a vein of comedy or parody, which bring the reader back to her again and again. She also freed the English novel from its predominantly episodic or epistolary form, and set new boundaries in literary style and narrative art. See *Selected Letters 1796–1817*, ed. R. W. Chapman, 1985; Mary Lascelles, *Jane Austen and Her Art*, new edn 1963; David Cecil, *A Portrait of Jane Austen*, new edn 1980.

**Aytoun, William Edmonstoune** (1813–65), Scottish poet and satirist, was born in Edinburgh, the son of a lawyer, and went to Edinburgh Academy and Edinburgh University, where he read law which, he later confessed, he had 'followed but could never overtake'. His first book of poetry was *Poland, Homer and Other Poems* (1832). From 1836 until his death, he contributed articles and poems to *Blackwood's Edinburgh Magazine*. He was elected Professor of Belles Lettres at Edinburgh University in 1845, and appointed Sheriff and Lord Admiral of Orkney and Shetland in 1852. Some of his parodies of traditional ballads and contemporary poets were included in *The Bon Gaultier Ballads* (1845), the rest being by Theodore Martin (1816–1909). His reputation was made by *Lays of the Scottish Cavaliers* (1849), in which 'The Execution of Montrose', 'The Burial March of Dundee', and 'The Widow of Glencoe', in particular, have fine feeling and resounding rhythms, while reflecting the more romantic aspects of the grim history of the Scottish Highlands. His most audacious literary exploit was to publish in 1854 a spoof review (with extracts) of *Firmilian* by Percy T. Jones, a poet of what he termed the 'Spasmodic school'. Neither the poem nor its author existed, and the Spasmodic school was an invention of Aytoun's to describe the ramblings of some contemporary poets who were attempting to write in the style of *Byron and Goethe (1749–1832). He then wrote the complete *Firmilian*, as a burlesque tragedy. See *Stories and Verse*, ed. W. L. Renwick, 1964.

**Bacon**, (Sir) **Francis** (1561–1626), prose writer, essayist, and jurist, was born in York House, the Strand, London, youngest son by his second marriage of Queen Elizabeth's statesman Sir Nicholas Bacon, and educated at home and at Trinity College, Cambridge, which he had to leave when he was 14 because of an outbreak of plague. After learning diplomacy in France, he studied law, graduating in 1582, and was elected to Parliament in 1584. After some years in subordinate posts, he was knighted by James I in 1603, and appointed Solicitor-General (1607), Attorney-General (1616), and Lord Chancellor (1618), becoming Baron Verulam in 1618 and Viscount St Albans in 1621. In that year he was accused of taking bribes from three suitors while their cases were being tried in his court. Though he had found against them, he was adjudged guilty of corruption in the House of Lords, dismissed from all his offices, and fined £40,000. He spent the rest of his life writing.

Throughout the whole of his professional career he wrote legal and political works which, with his frequent speeches in Parliament, form a sizable literary output on their own. Yet this extraordinary man, of whom *Pope wrote in *An Essay on Man* (IV. 281), 'If Parts allure thee, think how Bacon shin'd, / The wisest, brightest, meanest of mankind', also wrote several major philosophical and scientific treatises in Latin (the lingua franca of scholarship), including the unfinished *Instauratio Magna* (1620), and four literary works in English which are unique in his age. The first volume of his essays (ten in all) was published in 1597, and an enlarged edition in 1612. The definitive edition contains 58, including extended versions of ones already published. Didactic, aphoristic, incisively and clearly written, and often with striking openings, they are also a shrewd and objective picture of the manners and morals of the time. 'The Advancement of Learning' — *The Twoo Bookes of Francis Bacon: Of the Proficience and Advancement of Learning, Divine and Humane* (1605) — is a wide-ranging and systematic investigation into the knowledge of his era. *The Historie of the Raigne of King Henry the Seventh* (1622) is a landmark in English historical writing in that Bacon departs from the unselective chronicle approach to produce a coherent and balanced narrative, while bringing psychological insight to bear on his characters. *New Atlantis*, left unfinished and first published with *Sylva Sylvarum: or a Naturall Historie* (1626), is a philosophical, scientific and, in some respects, prophetic fable on the construction and methodology of society.

His enquiring mind caused his death. Keen to try refrigeration as a means of preserving food, he left his coach to buy a chicken, which he stuffed with snow. He caught a chill, of which he died so quickly that he could not be got home. See *The Essayes or Counsels, Civill and Morall*, ed. Michael Kiernan, 1985; Catherine D. Bowen, *Francis Bacon: Temper of a Man*, 1983 (biography); Brian Vickers, *Francis Bacon and Renaissance Prose*, 1968.

**Bagehot, Walter** (1826–77), economist, political philosopher, literary critic, and journalist, was born in Langport, Somerset, son of a banker and shipowner. He was educated in Bristol and at London University, where he excelled at mathematics, philosophy, and political economy. After studying for and being called to the Bar, he joined his father's business, while contributing articles to literary and economic journals and, in 1855, becoming joint-editor of the *National Review*. In 1858 he married a daughter of James Wilson, editor of the *Economist*, whom he succeeded as editor in 1860, holding the post until his death. Bagehot's *The English Constitution* (1867, rev. edn 1872) is a classic, often-cited study of government in which, among other recommendations, he advocates life-peerages. In *Physics and Politics* (1872) he applies *Darwin's theory of 'natural selection' to world politics, and in *Lombard Street* (1873) he examines the current financial market. Collected volumes of literary, economic, and biographical studies were published (1879–81) after his death. His article 'Wordsworth, Tennyson and Browning, or Pure, Ornate and Grotesque Art in English Poetry' (1864) is much quoted, and contains the coinage of 'literatesque' to describe 'that perfect combination in the *subject-matter* of literature, which suits the *art* of literature'. See *Collected Works*, ed. Norman St John-Stevas, 1986; Norman St John-Stevas, *Walter Bagehot: a Study of His Life and Thought*, 1959.

**Barbour, John** (*c*.1320–95), the earliest-known Scottish poet, was probably born in or near Aberdeen. He is first mentioned in 1357, when as Archdeacon of Aberdeen (a post he held until his death) he was granted a pass by Edward III to accompany three scholars to Oxford. In that year, too, he was the Bishop's proxy at the council in Edinburgh to raise the ransom for the release of David II from England. He held various posts in the royal household and was auditor of the exchequer in 1372, 1382, and 1383. Two lost poems are attributed to him, *The Brut* and *The Stewartis Original*. His surviving work, *The Bruce*, 13,550 lines long, and written in rhyming couplets of iambic tetrameters, is a patriotic panegyric both of Robert I (Robert the Bruce) and his successful fight to free Scotland from English domination, which culminated in the battle of Bannockburn (1314), and of the ordinary people of Scotland who played their part. It is remarkable for its attention to detail, for its attempt to present an authentic record, and for the poet's narrative power and insight. In 1377 Robert II (grandson of the Bruce and the first Stewart King of Scotland) granted Barbour £10 for writing the poem and a pension of 20 shillings a year, which the poet made over to the cathedral for a mass, to be said each year on his birthday, for him and his parents, which was done until the Reformation. Two fifteenth-century transcripts of *The Bruce* survive; the first printed edition was in 1571. See in Kurt Wittig, *The Scottish Tradition in Literature*, new edn 1978; and in Roderick Watson, *The Literature of Scotland*, 1984.

**Barrie,** (Sir) **J(ames) M(atthew)** (1860–1937), Scottish dramatist, novelist, and journalist, was born in Kirriemuir, Angus, ninth child of a handloom weaver, and educated at Glasgow, Forfar, and Dumfries academies, and at Edinburgh University. He was a leader-writer on the *Nottingham Journal* 1882–4, after which he returned home to write articles for London periodicals. In 1885 he moved permanently to London, and in 1894 embarked on a disastrous marriage to the actress Mary Ansell. His Scottish pieces, published as *Auld Licht Idylls* (1888) and *A Window in Thrums* (1889), give him the dubious distinction of being the earliest member of the Kailyard school of novelists, who tended to present cosy as well as rosy portraits of Scottish rural life. *The Little Minister* (1891), however, was hugely successful as a novel and then a play (1897). Barrie was the first major Scottish-born playwright, and *The Admirable Crichton* (1902), *Dear Brutus* (1917), and *Mary Rose* (1920) are still remembered if not often performed. There is more of Barrie (his closeness to his mother, his nostalgia for childhood, and his love for the five boys for whom he cared after their parents' deaths) in the perennially popular children's play about the boy who never grew up, *Peter Pan* (1904), which he rewrote as a story, *Peter Pan and Wendy* (1911). He was created a baronet (1913), awarded the OM (1922), and elected Chancellor of Edinburgh University (1930). See *The Works of J. M. Barrie*, 1925–32; Leonee Ormond, *J. M. Barrie*, 1987 (critical biography).

**Beaumont, Francis** (1584–1616), dramatist, was born at Grace Dieu, Leicestershire, son of a judge, on whose death in 1598 he and his two elder brothers had to leave Oxford without finishing their degree courses. He enrolled as a law student in London, was accepted by \*Jonson and his circle, and met \*Fletcher, with whom he struck up such a rapport that they shared the same lodgings and, according to \*Aubrey, 'one wench in the house between them'. The only play generally regarded to be by Beaumont alone is *The Knight of the Burning Pestle* (*c*.1608), a boisterous burlesque in which a grocer and his wife take their apprentice, Ralph, to the theatre, and get hilariously involved in the plot and the action of the play on the stage. Between 1607 and 1613, when Beaumont married, he and Fletcher collaborated on some ten plays, usually marked by complex plots and surprising revelations. They knew their market and the poetry of their plays suffers only in comparison with that of their more famous contemporaries. *Philaster* (*c*.1609) is a tragicomedy of frustrated love. In *The Maid's Tragedy* (*c*.1611) Amintor is forced by his king to break off his engagement and marry Evadne, who reveals on their wedding night that she is the royal mistress. The destinies of the main characters are resolved by violent deaths, but the play is notable for its initial situation and for the conflicts of loyalty which it depicts. See W. W. Appleton, *Beaumont and Fletcher*, 1956; and in Una Ellis-Fermor, *The Jacobean Drama*, 1936.

**Beckett, Samuel** (1906–89), Irish dramatist, novelist, poet, translator, and critic, was born in Foxrock, near Dublin, son of a quantity surveyor, and educated at Portora Royal School, Co. Fermanagh, and Trinity College, Dublin, where he got a first in French and Italian literature and excelled at sport. After teaching in Belfast and Paris, and at Trinity College, Dublin, he settled in Paris, where he had previously met and become closely associated with *Joyce. In the 1930s he published two volumes of verse, *Whoroscope* (1930) and *Echo's Bones and Other Precipitations* (1935); a collection of short stories, *More Pricks Than Kicks* (1934); a critical study of Proust (1931); and a novel, *Murphy* (1938). At the outbreak of World War II he returned to France from Ireland and joined the Resistance, while working as a farm labourer and writing a second novel, *Watt* (not published until 1953). Back in Paris after the war, between 1945 and 1950 he wrote three novels (all in French) — *Molloy* (English translation 1959), *Malone Meurt* (*Malone Dies* 1958), and *L'Innomable* (*The Unnamable* 1959) — and the play *En Attendant Godot*, which was performed in Paris in 1953 and made his reputation. In his own translation as *Waiting for Godot*, it was staged in New York in 1954 and London in 1955, and published in Britain in 1956. After a fallow period following the death of his mother, he wrote in English between 1956 and 1961 *All That Fall: a Play for Radio* (1957), *Embers* (a piece for radio), and the one-act play *Krapp's Last Tape* — published together as *Krapp's Last Tape and Embers* (1959) — and the two-act stage play *Happy Days* (1962). His other most significant drama in English is *Not I* (1973), first performed in New York in 1972. He was awarded the Nobel Prize for Literature in 1969.

Even if one includes *Waiting for Godot* and the one-act play *Endgame* — translated by himself from *Fin de Partie* and first published in Britain in 1958 — Beckett's total contribution to English literature comprises two slim volumes of verse, a book of short stories, five novels (of which three were originally written in French), a handful of short plays, and some even briefer pieces, and the concessions that he made to his readers tended to decrease in inverse proportion to the growth of his reputation. His poetry, though Joycean in essence, has an innocence underlying the bitterness, and an Anglo-Irish linguistic ring. The same character, Belacqua Shuah, appears in all the tales in *More Pricks Than Kicks*, among which 'Dante and the Lobster' stands out not only as a remarkable story in its own right, with an unforgettable and thought-provoking ending, but as descriptive prose at its tautest and most expressive. All these stories are set in Dublin. The protagonist of *Murphy* lives, and in the oddest way imaginable dies, in London, having just found the mental contentment towards which he has been blundering. With *Watt*, Beckett returns to Ireland. Watt himself is the archetypal fall guy, whose route to mental salvation ends in a lunatic asylum, not as a nurse, as Murphy had briefly been, but as an inmate. The experimental style had now become mannered, and it was as though having reached his particular philosophical periphery in narrative prose, Beckett now turned to French as his medium for the novel, and to drama, whose intellectual limits he redefined even more profoundly than *Osborne was to change the direction of its subject matter.

Beckett's relentless theme is depression, often verging on despair. With *Waiting for Godot*, he proved that it was possible dramatically to project the desolation and meaningless protraction of existence through characters who represent just these states in their actions and dialogue. In *Endgame* and *Not I*, he abandoned movement and other normal stage conventions even more radically. In *Happy Days*, his only moderately optimistic piece, the main character is immobilised up to the waist in sand in the first act and to the neck in the second, and her husband, the only other character, is hardly seen. Though the theatre presentation of *Krapp's Last Tape* is enhanced by visual devices built into the script, his economy and manipulation of timing as well as of language makes the piece just as effective on radio. See *Poems in English*, 1961; *The Complete Dramatic Works*, 1986; Deirdre Bair, *Samuel Beckett: a Biography*, 1978; A. Alvarez, *Beckett*, 1973 (critical study).

**Beckford, William** (1759–1844), novelist, was born at the family seat, Fonthill Abbey, Wiltshire, son of a wealthy alderman of the City of London, and educated by a private tutor, Rev. Dr Lettice. At 21, he inherited the family fortune (amassed largely from Jamaican plantations) of £1m, plus £100,000 a year. At 22, in one sitting of three days and two nights, he drafted in French, *Vathek, an Arabian Tale*. A pirated translation of the finished work was published in 1786, and an authorised English version and the original French edition in 1787. Though frequently abroad and from 1796 a virtual recluse, Beckford was elected to Parliament 1784–94 and 1806–20. He had Fonthill rebuilt by James Wyatt in 1796 as a half-ruined Gothic monstrosity, with a 275-foot tower which collapsed shortly afterwards and was as promptly replaced. Here he devoted himself to scandalous pursuits and the collection of books and objets d'art. In 1822, his fortune now reduced to a mere £80,000, he was forced to sell out and retire to Bath. *Vathek* is a fantasy-adventure of a sadistic caliph who sells himself to Eblis, the devil, in whose underground halls, lit with flaming pyramids, Vathek's heart and those of the newly damned finally burst into eternal fire. Beckford also wrote the satirical *Memoirs of Extraordinary Painters* (1780) and some witty and perceptive accounts of his travels. See James Lees-Milne, *William Beckford*, 1976.

**Beerbohm,** (Sir) **Max** (1872–1956), essayist, critic, broadcaster, parodist, and caricaturist, was born in London and educated at Charterhouse and Merton College, Oxford, without taking a degree. Known as 'the incomparable Max', he lived outwardly as a leisurely dandy, while at the same time doing many things very well. It was a sign of his impish and paradoxical nature to call his first book *The Works of Max Beerbohm* (1896), and his next two volumes of essays *More* (1899) and *Yet Again* (1909). In 1898 he succeeded *Shaw as drama critic of the *Saturday Review*, a post he held until 1910 when, having married the actress Florence Kahn, he retired to Rapallo, Italy, where except for the two world wars he remained for the rest of his life. His only novel, *Zuleika Dobson* (1911), describes delicately but uproariously the effect on undergraduate passions of the beautiful and predatory niece of the head of an Oxford college. *A Christmas Garland* (1912) is a collection of devastating parodies of notable authors of the time (including *James, *Kipling, *Hardy, and *Conrad) on the theme of Christmas, which are as incisively observed and executed as his pictorial caricatures of the famous, including members of the Royal Family. *Seven Men* (1919), later published as *Seven Men and Two Others* (1950), is a volume of short stories, among them '"Savonarola" Brown', which incorporates a memorable skit on Elizabethan stage drama. He was knighted in 1939. See David Cecil, *Max*, new edn 1970.

**Behn, Mrs Aphra** (or **Ayfara**) (1640–89), née Johnson, dramatist and novelist, was born in Wye, Kent. Her early life is an enigma. She may have visited Surinam with a member of her family or with a lover. If so, she then married a Dutchman who died soon afterwards. She may have been employed as a British spy in Holland in 1666 or have used knowledge gained from another lover, or the same lover, to try to obtain favours from the Government. What is certain is that in about 1670 she needed to earn a living and in doing so became the first English professional woman writer. Her comedies tend to be derivative and faintly indecent. *The Rover* (1677), an anonymous picaresque play about the amorous adventures in Europe of a band of Cavaliers, was her first major success: she wrote a second part in 1681 under her own name. *The City Heiress* (1682) is more typical of Restoration drama, and has a political message — the Commonwealth-sympathiser is bested by his Tory nephew. She also wrote fiction. *Three Histories* (1688) contained *Oroonoko: or the Royal Slave*. This is regarded as the first English philosophical novel, in that within an impressive adventure story of love and treachery is an expression of the meaning of nobleness and honour to those in whom the society of the time allowed there to be none, and an indictment of those who ran, or tolerated, the slave trade. See *Works*, ed. Montague Summers, 1915; *Five Plays*, 1990, and *Oroonoko and Other Stories*, 1986, ed. Maureen Duffy; Maureen Duffy, *The Passionate Shepherdess*, 1977 (biography).

**Belloc, Hilaire** (1870–1953), poet, novelist, travel writer, and journalist, was born in St Cloud, France, of Anglo-French Catholic parentage, and educated at the Oratory School, Birmingham. He did military service in the French army before being helped by his sister, the novelist Mrs Belloc Lowndes (1868–1947), to go to Balliol College, Oxford. He was a Liberal Member of Parliament 1906–10, but did not seek re-election after making an anti-Semitic remark in the House. He was literary editor of the *Morning Post* 1906–10, and founded the journal *Eye-Witness* in 1911. He was a prolific writer. He had to be, for his wife died in 1914 and he had five children to support. His more lasting works include his cautionary tales for children (e.g. 'The chief defect of Henry King / Was chewing little bits of string…'); some lyrics, including 'Tarantella' ('Do you remember an inn, Miranda?…'), 'Ha'nacker Mill', 'The South Country'; numerous epigrams (including 'When I am dead, I hope it may be said / His sins were scarlet and his books were read.'); *The Path to Rome*, a personal account of a journey on foot; biographies of Wolsey (1930), Napoleon (1932), Cromwell (1934), and Louis XIV (1938); *The Servile State* (1912), an attack on both socialism and capitalist industrial society; and some light novels, of which *Belinda* (1928) was the most notable in his time. See *Complete Verse*, new edn 1970; *Letters*, ed. Robert Speaight, 1958; A. N. Wilson, *Hilaire Belloc*, new edn 1986.

**Bennett, Arnold** (1867–1931), novelist, short story writer, dramatist, and journalist, was born in Hanley, Staffordshire, one of the five towns of the 'Potteries', the setting of many of his novels and stories. He was educated locally and given a sound background in the arts at home. In 1893 he gave up his solicitor's training in London to be assistant editor of the weekly journal, *Woman*, becoming editor in 1896. His first novel, *A Man from the North*, was published in 1898, and *Anna of the Five Towns* in 1902. He then spent ten years in Paris, where he got the inspiration for *The Old Wives' Tale* (1908), an intricate saga of two sisters from the Potteries whose inclinations take them in separate directions but who live out their final years together. *Clayhanger* (1910) has the same regional and social background, but its quality is not matched in its sequels, *Hilda Lessways* (1911) and *These Twain* (1915). During World War I, Bennett gave valuable service to the Ministry of Information. The post-war years, during which he lived in London in some style, were ones of increased activity but waning creativity, though the grim story of a London bookseller,

*Riceyman Steps* (1923), won him his first literary award. He was a tireless patron of the arts, and introduced many people to new and often unknown writers through his reviews in the *Evening Standard*. His lasting contribution, however, is as a regional novelist who reflected magnetically and with meticulous detail a whole way of life. See Margaret Drabble, *Arnold Bennet*, new edn 1985.

**Berkeley, George** (1685–1753), Irish philosopher and cleric, was born at Dysart Castle, Co. Kilkenny, and educated at Kilkenny College and Trinity College, Dublin, of which he became a Fellow in 1711. In 1707 he began a series of commonplace books (now referred to as *Philosophical Commentaries*) containing his beliefs about existence and perception. His first published works were *A New Theory of Vision* (1709) and *Principles of Human Knowledge* (1710). He was in England in 1713, where he joined the circle of *Addison, *Pope, and *Steele, and then travelled abroad until 1721, when he returned to Trinity College. In 1724 he was appointed Dean of Derry. A reformer as well as a visionary, he sailed for America in 1728 with the promise of government sponsorship for a college in Bermuda 'for the Christian civilisation of America', but had to return in 1731 when the grant failed to materialise. While he was there, he wrote *Alciphron, or the Minute Philosopher* (1732), a dialogue which is Platonic in both form and thought. He was created Bishop of Cloyne in 1734, retiring in 1752 because of ill health, which had earlier moved him to write a treatise on the medical properties of tar-water, *Siris* (1744). The basis of his philosophy is immaterialism: the belief that objects do not exist except in the mind, and that knowledge is confined to what can be perceived. His works are marked by clarity and dignity of style as well as of thought. See A. A. Luce, *The Life of Berkeley*, 1949; J. O. Urmson, *Berkeley*, 1982 (introduction to his thought).

**Betjeman,** (Sir) **John** (1906–84), poet and sage, was born in Highgate, London, only child of a successful manufacturer of furnishings. He was educated at Marlborough and Magdalen College, Oxford, where he failed to take a degree. An early interest in architecture became a lifetime's preoccupation with the Gothic revival, churches, and the social history of urban and rural England as it is illustrated by buildings large and small, and led to many elegantly written and effectively argued architectural and topographical works from *Ghastly Good Taste* (1933, rev. edn 1970) to *London's Historic Railway Stations* (1972). His first book of verse, *Mount Zion* (1932), comprised just eleven short poems; *Continual Dew* (1937) was more substantial. His poetry was regarded by some critics at the time as facile, with its jaunty rhymes and rhythms, middle-class suburban settings, muscular maidens, and expressions of innocent love. It was, however, hugely enjoyed by the public for its accessibility and wit, and for its evocation of places, past times, and situations.

Betjeman was a poet of compassion and humanity, whose fear of ultimate infirmity and death was counter-balanced by his Christian belief, and whose insight into such a range of themes repeatedly causes the reader to respond with recognition, and often with surprise. He was knighted in 1969, and appointed Poet Laureate in 1972. See *Collected Poems*, rev. edn 1979; *Summoned by Bells*, new edn 1977 (verse autobiography); Bevis Hillier, *Young Betjeman*, new edn 1989.

**Blackmore, R(ichard) D(oddridge)** (1825–1900), classicist and novelist, was born in Longworth, Berkshire, son of the curate. Three months after his birth, his mother died in a typhus epidemic. He was educated at Blundell's School, Devon, and Exeter College, Oxford, and was called to the Bar in 1852, but gave up the law in 1855 because of bouts of epilepsy and was briefly a schoolmaster. With a legacy from an uncle, he was able in 1858 to build a country house in Teddington, Middlesex, where he devoted the rest of his life to writing and to market-gardening. In 1855 he had two volumes of poetry published, *Poems by Melanter* and *Epullia*, followed by a verse translation of the first two books of Virgil's *Georgics*, infelicitously entitled *The Farm and Fruit of Old* (1862). He wrote 15 novels, of which the first, *Clara Vaughan* (1864), was published anonymously, and *The Maid of Sker* (1872) was his favourite. His literary distinction, however, rests entirely on his third, *Lorna Doone* (1869), a regional novel somewhat in the vein of *Scott, set on and around Exmoor and covering the events and aftermath of the rebellion of the Duke of Monmouth in 1685. It was not very well received by the critics, but it soon won enormous and continuing public acclaim for its melodramatic plot and for the lyrical intensity with which he evokes the romance between John Ridd and Lorna Doone, the blood feud between their families, and the rugged Devon landscape. See Kenneth Budd, *The Last Victorian: R. D. Blackmore and His Novels*, 1960.

**Blake, William** (1757–1827), poet, painter, illustrator, and engraver, was born in London, son of an Irish hosier. He attended a drawing school and at 14 was apprenticed to James Basire, engraver to the Society of Antiquities, after which he studied at the Royal Academy. At an early age he was given to visionary experiences, some of which he expressed in verses included in *Poetical Sketches* (1783). For *Songs of Innocence* (1789) he devised a novel method of book production by etching text and illustrations on to a plate, and colouring the printed sheets by hand with the help of his wife. In 1794 he added further poems through which the book could show 'the two contrary states of the human soul' and published it as *Songs of Innocence and Experience*. Only 24 copies of the original edition are recorded. In opposition to the radical thinking of the day, he had begun to issue his 'Prophetic Books', including *The French Revolution* (1791), *Visions of the Daughters of Albion* (1793), and *America: a Prophecy*

(1794), in all of which the different forces of revolution are interpreted in moral and cosmic terms, while in *The First Book of Urizen* (1794), *The Book of Ahania* (1795), *The Book of Los* (1795), and *The Song of Los* (1795), the tone and the vision become even more turbulent. The years 1799 to 1803 were spent on the estate of the minor literary figure William Hayley (1745–1820), at Felpham, Sussex, and were frustrating rather than fruitful, culminating in Blake being unsuccessfully prosecuted for sedition on the evidence of a drunken soldier whom he had removed from his garden. Between 1804 and 1808 he wrote and etched *Milton*, a complex work inspired by and related to *Paradise Lost*. In the preface occurs the hymn 'And did those feet in ancient time ...'. *Jerusalem: the Emanation of the Giant Albion* was written and etched between 1804 and 1820. In 1809, having been thwarted by the Royal Academy, which refused to exhibit what he termed his 'portable frescos' (done in a water-based medium), he held his own show. The enterprise was a financial failure, but the *Descriptive Catalogue of Pictures, Poetical and Historical Inventions* is a splendid example of evocative prose.

In *Jerusalem* (I.5) Blake wrote, '... I rest not from my great task! / To open the Eternal Worlds, to open the immortal Eyes / Of Man inwards into the Worlds of Thought ...'. An early and particularly intense but largely unheeded Romantic, his personal satisfaction came from the knowledge of his own eccentric, mysterious, and mystical genius, which he displayed in his early lyrics ('The Little Black Boy', 'The Chimney Sweeper', 'The Tyger') as clearly as he did, with enhanced symbolism and a mythology based on a dual vision of God and man, in his later works. See *Poetry and Prose*, ed. Geoffrey Keynes, new edn 1989; Mona Wilson, *The Life of Blake*, ed. Geoffrey Keynes, 1971; Alexander Gilchrist, *Life of William Blake*, ed. Ruthven Todd, 1982; Martin K. Nurmi, *William Blake*, 1975 (critical study).

**Blunden, Edmund** (1896–1974), poet, critic, and literary biographer, was born in Yalding, Kent, and educated at Christ's Hospital and The Queen's College, Oxford. His first book, *Poems, 1913 and 1914*, was published in 1914, the year he joined the Army. He served as a lieutenant at the front from 1916 to 1918, winning the MC. He was Professor of English Literature, Tokyo University 1924–7, and a Fellow of Merton College, Oxford, from 1931. In 1943 he joined the editorial staff of *The Times Literary Supplement*, but returned to the Far East after World War II and taught for a time at Hong Kong University. He was Professor of Poetry at Oxford 1966–8. Blunden's quiet and reflective nature is mirrored in his work. Even in his classic prose account, *Undertones of War* (1928), his personal reminiscences of the ghastly business conducted in Flanders, and in his war poems written at the time and afterwards, there is more expression of pity and ironic observation than of anger or outrage. Much of his poetry is concerned with the countryside and its traditional sights and sounds, as is suggested by the titles of some of his earlier volumes: *Pastorals* (1916), *The Waggoner* (1920), *The Shepherd* (1922). Like many countrymen, too, he was a fervent cricket enthusiast, and his *Cricket Country* (1943) is a notable and noble attempt to assess the nature and appeal of the game. He also wrote deft critical biographies of *Hunt (1930), *Lamb (1932), *Hardy (1941), and *Shelley (1946). See *Poems of Many Years*, ed. Rupert Hart-Davis, 1957.

**Borrow, George** (1803–81), linguist, prose writer, and traveller, was born in East Dereham, Norfolk, son of a regimental staff officer, and educated at the High School of Edinburgh and Norwich Grammar School. He was articled to a solicitor, but went to London on his father's death and worked as a publisher's editor and hack writer. Disillusioned, he spent the years 1825 to 1832 wandering through England, often with gypsies as companions. In 1833 he became an agent of the British and Foreign Bible Society, for whom he travelled to Russia, Spain, Portugal, and Morocco, gratifying his gift for languages — he published *Targum; or Metrical Translations from Thirty Languages* in St Petersburg in 1835. On his return in 1835, he married a widow whom he had met in Spain, and settled with her in Oulton Broad, Norfolk. He began his full-time literary career with *Zincali, or an Account of the Gypsies in Spain* (1841). He then used the letters he had written to the Bible Society as the basis of *The Bible in Spain* (1843), which was an instant success. This led him to write two accounts of his earlier life: *Lavengro* (1851) — the Romany for 'word-master' — and a sequel, *Romany Rye* (1857) — *rai* means 'gentleman'. More profitably read as picaresque fiction than as autobiography, they are discursive, racy, often comic, with sharp dialogue. Borrow's attitude to gypsies was over-romantic, but he influenced later Romany scholars such as John Sampson (1862–1931) and Dora Yates (1879–1974). See William I. Knapp, *Life, Writings and Correspondence of Borrow*, 1899; Martin Armstrong, *George Borrow*, new edn 1982.

**Boswell, James** (1740–95), Scottish prose writer and biographer, was born in Edinburgh, son of a barrister who in 1754 became a Lord of the Court of Session with the courtesy title of Lord Auchinleck, and was educated at Mundell's School, Edinburgh, and by private tutors, before going to Edinburgh University, where he took an arts degree and indulged his passion for poetry and the theatre. His subsequent free living led to the first of several breaches with his father and his being enrolled for a law course at Glasgow University, from which he quickly escaped to London in 1759. After failing to get a commission in a guards' regiment, he was persuaded to renew his law studies in Edinburgh. In 1762, having attained his majority, he left again for London, where he first met his literary idol *Johnson — see *Boswell's London Journal 1763–64*, ed. F. A. Pottle, 1952. After further studies in Utrecht and a Grand Tour of Europe (including Corsica), he was called to the Scottish Bar in 1766, and in 1768 published *An Account of Corsica*, an admirable description and an eloquent justification of Corsican nationalism. After numerous rebuffs, changes of heart and mind, and several torrid affairs, he married in 1769 Margaret Montgomerie, a cousin two years his senior, whom he had known for some years — she died in 1789, having borne him four children. Also in 1769, he bought an interest in the *London Magazine*, to which he contributed between 1777 and 1785 as 'The Hypochondriack' a regular series of essays on popular philosophical and practical issues.

In 1773 he managed to persuade Johnson, who was notoriously averse to anything Scottish, to accompany him on an exhausting but successful three months' trip, taking in Edinburgh, Aberdeen, and Glasgow, as well as the Western Isles, which he wrote up in a classic travelogue, *The Journal of a Tour to the Hebrides, with Samuel Johnson, LL.D.* (1785), a much superior account to that of his travelling companion. After Johnson's death, Boswell left his family in Scotland in 1786, and went to London to prepare his friend's biography, being admitted to the English Bar, at which he performed with even less success than in Scotland. His monumental *The Life of Samuel Johnson* was published in 1791, and reflects not only his dedication to his task and to his subject, but his brilliant eye for a telling detail, his skill as an interviewer, his recall of dialogue and his ability to reconstruct a conversation, and his flair for the dramatic situation. Boswell's death was hastened if not caused by his compulsive concupiscence. He was a failure at the law and was consistently rejected in his pursuit of public office; yet through his books, journals, and other writings, many of which were only discovered in Ireland and in Scotland between 1926 and 1950, he is the most vivid personality of his age. See 'The Yale Editions of the Private Papers of James Boswell', various eds, 14 vols 1955–89; Iain Finlayson, *The Moth and the Candle: a Life of James Boswell*, 1984.

**Bowen, Elizabeth** (1899–1973), Irish novelist and short story writer, was born in Dublin, brought up largely on the family estate at Bowen's Court, Co. Cork, and educated at Downe House, Kent. Of Anglo-Irish descent, she is regarded as combining the subtle observation of manners of Jane *Austen and the class-awareness of Maria *Edgeworth, with the Irish social comedy of the cousins Edith Somerville (1858–1949) and Martin Ross (1862–1915) — best known for *Some Experiences of an Irish R. M.* (1899) and sequels, but also recommended for their tragic novel, *The Real Charlotte* (1894). The carefully built-up and sustained situations and settings of Elizabeth Bowen's novels span both milieus. *The Last September* (1929) centres on a big house in Ireland during the 1920 'Troubles'. Wartime London and the blitz form the background to *The Heat of the Day* (1949), a highly intelligent novel of romantic love and suspected treachery. Recurrent themes are the loneliness and vulnerability of the young, a reflection of her own insecurity caused by her father's mental degeneration and her mother's death. These are most evident in *The House in Paris* (1936), *The Death of the Heart* (1938), and *Eva Trout* (1969). Her first book was the volume of short stories, *Encounters* (1923), and throughout her career she invested her short stories with similar themes and settings to those in her novels, with the added dimension of the supernatural. See *Bowen's Court*, 1942, rev. edn 1964 (early autobiography and family history); *Pictures and Conversations*, 1975 (unfinished autobiography); *Collected Stories*, 1980; Victoria Glendinning, *Elizabeth Bowen: Portrait of a Writer*, 1977; Edwin J. Kenney, *Elizabeth Bowen*, 1975 (critical study); P. Lassner, *Elizabeth Bowen*, 1989 (critical study).

**Bridges, Robert** (1844–1930), poet and critic, was born in Walmer, Kent, of aristocratic stock. His father died when he was ten, but left provision for his son's education at Eton and Corpus Christi College, Oxford. Bridges determined to practise medicine until he was 40, and then retire to write poetry: in the end an illness forced him to give up his profession in 1881. He married in 1884, and in 1907 moved to Boars Hill, Oxford, where he lived quietly for the rest of his life. His first volume of poetry had been published in 1873, and his collected *Shorter Poems* in 1890. He aimed to use form and words to create an object of beauty. He continually experimented with metre and line stress, employing poetic diction to enhance linguistic precision. He was the first to publish poems in 'sprung rhythm', a form developed by his friend *Hopkins, which particularly suits his topographical poems, notably 'London Snow' and 'The Downs'. His lyrics, especially 'The Linnet', 'Cheddar Pinks', and 'Christmas 1913', reveal his command of simple language as a medium of melody. His last major work, *The Testament of Beauty* (1927–9), is a long poem 'in loose Alexandrines' in which he attempts to reconcile idealistic philosophy with modern scientific thought and to relate beauty to reason. His criticism is best represented by the essay 'Milton's Prosody' (1893, rev. 1921). He was appointed Poet Laureate in 1910 and awarded the OM in 1929. See *Poetry and Prose*, ed. John Sparrow, 1955; Edward Thompson, *Robert Bridges*, 1944.

**Bridie, James**, pseudonym of O. H. Mavor (1888–1951), Scottish dramatist, was born in Glasgow, son of an engineer, and educated at Glasgow Academy and Glasgow University, where he read medicine and generally had a good time. He qualified as a doctor in 1913, and served in the Royal Army Medical Corps 1914–19, as he did again in World War II. After World War I, he was consulting physician to the Victoria Infirmary, Glasgow, and then Professor of Medicine at Anderson's College. His life changed dramatically after the performance in 1928 of *The Sunlight Sonata*, a preliminary excursion into what was to become his main motif, the morality play in modern terms. *Tobias and the Angel*, the first of several plays with biblical themes, was staged in London in 1930, and *The Anatomist*, about the body-snatchers Burke and Hare and their enigmatic master Dr Knox, in 1931. He wrote 42 plays, of which *Mr Bolfry* (1943) and *Daphne Laureola* (1949) were probably the most popular. His works are intricate and witty, with several layers of meaning. He was the first genuinely Scottish major playwright and, like many Scottish writers, was preoccupied with questions of good and evil, with the Presbyterian Church in its various forms, and with the contradictions of contemporary life. He was chairman of the Glasgow Citizen's Theatre and in 1950 founded the first Scottish college of drama. He was made CBE in 1946. See *One Way of Living*, 1939 (autobiography); Ronald Mavor, *Dr Bridie and Mr Mavor*, 1988 (biography); J. T. Low, *Devils, Doctors, Saints and Sinners*, 1980 (critical study).

**Brontë, Anne** (1820–49), novelist and poet, younger sister of *Charlotte and *Emily, was born at Thornton Vicarage, Yorkshire, and educated at home at Haworth, and for two years at Miss Wooler's school at Dewsbury Moor. She became a governess in 1839 but was forced to leave her second post in 1845, probably because of an impending scandal in which her brother Branwell, tutor in the same household, was involved. She died of consumption during a trip to Scarborough. Her first novel, *Agnes Grey* (1847), written under the pseudonym of Acton Bell, appeared as the third volume of a publication whose first two consisted of Emily's *Wuthering Heights*. *The Tenant of Wildfell Hall* was published on its own in 1848. Charlotte wrote: 'Anne's character was milder and more subdued [than Emily's]; she wanted the power, the fire, the originality of her sister...'. Anne was unable to invest her limited experience of life with the imagination required of a great novelist, and though *Agnes Grey* portrays faithfully and vividly the tribulations of a governess, and *The Tenant of Wildfell Hall* the degeneration of an alcoholic (based on her observation of Branwell), her place in fiction is largely founded on her being one of a remarkable family trio. The same is true of her poetry. Her religious verse reveals the extent to which Calvinism disturbed her consciousness, and how she tried to reconcile the notion of retribution with that of compassion. See *Poems*, ed. Edward Chitham, 1979; Winifred Gérin, *Anne Brontë: a Biography*, 1959; Elizabeth Langland, *Anne Brontë: the Other One*, 1989 (critical study).

**Brontë, Charlotte** (1816–55), novelist and poet, was born at Thornton Vicarage, Yorkshire, third child of Rev. Patrick Brontë, an Irish-born, Cambridge educated, Church of England minister with genuine literary pretensions. In 1820 he was appointed to Haworth. Mrs Brontë died of cancer in 1821, and the children, of whom there were now six, were looked after by her sister. In 1824 Charlotte and *Emily joined their elder sisters, Maria and Elizabeth, at the Clergy Daughters' School at Cowan Bridge. The following year Maria and Elizabeth were sent home with tuberculosis and died. Charlotte and Emily were removed from the school and stayed at home until 1831, when Charlotte went to Miss Wooler's school at Roe Head for 18 months, then came home to teach her two sisters. A year after the death of his two eldest children, Mr Brontë had brought home for his son Branwell (1817–48) a box of wooden soldiers, which were the immediate inspiration for a fantasy world called the Glass Town Confederacy, documented in prose, drama, and verse, and developed later by Charlotte and Branwell as the kingdom of Angria — see Fannie E. Ratchford, *The Brontës' Web of Childhood* (1941). Charlotte returned to Roe Head (the school moved to Dewsbury Moor in 1837) from 1835 to 1838, when she came home, ill and dispirited. In the next two years she had two posts as governess and turned down two proposals of marriage. She then took the momentous step of going with her sister to the Maison d'Education pour les Jeunes Demoiselles in Brussels, where she developed a profound but unrequited passion for the husband of the proprietor. Back at Haworth, she discovered in 1845 some poems by Emily, which gave her the idea of offering for publication a book of verse by the three sisters. *Poems by Currer, Ellis and Acton Bell* (1846), subsidised by the authors, got three reviews and sold two copies.

Meanwhile they were each finishing a novel. *Anne's and Emily's were accepted for publication together, but Charlotte's *The Professor* (an attempt to reconstruct her Brussels' experience of love with the roles reversed) was rejected seven times. In 1847 she sent another manuscript to the publisher who had been most constructive about *The Professor*. He published it as *Jane Eyre: an Autobiography, edited by Currer Bell* (1847) with immediate success. By the time she had finished *Shirley* (1849), Anne, Emily, and Branwell were dead. In 1850 she first met Mrs *Gaskell, which led to a close friendship with her ultimate biographer. When her publisher again refused to bring out *The Professor* (it was finally published posthumously in 1857), she began *Villette* (1853), a further reworking of her romance, which virtually exhausted her remaining materials for realistic fiction. In a depressed state she accepted a proposal of marriage from her father's curate, Arthur Bell Nicholls. Mr Brontë, furious at an impecunious parson marrying his now famous daughter, refused to attend the wedding in June 1854. Later that year, Charlotte wrote two chapters of *Emma*, which her husband feared might be criticised as repetitious — the fragment was published in 1860 in *Cornhill Magazine* with an introduction by *Thackeray. On 31 March 1855, already weakened by a chill caught on the moors, she died of excessive pregnancy sickness.

Charlotte's failings as a writer outnumber but do not outweigh her virtues — Professor Lord David Cecil in *Early Victorian Novelists* (new edn 1964) describes her as a 'freak genius'. Her range is constricted by her own experience, except in *Shirley*, where the Luddite episodes are drawn from her father's recollections. The development of the dramatic action is frequently broken (one romance in *Villette*, rather than three, might have proved more effective, and the several themes in *Shirley* are imperfectly blended), and the plot often turns on the most improbable coincidences. Yet she succeeds through the very vigour of her story-telling, the way she brings opposites into conflict and also into relationship with each other, the depth with which she explores feelings, and the unity imposed, as it is to such advantage in *Jane Eyre*, by concentration on the experience of the main character. As a poet, however, she lacked the intensity of feeling and expression of either of her sisters, and was inhibited by the restrictions of the verse forms she used as a child and adult. See Rebecca Fraser, *Charlotte Brontë*, new edn 1989 (biography); Helene Moglen, *Charlotte Brontë: the Self Conceived*, new edn 1984 (critical study from feminist viewpoint).

**Brontë, Emily** (1818–48), novelist and poet, younger sister of *Charlotte, was born at Thornton Vicarage and educated briefly at Cowan Bridge, then at home by her father, and for three months in 1835 at Roe Head, where the restrictions on her freedom made her so ill that she was brought home. The freedom that she enjoyed at Haworth was embodied in the moors, over which she roamed and ran, while the dramatic terrain and skyscapes, and the companionship of animals and birds in the wild, were immediate sources of inspiration in her childhood literary pursuits and a formative influence on her adult writing. By the time Charlotte went to Roe Head in 1831, Emily and *Anne had abandoned any further development of the Glass Town saga for their own creation, the kingdom of Gondal. Emily contributed throughout her life to the growth of its mythology, and the main characters, notably the strong, wilful, passionate, criminally-inclined heroine, Augusta Geraldine Almeda, frequently recur in her verse. Her re-establishment at home after Roe Head coincided with the ignominious return of Branwell from London, where he had gone in hopes of making a mark in the arts, and he was a stimulus to her reading and writing. In 1837–8 she spent a few depressing months as a teacher at Law Hill, Halifax, her unhappiness, homesickness, and continuous search for freedom of mind and body being especially reflected in the poems she wrote at the time or soon after, such as 'I'll come when thou art saddest', 'Gleneden's Dream', 'Loud without the wind was roaring', and 'A little while, a little while...'.

In 1841, with Branwell in the unlikely job of clerk to the railways, and Charlotte and Anne unsettled as governesses, it was proposed that the three sisters should open a school. The scheme was abandoned, or postponed, in favour of Charlotte and Emily's educational sojourn in Brussels, which was cut short by the death of their Aunt Branwell in October 1842. Charlotte returned to Brussels as pupil-teacher; Emily

remained at Haworth to look after their father. The discovery by Charlotte in 1845 of Emily's poems and her decision to get them published
along with hers and Anne's must be seen also in the light of the family
financial circumstances. Mr Brontë was going blind; Branwell, having
lost his job on the railways, had now also been dismissed from his post as
tutor to the family to which Anne had been governess, and was showing
signs of disintegration. Emily wrote *Wuthering Heights* between the
autumn of 1845 and July 1846, but it was a year before it was accepted by
T. C. Newby. Even so, Charlotte's *Jane Eyre*, which was then not even
finished, was published by Smith, Elder, before *Wuthering Heights: a
Novel by Ellis Bell* appeared in December 1847 in two volumes, with
Anne's *Agnes Grey* making a third. They were full of misprints, and
*Wuthering Heights* got such a bad press that Newby decided to boost his
sales by encouraging the prevailing rumour that all three novels were the
work of a single author. While Emily stayed at home, hoping to retain her
anonymity, Charlotte and Anne caught the night train to London and
resolved the confusion in person. These circumstances contributed to
Emily's decision to abandon, and probably to destroy, a second novel.
Branwell died in September 1848. Emily, easily the most athletic and
usually the healthiest of the family, caught a cold at his funeral. On 19
December she died of consumption.

*Wuthering Heights* is an extraordinary book by any criteria. To have
been written by a young woman of just 27 whose life was constricted even
by Victorian standards makes it arguably the most powerfully imaginative novel in the English language. From its violent and supernatural
opening it moves inexorably through the present and the dark and stormy
past to the ghostly reunion of Heathcliff and the lost but ill-used love of
his youth. The mystical vision which enabled Emily to write it, and the
strange passions, conflicts, and forces which motivate the characters, are
easier to comprehend in the light of her poetry, much of which is concerned with just these elements in the Gondal world. Heathcliff and
Catherine's death-wish has its parallel, too, in many of her finest poems,
notably 'No coward soul is mine...' and 'Silent is the House...' (sometimes called 'The Prisoner'), both written while she was working on
*Wuthering Heights*. See *Wuthering Heights,* ed. Hilda Marsden and Ian
Jack, 1976; *The Complete Poems,* ed. C. W. Hatfield, 1941; Winifred
Gérin, *Emily Brontë*, new edn 1978 (biography); Muriel Spark and Derek
Stanford, *Emily Brontë: Her Life and Work*, new edn 1985.

**Brooke, Rupert** (1887–1915), poet, was born in Rugby, and educated at
Rugby School, where his father was a housemaster, and King's College,
Cambridge, of which he then became a Fellow. His first book, *Poems*
(1911), revealed a sardonic wit as well as a lyrical bent. While in Berlin in
May 1912 he wrote, or according to some sources 'dashed off', a series of
nostalgic octosyllabic couplets which appeared the following month in

the Cambridge journal *Basileon H* as 'The Old Vicarage, Grantchester', with the final lines: 'Stands the Church clock at ten to three / And is there honey still for tea?' It was also published in *Georgian Poetry 1911–1912*, the first of five anthologies edited by Edward Marsh, to whom Brooke had suggested the idea — the 'Georgian Poets' comprised not so much a movement as a group of younger poets whose work needed a forum. In 1913 Brooke went on a world tour and in Tahiti wrote some love poetry, notably 'Retrospect' and 'Tiare Tahiti', which ranks among his best. On the outbreak of war, he was commissioned in the Royal Naval Volunteer Reserve and saw action at Antwerp in October 1914, after which he wrote five jingoistically-inspired war sonnets. The last of these, 'The Soldier' ('If I should die, think only this of me...'), earned him immortality as a poet-figure. In 1915 his division was posted to the Dardanelles, but he died *en route* at Scyros, of blood poisoning. He was a fine prose writer — see especially *Letters from America*, ed. Henry James (1916) — and also wrote a one-act play, *Lithuania* (1915). See *Collected Poems*, new edn 1987; Christopher Hassall, *Brooke: a Biography*, new edn 1972.

**Brown, George Mackay** (*b*.1921), Scottish poet, novelist, short story writer, and dramatist, was born in Stromness, Orkney, son of a postman, and educated at Stromness Academy. Illness prevented him from continuing his education until 1957, when he went to Newbattle Abbey College (of which *Muir was warden), and again until 1962, when he went to Edinburgh University as a student. Since then he has lived in Stromness. He has been to England just once, in 1989, when he saw the sights of London and Oxford, witnessed the election of *Heaney as Professor of Poetry, and visited some of the haunts of *Newman. He has written: 'Most islands... have a rich tradition of song and music. This is not so in Orkney.... Art in Orkney has devoted itself in the main to the production of stories: the noises and sounds come from the grave mouth of the storyteller.' Orkney belonged to Norway until 1468, and its unusual Pictish/Viking history and folklore, its communal and religious life, its rugged landscape and changeful skies, and the continual presence of the sea which is both a friend and an enemy, provide the themes for his two novels, *Greenvoe* (1972) and *Magnus* (1973); a book of essays, *An Orkney Tapestry* (1969); and many of his short stories and poems — his first volume of verse was appropriately called *The Storm* (1954), and his second *Loaves and Fishes* (1959). Much of his poetry is concerned, too, with the rituals and rhythms of life, death, and resurrection — he became a Catholic in 1961. *The Golden Birds* (1987), two novellas, won the James Tait Black Memorial Prize. His latest volume of stories is *The Masked Fisherman* (1989), and of verse, *The Wreck of the Archangel* (1989). He was awarded the OBE in 1974. See *Selected Poems*, 1977; *Witch and Other Stories*, 1977 (includes 'Master Halcrow, Priest' and 'The Whaler's Return'); Alan Bold, *George Mackay Brown*, 1978.

**Browne,** (Sir) **Thomas** (1605–82), prose writer, was born in London, only son of a silk dealer, and educated at Winchester College and Pembroke College, Oxford, then studied medicine on the Continent, graduating at Oxford in 1635. He set up practice in Norwich, where he remained for the rest of his life, being knighted in 1671 by Charles II as the most distinguished citizen of the town. His major work, *Religio Medici*, which he wrote in about 1636, attempts to reconcile science with religion, and other apparently contradictory elements with each other. It was published in an authorised version in 1643. *Pseudodoxia Epidemica: or Enquiries into Very many received Tenets And commonly presumed Truths* (1646), more usually referred to as 'Vulgar Errors', ranges widely in science, medicine, ritual, and biblical history. *Hydriotaphia: Urne-Buriall* (1658) is a treatise on cremation, inspired by the discovery in Norfolk of some ancient funerary urns. It was published with *The Garden of Cyrus*, an extraordinary speculation into the existence of the 'quincunx' pattern in heaven and on earth, using as its starting point the pattern in which Cyrus is said to have planted trees. The distinction of Browne's writing lies not only in the breadth of thought and learning, but in the style: clauses are intricately fashioned like linguistic bricks and built up into resounding periods. See *Religio Medici and Other Works*, ed. L. C. Martin, 1964; *Major Works*, ed. C. A. Patrides, 1977; Joan Bennett, *Browne*, 1962 (critical study).

**Browning, Elizabeth Barrett** (1806–61), née Moulton Barrett, poet, was born at Coxhoe Hall, Co. Durham, eldest of eleven children of an autocratic West Indian plantation owner. Initially educated alongside her brother, she became a proficient classicist and acquired several modern languages. Some of her early verse was privately printed, but the publication of *Poems* (1844), written at home in London during a period of seclusion caused by ill-health, led to a correspondence with *Browning. Fearing a confrontation with her father, the couple married secretly in 1846 and eloped to Italy, where they settled in Florence. There she took a strongly partisan interest in the struggle for the unification of the Italian states, which took poetic form in *Casa Guidi Windows* (1851) and *Poems before Congress* (1860). Admired in her lifetime, when she was more highly regarded than her husband, she has suffered a decline in reputation, although the case for a reappraisal is well argued by Alethea Hayter in *Mrs Browning: a Poet's Work and Its Setting* (1962). *Aurora Leigh* (1856), a lengthy romantic novel in verse, has recently received attention as a feminist work, but Elizabeth's reputation rests mainly on *Sonnets from the Portuguese* (1850), a technically near-perfect celebration of her love for Browning, and some late lyrics, notably 'A Musical Instrument' and 'Bianca among the Nightingales'. See *Selected Poems*, ed. Margaret Forster, 1988; Margaret Forster, *Elizabeth Barrett Browning*, 1988 (biography).

**Browning, Robert** (1812–89), poet, was born in Camberwell, London, and educated at Peckham School until he was 14, and later at London University, from which he dropped out after six months. His father, a mild man who had become a Bank of England clerk, gave him a firm base in classics and literature and the run of his library of 6000 volumes, while his mother, to whom he was deeply attached, instructed him in religion and music. Until he was 34, he lived at home, financed by his father. In 1833 his family's faith in his poetic destiny was justified by *Pauline*, a piece of romantic soul-baring, parts of which he later regretted. *Paracelsus* (1835), verse dialogues in which he used settings in medieval Europe for an exposition of the conflict between love and knowledge, was admired by the critics. His passion for Italy inspired *Sordello* (1840), an excursion into the philosophy of the poetic soul against a background of the wars of the Guelphs and Ghibellines. That the poem is obscure is due to Browning's conviction that his audience was as widely read as he was and to his reluctance to reveal his inner self. In the meantime his play *Strafford* (1837) had run for only five nights. Two more historical dramas were rejected by the actor-manager W. C. Macready (1793–1873), who accepted *A Blot in the 'Scutcheon* with misgivings — it was performed just three times in 1843 and marked Browning's end as a dramatist (*Colombe's Birthday*, written at the same time, had a week's run in 1853), but not as a dramatic poet.

Between 1841 and 1846 he published eight books of verse under the series title of *Bells and Pomegranates*. *Pippa Passes* (No I) comprises four Italianate scenes in which evil plots are contrasted with the innocence of the silk-worker, Pippa, who appears on the scene but does not intervene in the action. *Dramatic Lyrics* (II), which marked his greatest change of attitude and form, included the monologues, in different metres and rhythms, 'My Last Duchess' and 'Soliloquy of the Spanish Cloister', 'The Pied Piper of Hamelin', written to amuse Macready's son Willy when he was ill, the allusive dialogue 'In a Gondola', and the grim story-poem 'Porphyria's Lover'. *Dramatic Romances and Lyrics* (VII) contained the fine religious monologue 'The Bishop Orders His Tomb at St Praxed's Church', the lyrics 'Home-Thoughts from Abroad' and 'Meeting at Night', and the galloping but wholly imaginary 'How They Brought the Good News from Ghent to Aix'. After his marriage in 1846 (see E. B. *Browning), he and his wife lived in Florence until her death in 1861, during which time, in spite of the distraction of the hyperactive childhood of their son, the sculptor Robert 'Pen' Browning (1849–1912), it was she who was the most productive. Apart from *Christmas-Eve and Easter-Day* (1850), which vividly explores the threefold choice of worship then exercising Christians, his only new work was *Men and Women* (1855), 50 poems (plus 'One Word More: to E.B.B.') which include his most outspoken statements of sexual love, as well as 'Fra Lippo Lippi' and 'Andrea del Sarto', and the romance, 'Childe Roland to the Dark Tower

Came'. After Elizabeth died, he returned with Pen to London, where on his father's death in 1866 his sister Sarianna came to keep house for him — his proposal of marriage to Lady Ashburton in 1871 was couched so tactlessly that it could only be refused. *Dramatis Personae* (1864) contains the last of his shorter poems of quality, but *The Ring and the Book* (1868–9) placed him in popular acclaim second only to *Tennyson among living poets. Through dramatic monologues in blank verse, it retells the case of Count Guido Franceschini, accused in 1698 of murdering his teenage wife. Browning found the lurid and the legal details in a 'square old yellow book' he had picked up on a Florentine market stall in 1860. He died in Venice the day his last book, *Asolando: Fancies and Facts* (1890), was published, and was buried in Westminster Abbey.

Just as the speaker in a Browning monologue masks the poet from the reader, so Browning's outer persona obscured a character which puzzled his contemporaries. He was concerned to use grotesque as well as conventional subjects, and broken rhythms, discordances, and colloquialisms as well as passages of beauty, to demonstrate the devious workings of the mind, particularly under stress, and in doing so he brought Victorian poetry into the twentieth century. See Donald Thomas, *Robert Browning: a Life Within Life*, new edn 1989; Philip Drew, *The Poetry of Robert Browning: a Critical Introduction*, 1970.

**Buchan, John** (1875–1940), Scottish novelist, biographer, and statesman, was born in Perth, son of a Free Church minister, and educated at Hutcheson's Boys School and Brasenose College, Oxford, where he won the Stanhope historical essay prize and the Newdigate Prize for poetry, was President of the Union, and got a first in Greats. He was called to the Bar, worked in South Africa on the staff of the High Commission and, on his return, became a journalist. In 1927 he was elected Conservative MP for the Scottish universities, a seat he held until 1935 when, as Lord Tweedsmuir of Elfield, he was appointed Governor-General of Canada. He wrote his first novel, *Prester John* (1910), because he was 'appalled by the dullness of most boys' books'. His subsequent success as a writer of adventure stories, the first of which, *The Thirty-Nine Steps* (1915), was written while he was confined to bed by illness, was due not only to his plots and settings, but to the realistic detail with which he delineates his various heroes. These books have tended to obscure his influence in other fields of literature. *Poems, Scots and English* (1917) contains some fine nature poetry in Scots, while his anthology of Scottish verse, *The Northern Muse* (1924), was the first of its kind. He wrote several fine biographies, of which *Montrose* (1928) is the classic study of that unfortunate Scottish general, and *Sir Walter Scott* (1932) contains good if sometimes unnecessarily apologetic criticism. See *Memory Hold-the-Door*, new edn 1984 (autobiography); Janet Adam Smith, *John Buchan*, 1965 (biography).

**Bunyan, John** (1628–88), preacher and prose writer, was born in Elstow, near Bedford, son of a travelling tinker, and learned to read and write at a local school. He was conscripted into the Parliamentary army in 1644, serving mainly on garrison duty until discharged in 1647. In about 1655 he joined the Nonconformist church at Bedford of John Gifford, where he soon became a prominent member and then a preacher, while from 1656 he published numerous tracts and pamphlets. His first wife died in 1658, leaving him with four children, the eldest of whom was blind. He married again in 1659. At the Restoration of the monarchy and of the bishops in 1660, he was charged with preaching illegally, and was offered the choice of stopping his religious activities or going to jail. He chose the latter, and was sentenced to twelve years, during which he wrote a spiritual autobiography, *Grace Abounding to the Chief of Sinners* (1666), and much if not all of the first part of *The Pilgrim's Progress, From This World to That Which is to Come* (1678). This rehearses Bunyan's own spiritual struggles in allegorical form, as Christian, in the author's dream, sets out from the City of Destruction, having failed to convince his family to accompany him. He extricates himself from the Slough of Despond, and journeys through various hazards, including the Valley of the Shadow of Death, Vanity Fair, and Doubting Castle, to the Gates of Heaven, meeting on the way Obstinate, Pliable, Mr Worldly Wiseman, the monster Apollyon, Giant Despair, Ignorance, and others, and helped along by sundry more pleasing qualities. *The Pilgrim's Progress* is more than just an allegorical quest romance or even an expression of Puritanism. It is a statement, founded on the author's experience as well as his beliefs, of support for the English poor, set in a recognisable English landscape, and a suspenseful story, written in a straightforward, basically monosyllabic but beautifully expressive prose which the English labouring man, and his wife, could readily appreciate.

The rest of Bunyan's life was one of heavy pastoral duties (he was elected to lead the congregation in 1671), but included a further short term of imprisonment in 1677 and periods spent hiding from arrest. In 1685, fearing a further term or perhaps even a sentence of death, he made over his meagre property to his wife. He still found time, however, for several further literary works, including *The Life and Death of Mr Badman, Presented to the World in a Familiar Dialogue between Mr Wiseman and Mr Attentive* (1680), which can almost be classed also as a realistic novel of social life; *The Holy War* (1682), in which the field of battle is a town rather than the mind of man; and the second part of *The Pilgrim's Progress* (1684), in which Christian's aged wife and her children make their own journey. He probably died from pneumonia caught while preaching in London. Of his posthumously published works, *Of Antichrist and His Ruin* (1692) is the most notable. See Christopher Hill, *A Turbulent, Seditious and Factious People: John Bunyan and His Church*, new edn 1989; Roger Sharrock, *John Bunyan*, new edn 1984 (critical study).

**Burke, Edmund** (1729–97), Irish political philosopher, was born in Dublin (his father was a Protestant attorney and his mother a Catholic), and educated at a Quaker school in Co. Kildare and at Trinity College, Dublin. In 1750 he began studying law in London, but gave it up for literature against the will of his father. His first two books were published anonymously. *A Vindication of Natural Society* (1756) is an ironic attack on the views of the 1st Lord Bolingbroke (1678–1751). In *A Philosophical Enquiry into the Origin of our Ideas of the Sublime and Beautiful* (1757) he distinguishes between the sublime (which can be born of mystery or even horror) and beauty (which is founded on love). He entered Parliament in 1765, and was a leading light of the Whigs until his retirement in 1794. A halting delivery made him a poor speaker, but there is little wrong with his eloquence or ideals when cast in print. He was an empiricist who believed in the constitutional right of Parliament to govern, expressed in *Thoughts on the Cause of the Present Discontents* (1770); in a unified America; in free trade with Ireland and toleration of Catholicism; in reform of the Indian administration (with *Sheridan he formulated and delivered the case for the impeachment of the Governor-General, Warren Hastings); and in peace and change in France, not revolution (advocated in 1790 in *Reflections on the Revolution in France*). See *The Writings and Speeches of Edmund Burke*, various editors, 1981– ; Stanley Ayling, *Edmund Burke: His Life and Opinions*, 1988.

**Burney, Fanny** (1752–1840), novelist and diarist, was born in King's Lynn, daughter of a distinguished musical scholar, and was largely self-educated at home in Norfolk and London through reading, writing, and meeting her father's acquaintances. *Evelina: or, The History of a Young Lady's Entrance into the World* (1778), written in the form of letters and set in the social climate which its author had so acutely observed, was highly praised and enormously successful. She was invited to join the formidable literary coterie of both sexes, the Blue Stocking Circle, about whose members she wrote a satirical play, *The Witlings,* which her father refused her to allow to be performed. By contrast with *Evelina,* the heroine of *Cecilia* (1782) starts as an heiress but achieves her true love only after some extraordinary adventures. More dramatic and less comic than *Evelina,* it was equally well received. Fanny had a position at court from 1786 to 1791 and in 1793 married a French refugee, General d'Arblay, who died in 1818. In the meantime she had written *Camilla* (1796), which revealed that she had lost her touch as a novelist but which earned her enough to build a cottage. *The Wanderer* (1814), enormously long and unevenly written, was savagely treated by the critics but made her some welcome money. *The Diary and Letters of Madame d'Arblay 1778–1840,* published shortly after her death, and *The Early Diary of Frances Burney 1768–78* (1889) demonstrate her discerning eye and command of dialogue. See Joyce Hemlow, *The History of Fanny Burney*, 1958.

**Burns, Robert** (1759–96), Scottish poet, was born in Alloway, Ayrshire. The eldest son of a poor farmer, he went to school at the age of six, and was later educated at home by a teacher hired by the families in the district. At 15, he was the farm's chief labourer. He supplemented his education by voracious reading, wrote poetry, and indulged enthusiastically in the rural pursuits of drinking, dancing, singing, and fornication. When his father died in 1784, he and his brother Gilbert rented a farm at Mossgiel, which failed. By 1786 he had so many financial and domestic problems that he seriously considered emigrating to Jamaica — two girls were pregnant by him, and the father of one of them, while refusing to let him marry his daughter, whose name was Jean Armour, was bent on retribution. Burns managed to raise the money from potential purchasers to have some of his poems printed. This Kilmarnock edition of *Poems, Chiefly in the Scottish Dialect* (1786) changed his life. He became the toast of Edinburgh society — it is to this period that his celebrated correspondence with Mrs MacLehose ('Clarinda') belongs — and he married Jean, though not before she had borne him two sets of twins. Mere fame, however, did not pay the bills, and after trying farming again, Burns became a customs official in Dumfries. His main literary task from 1787 until his death from rheumatic fever was to contribute to and edit (unpaid) two compendia of songs, *A Select Collection of Original Scottish Airs* (published from 1793) and *The Scots Musical Museum* (1787–1803). In 1790, to oblige a friend, he wrote a version of a scary folktale, 'Tam o'Shanter'. This narrative poem of sustained intensity is today recited at celebrations all over the world on Burns's birthday.

Burns is a poet of simple concepts, simply expressed. He employed a variety of metres to suit different poetic forms. His range is as prodigious as his output: satire ('Holy Willie's Prayer'), scenes of rustic life ('The Holy Fair', 'Poor Mailie's Elegy'), epistles to friends, epigrams, nature poems ('To a Mouse'), and songs — love songs ('A Red, Red Rose', 'O, Wert Thou in the Cauld Blast', 'Ye banks and braes o' bonie Doon'), and songs of the countryside ('The Birks of Aberfeldy'). He was concerned not only with Scottish themes and with promoting his area of the country as a source of poetry, but with the Scottish language, in which he was influenced by reading Robert Fergusson (1750–74), who in his short but productive life had developed a composite, poetic Scots, employing words from different Scottish dialects. Unlike Fergusson, Burns wrote equally well in English and in Scots, and even uses both in the same poem ('The Cotter's Saturday Night', 'To a Mountain Daisy'). He is one of the few major poets in any language to have overcome the handicap of an indigent upbringing — he was called 'the ploughman poet'. He was also an outspoken opponent of hypocrisy and a champion of the rights of the poor. See *Letters of Robert Burns*, 2nd edn ed. G. Ross Roy, 1985; David Daiches, *Robert Burns*, 3rd edn 1981 (critical biography); Richard Hindle Fowler, *Robert Burns*, 1988 (critical study).

**Butler, Samuel** (1612–80), poet, was born in Strensham, Worcestershire, son of a well-to-do farmer, and educated at King's School, Worcester. He is said to have served in various aristocratic households. By his own account, he met a colonel of the Parliamentary army and his clerk in London during the Civil War, and used them as the basis for the pedantic Presbyterian knight and the argumentative Nonconformist squire of his mock-heroic poem, *Hudibras*. After the Restoration of the monarchy in 1660, Butler became secretary to the Lord President of Wales and steward of Ludlow Castle. The first two parts of *Hudibras* were published in 1663 and 1664. Between 1667 and 1669 he wrote his 'Characters', a series of satirical sketches on the failings and foibles of the times, which were not published until 1759. *Hudibras* Part III was published in 1678, earning him £100 from Charles II and a pension, which belies the poet's own claim that his reward for supporting the King with his satire was penury. *Hudibras,* written in rough-hewn octosyllabic couplets, has every claim to be ranked among the great English satirical poems, but where *Dryden and *Pope take a rapier, Butler employs a pikestaff. Those of the persuasion of Hudibras, for instance, 'Call fire, and sword, and desolation / A godly, thorough reformation'. His images are deliberately base, too: 'And like a lobster boil'd, the morn / From black to red begins to turn.' See *Hudibras Parts I and II and Selected Other Writings*, ed. John Wilder and Hugh de Quehen, 1973.

**Butler, Samuel** (1835–1902), novelist, prose writer, poet, philosopher, and painter, was born in the rectory of Langar, Nottinghamshire, son of a future canon of Lincoln and grandson of the Bishop of Lichfield and Coventry. After accompanying his parents on a tour of Europe by rail (a new phenomenon) in 1843, he was educated at Shrewsbury School and St John's College, Cambridge. Religious doubts, expressed in a correspondence with his father which is accurately but not fully reproduced in *The Way of All Flesh*, led him to abandon his family's intention that he should study for the ministry, and when they opposed his ambition to become a painter instead, he emigrated to New Zealand in 1859, where he made a small fortune by breeding sheep — his accounts of his experiences, edited by his father, were published in 1863 as *A First Year in Canterbury Settlement*. In 1864 he returned to England, settled in London, and studied painting, later exhibiting on several occasions at the Royal Academy. While he was in New Zealand, he had contributed a witty article to the *Christchurch Press* on 'Darwin and the Machines', which became the basis of *Erewhon, or Over the Range* (1872), published anonymously. The state which the traveller finds (Erewhon is an anagram of 'nowhere') is not so much a Utopia as a parody of Victorian society. It was his only book which enjoyed any success in his lifetime. *The Fair Haven: a Work in Defence of the Miraculous Element in Our Lord's Ministry* (1873), also published anonymously, was based on a pamphlet privately printed in

1865, and is in point of fact a cleverly presented and amusing argument *against* the Resurrection.

Unwise investments in Canadian stocks led to several visits there to try and recover his funds, on one of which (in 1875) he composed 'A Psalm of Montreal', with the immortal refrain 'O God! O Montreal!', satirising the treatment afforded by the local museum to a statue of a Greek discus-thrower. In 1877 he published *Life and Habit*, the first of several works in which he questioned *Darwin's line of reasoning. His wide interests are reflected also in two Alpine travel books, two published oratorios, prose translations of the *Odyssey* and the *Iliad*, and two bizarre critical studies, *The Authoress of the Odyssey* (1897) and *Shakespeare's Sonnets Reconsidered* (1899). In *Erewhon Revisited* (1901) his society founds its own religion. *The Way of All Flesh*, on which he worked for 30 years, was published posthumously in 1903. Technically a novel, it is also a blend of autobiography (particularly describing an unhappy childhood and rebellious youth, of which genre it was a forerunner), social satire, and eccentric interpretation of the scientific, psychological, and religious theories of the age. His own views on evolution were inspired by the French naturalist, Chevalier de Lamarck (1744–1829), and these, his stance on religious matters, and his attitude to money and wealth, influenced *Shaw, who refers to his debt in the Preface to *Major Barbara*. See Philip Henderson, *Samuel Butler: the Incarnate Bachelor*, 1953.

**Byron, (George Gordon), 6th Lord** (1788–1824), poet, was born in London, but spent his childhood in Scotland, and inherited the title from his great-uncle in 1798. He was educated at Harrow, where a club-foot did not hamper his athletic pursuits, and Trinity College, Cambridge. A selection of poetic juvenilia, *Hours of Idleness* (1807), was not unjustifiably savaged in the *Edinburgh Review*, which nettled Byron into responding with *English Bards and Scotch Reviewers* (1809). Between 1809 and 1811 he travelled in and around the Mediterranean and wrote the first two cantos of a spiritual travelogue, *Childe Harold's Pilgrimage*, which were an immediate success when published in 1812. Byron promptly turned out four dramatic tales — *The Giaour* (1813), *The Bride of Abydos* (1813), *The Corsair* (1814), and *Lara* (1814) — which contain some passages of fine poetry. He also indulged in two spectacular affairs — with Lady Caroline Lamb, wife of the future Prime Minister, Lord Melbourne, and with Augusta Leigh, his own half-sister, the daughter of his profligate father by a first marriage to Lady Carmarthen. The daughter born to Mrs Leigh in 1814 is generally regarded to have been Byron's. In 1815 he embarked on a disastrous marriage with Annabella Milbanke, who walked out on him soon after the birth of their daughter Ada, claiming he was insane. In 1816, hounded by creditors and ostracised by society, he left England for good.

For a few months Byron lived on Lake Geneva, next door to *Shelley, his mistress Mary Godwin, and Mary's step-sister Claire Clairmont, with whom Byron continued an affair which had begun in London — a daughter, Allegra, was born in 1817. During this time he wrote Canto III of *Childe Harold*. Canto IV was finished in Venice in 1817. In the Italian burlesque poetry of Luigi Pulci (1432–84) Byron now found the form and metre (*ottava rima*, stanzas of eight iambic pentameters rhyming *abababcc*) for the kind of epic satire he was contemplating. He experimented with *Beppo* (1817), a slender tale of technical infidelity. The 16 cantos of his unfinished masterpiece, *Don Juan*, were published in parts from 1819. In 1819 he met, in Venice, Teresa, Countess Guiccioli, and moved to Ravenna to be near her. She left her husband for him in 1821. Through her brother he met the Carbonari, a secret society for the liberation of Italy, which inspired two Venetian dramas, *Marino Faliero* (1820) and *The Two Foscari* (1821). The former was staged at Drury Lane in 1821 against his wishes, and failed, much to his annoyance. *Don Juan* was attacked in 1821 in the preface to the Poet Laureate Robert Southey's lamentable elegy on the late King George III, *A Vision of Judgement*. Never one to suffer fools or critics gladly, Byron produced his own version, *The Vision of Judgement* (1822), a satire so devastating that it had to be published anonymously and the publisher was fined £100 for 'calumny'. In 1823, bored with Italy, and even with Teresa, and suspecting a falling-off in his poetic reputation, Byron went to Greece, offering his services, and money, to the local freedom-fighters against the Turks. He saw no action, dying of malaria at Missolonghi in April 1824.

For many years the more romantic and notorious aspects of Byron's life overshadowed his poetic reputation. He wrote some memorable short poems, including 'When We Two Parted', 'So We'll Go No More A-Roving', 'She Walks in Beauty', and 'The Destruction of Sennacherib' — the last two published in *Hebrew Melodies* (1815) — and 'The Isles of Greece', which appears in *Don Juan* Canto III. His true *métier*, however, was satire. *Don Juan* is also the most genuinely funny major poem in the English language. Its picaresque hero is sent abroad at 16, having been discovered *flagrante delicto* in a married woman's bed. After a dramatic and romantic Odyssey to Greece, Constantinople, and Russia, he is sent by the Empress Catherine to England as her special envoy. The tale is cut short at the intriguing point at which a ghostly friar materialises in Juan's bedroom in a Gothic mansion and is revealed as one of his fellow-guests: 'In full, voluptuous but *not o'er*grown bulk, / The phantom of her frolic Grace — Fitz-Fulke'. The form and metre gave Byron freedom to digress on all manner of topics, and to use outrageous rhymes and familiar, often down-to-earth, diction and images, while the couplet at the end of each stanza invited the pithy epigram which had been such a feature of the satire of *Dryden and *Pope. See Leslie A. Marchand, *Byron: a Portrait*, new edn 1987; Andrew Rutherford, *Byron: a Critical Study*, 1961; Leslie A. Marchand, *Byron's Poetry: a Critical Introduction*, 1965.

**Carleton, William** (1794–1869), Irish novelist and short story writer, was born in Prillisk, Co. Tyrone, youngest of 14 children of a small farmer. Bilingual, he had a rudimentary hedge-school education, but enjoyed a rich background of songs and stories from his parents. He was destined for the priesthood, but instead, after trying various jobs, he began writing for the Protestant paper, *Christian Examiner*, in 1828. Two series of *Traits and Stories of the Irish Peasantry*, which had appeared in a number of journals, were published in book form in 1830 and 1833. They deal with a wide variety of aspects of rural life — funerals, wakes, weddings, folklore, religion, sports, fights — and considering that he had no literary tradition from which to work, they are remarkable for their exuberance, wit, descriptive power, and dialogue. They are also the first genuine accounts of peasant life in Ireland before the Famine of 1845 to 1848. *Tales of Ireland* followed in 1834. Subsequently he wrote more than fifteen novels, of which *Fardorougha the Miser* (1839) is the most notable. *The Black Prophet* (1847), *The Red Hall, or the Baronet's Daughter* (1852), afterwards published as *The Black Baronet*, and *The Squanders of Castle Squander* (1852) deal gloomily and in lurid detail with the effects of the Famine. They are not at all as appealing as his shorter stories and pieces, and are written as though didactically directed to an audience who would know nothing of the background. See *Autobiography*, 1896 (published with his letters); Benedict Kiely, *Poor Scholar: a Study of the Works and Days of William Carleton*, new edn 1972.

**Carlyle, Thomas** (1795–1881), Scottish historian, biographer, critic, translator, and thinker, was born in Ecclefechan, Dumfriesshire, son of a stonemason, and educated at Annan Academy and Edinburgh University. Having given up the idea of the ministry, he taught for several years, took up and then abandoned the law, and studied German literature. In 1825 he published *The Life of Friedrich Schiller*, and in 1826 he married Jane Baillie Welsh, a girl of considerable intellect and owner of the small, remote estate of Craigenputtock, near Dumfries, where they lived from 1828 to 1834. Here he wrote *Sartor Resartus*, first published in *Fraser's Magazine* 1833–4, a witty 'symbolic myth' in the form of a philosophical treatise on clothing. In 1834 the couple moved to Cheyne Row in London. *The French Revolution* (1837) plants the reader vividly in the midst of the events described. *On Heroes, Hero-Worship and the Heroic in History* (1841), and a six-volume biography of Frederick the Great (1858–65), enabled Carlyle to indulge in his favourite intellectual pastime of transcendentalism, finding precedents in the past to explain events and characters in recent history, which in turn offer pointers to the future. After Jane died in 1866 he wrote little. Apart from his breadth of vision, his appeal lay in the distinctive style he developed in mid-career, which has been called 'ejaculatory': a vast vocabulary backs conventional speech-patterns. See *Sartor Resartus*, ed. Peter Sabot and Kerry

McSweeney, 1987; Ian Campbell, *Thomas Carlyle*, 1974 (biography); A. L. Le Quesne, *Carlyle*, 1982 (introduction to his ideas).

**Carroll, Lewis**, pseudonym of Charles Lutwidge Dodgson (1832–98), author and mathematician, was born in Daresbury, Lancashire, son of the future Archdeacon of Richmond, and educated at Rugby School and Christ Church, Oxford, where he then became a lecturer. Diffident and shy, he was able best to communicate with children. A story first told on the river to the daughters of the Dean of Christ Church was published in 1865 as *Alice's Adventures in Wonderland*, and for its wit, weird logic, linguistic fun, and wild rhymes, has remained popular with children and adults ever since. *Through the Looking-Glass and What Alice Found There* (1871) is slightly more contrived (as though the mathematician had influenced the story-teller), but in Humpty Dumpty, Tweedledum and Tweedledee, the White Knight, and the Red Queen, it contains characters as memorable as any in the earlier book. His other venture into fiction, *Sylvie and Bruno* (1889) and a sequel, was not much appreciated even by his contemporaries, unlike *The Hunting of the Snark* (1876), a sustained nonsense-poem, many of whose witty allusions are just as valid today. Of a number of mathematical treatises, *Euclid and His Modern Rivals* (1879) was the most influential, though E. V. Lucas (1868–1938) records: 'Scattered up and down it were many jokes, which would have been more numerous but for the criticisms of friends'. Dodgson was an accomplished photographer, especially of little girls. See *The Complete Works*, introduction by Alexander Woolcott, new edn 1989; Derek Hudson, *Lewis Carroll: an Illustrated Biography*, new edn 1981.

**Cary, Joyce** (1888–1957), Irish novelist, short story writer, and poet, was born in Londonderry, but spent most of his life in England. He was educated at Clifton College and, after two years studying art, at Trinity College, Oxford. He served with the Red Cross in the first Balkan War 1912–13, and was from 1913 to 1920 a member of the Nigerian Political Service — he saw action with the Nigerian Regiment in the Cameroons in 1915. In 1920 he and his wife settled in Oxford. Beginning with *Aissa Saved* (1932), he wrote four novels with African settings, of which the most notable, and memorable, is the tragicomic *Mr Johnson* (1939). *Charley is My Darling* (1940) echoes his own youth, and *A House of Children* (1941) is an autobiographical evocation of a childhood holiday in Ireland. *Herself Surprised* (1941), *To Be a Pilgrim* (1942), and *The Horse's Mouth* (1944) are novels about the world of the artist which are designed as a trilogy — in each, the narrative is told and the other characters observed by a different one of the three main protagonists. He deals in the same way with aspects of politics in *Prisoners of Grace* (1952), *Except the Lord* (1953), and *Not Honour More* (1955). In these six works in particular, he is concerned with the place, and problems, of the creative individual trying to make his own world out of, and his own way through, the repressions and contradictions of a changing contemporary society. See Alan Bishop, *Gentleman Rider: a Biography of Joyce Cary*, new edn 1989; Andrew Wright, *Cary: a Preface to His Novels*, 1958.

**Causley, Charles** (*b*.1917), poet and anthologist, was born in Launceston, Cornwall, and educated locally. He served in the Royal Navy in World War II, returning afterwards to his career as a local primary school teacher, which he remained until his retirement. His first volume of poetry was *Farewell, Aggie Weston* (1951), but his reputation was confirmed by his third, *Union Street* (1957), with a preface by Edith *Sitwell. Causley excels at the ballad form, taking his images from things he knows well — the sea, the Cornish countryside and folklore, Christianity, children. He often uses popular diction and reworks traditional rhythms and rhymes to create effects of intensity and surprise, as in 'Innocent's Song': 'Watch where he comes walking / Out of the Christmas flame, / Dancing, double-talking: — / Herod is his name.' (Innocence is a recurring theme in his poetry.) His narrative poems, outwardly artless but constructed and finished with precision, often reveal disturbing truths. 'The Ballad of Charlotte Dymond', 'Mother, get up, undo the door', and 'Ballad of Jack Cornwall' are good examples of this. Much of Causley's poetry is accessible also to children, for whom he has compiled several anthologies, the first of which, *Dawn and Dusk* (1962), broke new ground in that it comprised exclusively contemporary poetry originally written for adult audiences. He has also written poetry and plays especially for children. He was awarded the Queen's Gold Medal for Poetry in 1967 and was made CBE in 1986. See *Collected Poems 1951–1975*, new edn 1988.

**Chapman, George** (1559–1634), poet, dramatist, and translator, was born near Hitchin, Hertfordshire, and probably studied at Oxford or Cambridge, but without taking a degree. He is mentioned in the 1590s as a writer of comedies, but his first known published work, *The Shadow of Night* (1594), consists of two poems of obscure meaning. *Ovid's Banquet of Sense* (1595), however, demonstrates the qualities which enabled him to finish gracefully *Marlowe's *Hero and Leander* (1586). His translation of seven books of Homer's *Iliad* (1598) was the first instalment of *The Whole Work of Homer* (1616), the *Iliad* in rhyming lines of 14 syllables, the *Odyssey* in heroic couplets. His grasp of Greek was tenuous, and his interpolations inappropriate, but this was a monumental achievement which thrilled his contemporaries and inspired one of *Keats's most quoted sonnets, beginning, 'Much have I travelled in the realms of gold...'. Chapman's comedies, of which *All Fools* (1599) still reads well, are based largely on Roman or continental models, with a dash of ethics and topical satire — *Eastward Ho* (1605), written with *Jonson and John Marston (1576–1634) resulted in his being jailed for insulting the Scots.

His tragedies *Bussy D'Ambois* (1607) and its sequel (1613), and the two parts of the *The Conspiracy and Tragedy of Charles Duke of Byron* (1608), are based on near-contemporary figures from French history. As a dramatist, Chapman is regarded as a gifted intellectual whose works lack commercial instinct. See M. C. Bradbrook, *George Chapman*, 1977 (profile).

**Chatterton, Thomas** (1752–70), poet, was born in Bristol shortly after the death of his father, a schoolmaster. His mother, then 21, earned a living by keeping a dame school and taking in sewing. The boy was educated at a charity-school, and in 1767 was apprenticed to a lawyer. He had begun to write verse when he was ten, and soon afterwards he forged a 'medieval' poem which he presented to his teacher. Further forgeries of ancient documents followed, which he sold to local worthies, including a verse tragedy, *Aella*, purporting to be by a priest called Sir Thomas Rowley. Chatterton now invented a complete corpus of medieval poetry for Rowley, in which he tried unsuccessfully to interest *Walpole. In 1770 he broke his indentures by threatening to commit suicide, and went to London to earn his living as a writer. He succeeded for only a few weeks. On 24 August, exhausted and near starving, he poisoned himself in his lodgings. He was not yet 18. His own verses, mainly satirical, are largely of a juvenile nature. The 'Rowley' poems, however, though written in a pseudo-medieval English, with many spurious or misused archaisms, contain much of genuine lyrical excellence, and it is these and the circumstances of his death which led to his being regarded as one of the forerunners of the Romantic poets, and inspired *Wordsworth's reference in 'Resolution and Independence' to 'Chatterton, the marvellous boy, / The sleepless soul, that perished in his pride…'. See *Complete Works*, ed. D. S. Taylor and B. B. Hoover, 1971; Linda Kelly, *The Marvellous Boy: the Life and Myth of Thomas Chatterton*, 1971.

**Chaucer, Geoffrey** (*c*.1343–1400), poet, public servant, and courtier, was the son of a prosperous London wine-merchant. He may have attended St Paul's Cathedral School, and he almost certainly studied law between 1361 and 1367. The earliest record of him is in 1357 as a page in the household of Elizabeth, Countess of Ulster, wife of Lionel, third son of Edward III. He served with the army in France in 1359, being taken prisoner and then released for a ransom, £16 of which was paid by the King, in whose service he appears in 1367 as valet. In this capacity he undertook the first of many diplomatic missions to the Continent which continued into the reign of Richard II. In 1372–3 and 1378 he was in Italy, the physical and intellectual environment of which did much to inspire his poetic imagination. In about 1366 he had married Philippa (*d.c.*1378), daughter of Sir Payne Roet and sister of Katherine Swynford, mistress and, later, third wife of John of Gaunt. Chaucer was Controller of

Customs and Subsidy of Wools, Skins, and Hides in the port of London 1374–86, and Clerk of the King's Works 1389–91. His last public office was Deputy Forester of the royal forest of North Petherton in Somerset. On 4 December 1399 he took out a 53-year lease on a house in the garden of Westminster Abbey, where Henry VII's chapel now stands, and he was buried in the Abbey on his death the following year — his monument was set up in 1555 in what later came to be known as Poets' Corner. From internal evidence, the order in which he wrote his main poetical works is as follows:

*The Book of the Duchess*: written in octosyllabic couplets to commemorate the death of Blanche, first wife of John of Gaunt, in 1369. First printed in 1532 in Chaucer's works, ed. William Thynne (*d.*1546).

*The House of Fame*: an entertaining, unfinished dream poem in octosyllabic couplets, written between 1374 and 1385, and first printed in 1477/8 by William Caxton (*c.*1422–91).

*The Life of St Cecilia*: written in rhyme royal soon after 1373 and afterwards incorporated in *The Canterbury Tales* as the 'Second Nun's Tale'; it marks the beginning of the Italian influence on his work.

*The Parlement of Foules*: an imaginative treatment in rhyme royal of the dream poem, the Old French device of argument among birds, and the courtly disputation on questions of love, probably written for St Valentine's Day 1383. It is unusual and all the more lively in that the birds represent different strata in the human social hierarchy of the time, and the debate assumes the trappings of the English Parliament. First printed by Caxton in 1477/8 as *The Temple of Bras*.

*Troilus and Criseyde*: Professor F. N. Robinson in his edition of the works calls this 'Chaucer's supreme example of sustained narration... unsurpassed in its kind in later English poetry'. Written in rhyme royal not before 1385, it has more characterisation, tragic passion, and feeling for plot and setting than its immediate source, *Filostrato* by Giovanni Boccaccio (1313–75). First printed by Caxton in about 1482. (See also *Henryson.)

*The Legend of Good Women*: unfinished accounts of famous legendary and historical women, written between 1382 and 1394 and first printed in Thynne's edition. It marks the first use in English of the decasyllabic (heroic) couplet, in which *The Canterbury Tales* is mainly composed.

*The Canterbury Tales*: originally projected in about 1386, less than a fifth of its tales were completed, and they were never put into any proper order. Even so, the result is one of the most sublime and enjoyable works in English literature, and though there are precedents for the format, Chaucer's treatment is unique in that the story-tellers represent a wide variety of social classes, they interact with each other, and their characters are developed through their stories. The first printed edition was by Caxton in 1477/8. There are good modern verse translations by Nevill Coghill (1951) and David Wright (1985).

*The Romaunt of the Rose* is only attributed to Chaucer, but may partly be his. He wrote two prose works, *Boece*, a translation of *De Consolatione Philosophiae* of Boethius (*c*.475–524), and *A Treatise on the Astrolabe*, a simplified translation from the Latin made in 1392 for a boy who may have been his own son. It is significant that he always wrote in English, rather than French. In doing so he developed the language as a literary medium, while contributing to the dominance of the South-East Midland dialect on its way to becoming standard English. See *The Works*, ed. F. N. Robinson, new edn 1957; *The Riverside Chaucer*, ed. L. D. Benson, 1988; H. S. Bennett, *Chaucer and the Fifteenth Century*, 1947; S. S. Hussey, *Chaucer: an Introduction*, 1981.

**Chesterfield, (Philip Dormer Stanhope), 4th Earl of** (1694–1773), statesman and prose writer, was born in London and educated privately and, for a year, at Trinity Hall, Cambridge, before doing the Grand Tour of Europe. He was elected to Parliament while still only 20, and succeeded to his father's title in 1726. He was Ambassador to Holland 1728–32, from where he returned with his mistress. She bore him a son soon afterwards, called Philip, to whom from the age of five Chesterfield addressed a voluminous series of letters of elegant exhortation (published in 1774). On Philip's death in 1766, he transferred his epistolary attentions to his godson and heir, another Philip. Chesterfield had a long and distinguished political career. Apart from his journalistic and political writings, he allowed little to be published in his lifetime. *Miscellaneous Works* (including 'Letters to His Friends') appeared in 1777, as did *Characters of Eminent Personages of His Own Time*, including George I and Queen Caroline. Among the coinages and dicta in his letters to his illegitimate son are: 'An injury is much sooner forgotten than an insult' (1746); 'Take care of the minutes, for the hours will take care of themselves' (1747); 'Do as you would be done by is the surest method of pleasing' (1747); 'I should be sorry if you were an egregious fop; but I profess that, of the two, I would rather have you a fop than a sloven' (1749); '…a chapter of accidents…' (1753). See *Letters to His Son and Others*, new edn 1984.

**Chesterton, G(ilbert) K(eith)** (1874–1936), novelist, poet, critic, and journalist, was born in London, elder son of a prominent estate-agent, and educated at St Paul's School and the Slade School of Art. After a spell in publishing, he became a journalist, a designation he never abandoned even at the height of his fame. His first book, a volume of verse called *The White Knight*, appeared in 1900, and his first novel, *The Napoleon of Notting Hill*, a fantasy of the future, in 1904. At the same time he was writing critical studies of *Browning (1903) and *Dickens (1903), while also contributing to a number of journals. He was associated with *Belloc and his paradoxical ideas of a neo-medieval socialism. (So close was this association that *Shaw coined for them the name 'Chesterbelloc'.) He became a convert to Catholicism in 1922, as had been presaged in his critical articles and in the controversial *Orthodoxy* (1909). *The Innocence of Father Brown* (1911) was the first of five collections of detective stories about that unassuming priest, whose character was based on Chesterton's Yorkshire friend, Father O'Connor. As a poet, he had a fine command of rollicking rhythm, which he exploits to good effect not only in 'Lepanto' and 'The Rolling English Road', but also in more reflective poems such as 'The Secret People' and 'A Song of Gifts to God'. See *The Essential G. K. Chesterton*, introduction by P. J. Kavanagh, new edn 1986; *Autobiography*, new edn 1986; Michael Coren, *Gilbert: the Man Who Was G. K. Chesterton*, 1989.

**Churchill,** (Rt Hon. Sir) **Winston S(penser)** (1874–1965), statesman, historian, and biographer, was born at Blenheim Palace, son of the politician, Lord Randolph Churchill, and educated at Harrow. From 1895 to 1900 he combined the functions of war correspondent and army officer, performing both with distinction in Cuba, India — about which he wrote *The Story of the Malakand Field Force* (1898) — Sudan (where he took part in the last great cavalry charge of the British army and won a second medal for bravery), and South Africa (during the Boer War). He was elected to Parliament in 1900, in which year he published a loosely autobiographical novel, *Savrola*, followed in 1906 by his biography of his father. From then until his death he was both politician and author. His posts included First Lord of the Admiralty 1911–15, Chancellor of the Exchequer 1924–9, Prime Minister 1940–5 and 1951–5. Notable books are *The World Crisis* (1923–31), *Marlborough: His Life and Times* (1933–8), *The Second World War* (1948–54), and *A History of the English-Speaking Peoples* (1956–8). If his history of World War II is somewhat one-sided, that is because there was so much to be written about his conduct of it. He was able to use his own wide experience to illuminate his studies of people and events, and it is a measure of the quality of his prose that it almost demands to be read aloud. See the official biography, begun (1966–7) by his son Randolph and completed (1971–88) by Martin Gilbert.

**Clare, John** (1793–1864), poet, was born at Helpstone, near Peterborough, son of a barely literate countryman. He attended school, but was taught to read and write by a local farmer's son. The education which inspired his poetry was his observation of nature and of the daily routines of country life. A bookseller in Stamford published his *Poems Descriptive of Rural Life and Scenery* in 1820, the year the poet married not the love of his youth, whom he never forgot, but a girl he had got pregnant. *The Village Minstrel* (1821) and *The Shepherd's Calendar* (1827) were published in London but were financial disasters. The latter was violently and unsympathetically edited by the publisher, John Taylor (1781–1864) —

the original version, edited by Eric Robinson and Geoffrey Summerfield, was published in 1964 and reveals the true feeling of a village community. *The Rural Muse* (1835) earned Clare £40, but by now his spirit and mind were broken by poverty and privation, and in 1837 he entered a private asylum, from which he ran away four years later. He was then committed to the Northampton county asylum, where he spent the rest of his life, kindly treated and still writing. His poetry, which he never learned to punctuate and left unrevised, is shot through with penetrating insights and happy choices of phrase. His bird poems represent a corpus of nature poetry which is unique. See *Autobiographical Writings*, 1983, and *Selected Poems and Prose*, 1967, both ed. Robinson and Summerfield; J. W. and Anne Tibble, *Clare: His Life and Poetry*, 1956.

**Clarke, Austin** (1896–1974), Irish poet, novelist and dramatist, was born in Dublin, and educated at the Jesuit Belvedere College and University College, Dublin. In two early books of verse, *The Vengeance of Fionn* (1917) and *The Sword of the West* (1921), he attempted to recreate the Celtic ethos. A more lively representation of Ireland past is *The Cattle Drive in Connaught* (1925). Clarke worked as a journalist in England from 1929 to 1937, when he returned to Co. Dublin. *Pilgrimage* (1929) and *Night and Morning* (1938) still reflect the past, but are concerned, too, with matters of the present, in particular the conflicts betwen asceticism and natural desire, and between faith and reason. His defiance of artistic censorship both motivated and provided the subject of his first novel, *The Bright Temptation* (1932). With Robert Farren (1909–84) he founded the Dublin Verse-Speaking Society in 1940 and the Lyric Theatre in 1944, and for a time he concentrated on writing verse drama. With *Ancient Lights* (1955) he returned to his commitment to poetry and to speaking out about the various deprivations of life in Dublin. *Mnemosyne Lay in Dust* (1966) is a disturbing collection which recalls his incarceration in an asylum in his youth. He is essentially a national poet because of his concern about (and latterly satire on) the contradictions of modern Irish life and because he used, adapted, and breathed fresh life into traditional poetic forms. See *Twice Round the Black Church*, 1962, and *Penny in the Clouds*, 1968 (autobiography); and in A. Norman Jeffares, *Anglo-Irish Literature*, 1982.

**Clough, Arthur Hugh** (1819–61), poet, was born in Liverpool and stayed in England when his parents emigrated to America. He was educated at Rugby School, where he excelled at everything, and Balliol College, Oxford, where he did less well. In 1848 he resigned a fellowship at Oriel College rather than take holy orders, which religious doubts, implanted when an undergraduate, now made unthinkable. After two years as head of a college in London and three in America, he married and took a job in the Education Office in London. He died in Florence after a bout of malaria. *The Bothie of Tober-na-Voulich*, the revised title of a verse novel in hexameters first published in 1848, is an amusing and tender account of a Highland holiday romance between an English undergraduate and a local girl, with a happy ending. 'Amours de Voyage', first published in an American journal in 1858, is told in letters — Claude, who cannot crystallise his attitude to the short-lived Republic of Rome, dithers across Europe after the object of his affections, only to lose her in the end. Clough's other long poem, 'Dipsychus' (a reference to someone of a double-sided nature), is a drama in a variety of metres, comprising a dialogue with a tempting spirit. The best-known of his shorter poems are 'Say Not the Struggle Nought Availeth' and his skit on the Ten Commandments, 'The Last Decalogue'. It was unusual for a poet of his time to express personal doubts and intellectual tussles, which he does with a refreshing air of enquiring innocence. See *Selected Poems,* ed. Shirley Chew, 1987; Robindra Biswas, *Arthur Hugh Clough: Towards a Reconsideration,* 1972.

**Cobbett, William** (1763–1835), prose writer and political journalist, was born in Farnham, Surrey, son of a small farmer, and had little formal education. He enlisted in the Army in 1784, and during a year at Chatham devoured the contents of a local circulating library and taught himself grammar. He was a sergeant-major in Nova Scotia and New Brunswick between 1785 and 1791. After his discharge he accused his former officers of embezzlement, and he and his wife took refuge in France and then in America, where as Peter Porcupine he wrote fierce criticism of the local Democrats. After two prosecutions for libel, he prudently returned to England before the publication of *Porcupine's Works* (1801). In 1802 he began the weekly *Political Register.* His views veered from Tory to Radical, and in 1810 he was jailed for an article on army flogging. He repeatedly stood for Parliament, and was finally elected in 1832. A farmer as well as a writer, he had toured southern England in 1822 to observe agricultural conditions. His accounts were published in volume form as *Rural Rides* (1830), an eccentric but engaging mixture of autobiography, rural impressions, polemic, and lexical digressions. Other works include *Cottage Economy* (1822) and *Advice to Young Men* (1830). *Hazlitt wrote of him in *The Spirit of the Age* (1825): 'He is not only unquestionably the most powerful political writer of the present day, but one of the best writers in the language.' See Daniel Green, *Cobbett: the Noblest Agitator,* 1985.

**Coleridge, Samuel Taylor** (1772–1834), poet, philosopher, and critic, was born in Ottery St Mary, Devon, tenth and youngest child of the vicar and grammar school master and his second wife. A precocious boy who read and was deeply influenced by *Arabian Nights' Entertainments* at the age of six, he was educated at Christ's Hospital, which he found a traumatic experience, and Jesus College, Cambridge, where in 1791 he first took opium, for rheumatism. During his final year he got into debt and disappeared for four months to be an ineffective trooper in the Dragoons under an assumed name, and finished without a degree. He had already begun publishing his poems in newspapers when, on a vacation walking tour in 1794, he was introduced to the young poet Robert Southey (1774–1843). A close friendship was forged, founded on the idea of establishing a 'Pantisocracy' in a remote part of America. The scheme did not materialise but led to his marriage to Sarah Fricker, sister of Southey's fiancée. In 1796 he started a political journal, *The Watchman*, which survived for ten issues, and published *Poems on Various Subjects*, the second edition of which (1797) contained poems by *Lamb, a friend from Christ's Hospital days, and Charles Lloyd (1775–1839). The next few years were momentous and productive. He wrote a play, *Osorio*, which was rejected by *Sheridan but ultimately staged in 1813 as *Remorse*. A friendship with *Wordsworth had in 1797 grown into such a bond that the poet and his sister moved to Alfoxden near the Coleridges in Nether Stowey, Somerset. Between November 1797 and May 1798, he wrote the three works on which his reputation as a major poet is founded: the first part of the weird ballad, 'Christabel' (the second was composed in 1800, and the rest never at all); the opium-inspired fragment, 'Kubla Khan'; and 'The Rime of the Ancient Mariner', included in *Lyrical Ballads* (1798). This joint publication with Wordsworth expressed the theory of poetic sensation towards which they had been working, and spearheaded the Romantic Movement. With the Wordsworths he then undertook a study-tour in Germany, after which they moved north, and he spent some months in London as a journalist on the *Morning Post*. In 1800 he took his family to Greta Hall in the Lake District, into which the Southeys also moved.

Coleridge was now addicted to opium and emotionally entangled with Sara Hutchinson, Wordsworth's sister-in-law — the poem 'Dejection: an Ode' was in its original form written for her in 1802 under the title 'A Letter to…'. In 1804 he went to Malta for his health, and successfully took on the post of temporary Public Secretary of the island, only to return to England in 1806 more addicted to drugs than before. Between 1808 and 1814 he earned fame, and some money, by giving courses of literary lectures, some of which have been reconstituted in *Shakespearean Criticism*, ed. Thomas M. Raysor (2 vols new edn 1960). In 1816 he put himself in the hands of Dr James Gillman, into whose house in Highgate, London, he moved for what was intended to be a month. He stayed for 18 years until his death. The control of his addiction enabled him to attract a wide circle of disciples and friends, and to complete *Biographia Literaria* (1817), a critical study of poetry and philosophy with autobiographical digressions. He also published a new book of verse, *Sibylline Leaves* (1817), and a collected edition of his poetry (1828); and continued to write prose, though more discursively than before, and poetry, which by contrast was tighter and had lost its power to surprise.

Of his three children who survived infancy, Hartley (1796–1849), referred to in the poems 'Frost at Midnight' and 'The Nightingale', both written in 1798, had poetical talent but, having been sent to Oxford by Southey, lost his subsequent fellowship through drunkenness, failed as a school proprietor, and died a literary vagrant. Derwent (1800–83) became the first head of St Mark's College, Chelsea, and edited some of his father's and brother's works. Sara (1802–52), a notable scholar and translator, as well as a beauty and the model for 'Highland Girl' painted by William Collins, married her cousin Henry Coleridge. Her fantasy *Phantasmion* (1837) is interspersed with pleasant lyrics.

See *Coleridge's Verse: a Selection*, ed. William Empson and David Pirie, 1972 (critical edition of all the best poetry); *Selected Letters*, ed. H. J. Jackson, 1987; John Livingstone Lowes, *The Road to Xanadu: a Study in the Ways of the Imagination*, new edn 1980; Molly Lefebure, *Samuel Taylor Coleridge: a Bondage of Opium*, 1974 (biography); Richard Holmes, *Coleridge: Early Visions*, 1989 (biography to 1804); Richard Holmes, *Coleridge*, 1982 (introduction to his thought and works).

**Collins, Wilkie** (1824–89), novelist and dramatist, was born in London, eldest son of William Collins (1788–1847), the landscape painter. He was educated privately, and at the age of twelve accompanied his parents to Italy for three years. While working as a clerk in a London tea warehouse, he secretly wrote a novel of ancient Rome (published later in 1850 as *Antonina*) which so impressed his father that he entered the boy for the law. His father died in 1847, and Collins's biography of him appeared the following year. In 1851 he met *Dickens, to whose magazine, *Household Words*, he regularly contributed stories while also writing novels, which include *Hide and Seek* (1854), a study of deaf-and-dumbness, and *The Dead Secret* (1857), about blindness. *The Woman in White* (1860), first published as a serial, is a sensational mystery novel, with a complex plot, several secrets, and two villains. It was an immediate success, and was reprinted six times in six months. Collins wrote in all over thirty novels, of which the most famous, and best, is *The Moonstone* (1868), in which Sergeant Cuff is the first detective in English fiction to play a major role in the action. The story is told from several points of view and thus has a depth unusual in novels of this genre, though characterisation is secondary to plot, suspense, and revelation. Collins never married, but lived with a widow, and had three acknowledged illegitimate children by another woman. See Kenneth Robinson, *Wilkie Collins: a Biography*, new edn 1973.

**Collins, William** (1721–59), poet, was born in Chichester, son of a hatter who was twice Mayor of the city, and educated at Winchester College and

The Queen's College, Oxford, transferring to Magdalen as a scholar in 1741. In 1742 he published anonymously *Persian Eclogues*, four short extravaganzas in heroic couplets. His father died in 1744, and Collins, in debt and without a job, visited his uncle, Colonel Martin, serving in Flanders, who concluded that he was 'too indolent even for the army'. *Odes on Several Descriptive and Allegorical Subjects* (1746), his most substantial work, albeit containing only twelve poems, was neglected by the public. A plan sponsored by *Johnson, who got him a commission to translate Aristotle's 'Poetics', foundered in 1749 when Colonel Martin died, leaving the poet £2000, whereupon he repaid his debts and abandoned the project. His last known poem, 'An Ode on the Popular Superstitions of the Highlands of Scotland', was written in 1749. In the final years of his life depression became insanity. After his death his sister destroyed his surviving manuscripts. As befits his feckless way of life and his mercurial nature, true poetry flashes only intermittently in his works, of which the deeply-felt lyric, 'Ode: Written in the Beginning of the Year 1746' ('How sleep the brave...') and the unrhymed 'Ode to Evening' are regarded as his most accomplished. See Edward G. Ainsworth, *Poor Collins*, 1937 (critical biography). See also *Gray.

**Compton-Burnett, Ivy** (1884–1969), novelist, was born in Pinner, Middlesex, daughter of a doctor, and educated at home with two of her brothers and at Royal Holloway College, where she took a degree in classics. After *Dolores* (1911), written in collaboration with one of her brothers in the style of a Victorian novel, she wrote nothing until *Pastors and Masters* (1925). This established the distinctive ethos and literary style which pervade 18 further novels — *The Last and the First* (1971) was published posthumously. All are set at the end of the Victorian age and depict an enclosed community, such as a decayed country house or a school. In each, a tyrant, male or female, dominates the lesser characters (teachers, servants, companions or, most often, children), while a subsidiary group of hangers-on (solicitors, doctors, friends, relations) make up the complement. Crimes, carnal sins, and human failings (especially jealousy and acquisitiveness) motivate the plots, and the villains are more often condemned out of their own mouths than suffer at the hands of society or of their fellows. The actions are carried through almost entirely in dialogue, sometimes overheard through a key-hole or by a similar device, giving full play to the author's brilliant but austere wit. Especially recommended are *A Family and a Fortune* (1939), *Manservant and Maidservant* (1947), and *Mother and Son* (1955). She was made CBE in 1951 and DBE in 1967. See Hilary Spurling, *A Critical Biography of Ivy Compton-Burnett*, 1971.

**Congreve, William** (1670–1729), dramatist, was born in Bardsey, Yorkshire, son of an army officer who was soon afterwards appointed commander of the garrison at Youghal in Ireland. The boy was educated at Kilkenny College and Trinity College, Dublin (at both of which he was a contemporary of *Swift), and then studied law in London, for which he had little inclination. His first published work was a novel, *Incognita, or Love and Duty Reconciled* by 'Cleophil' (1693), according to him 'written in the idler hours of a fortnight's time'. A comedy, *The Old Batchelour* (1693), written four years earlier to amuse himself 'in a slow recovery from a fit of sickness', was an immediate success in 1693, running for 14 days and being declared by *Dryden to be the best first play he had ever seen. *The Double-Dealer*, performed later the same year and published in 1694, though also termed 'a comedy', has a darker side, which may account for its failure. *Love for Love* (1695), however, his best-plotted piece, restored his reputation and has remained the most frequently performed of his plays. *The Mourning Bride* (1697) is an out-and-out tragedy, but still packed the houses.

In 1698 there appeared an attack on the prevailing spirit of theatrical comedy, *Short View of the Immortality and Prophaneness of the English Stage*, by a Nonconformist minister called Jeremy Collier (1650–1726). Congreve replied with *Amendments of Dr Collier's False and Imperfect Citations* (1698), but he appears to have got the worst of the argument. *The Way of the World* (1700) contains some of the most dazzling wit and repartee in Restoration drama, scenes of brilliant inventiveness, and cleverly drawn and contrasted characters, notably the two pairs of lovers, Mirabell and Millamant on the one hand, and the scheming adulterers Fainall and Marwood on the other. Though it was not quite the total failure often ascribed to it, and it reads the best of all comedies of manners, its initial reception was such that Congreve gave up writing for the stage at the age of 30. He was for a time *Vanbrugh's colleague in the management of the new Haymarket Theatre, built in 1705, but his masque, *The Judgement of Paris* (1701), was never performed. The rest of his life was spent enjoying a series of near-sinecures — he was Commissioner for Licensing Hackney Coaches until 1705, when he became Commissioner of Wine Licences, and was appointed Secretary for Jamaica in 1714 — and delighting in his many friends, for unlike the main body of wits of the time, he is said never to have given offence to anyone. Latterly he suffered much from blindness and gout, but basked in the regular company, and favours, of Henrietta, Duchess of Marlborough, to whom he left the bulk of his estate on the understanding that it would ultimately go to her (and supposedly his) daughter, Lady Mary Godolphin. See *Complete Plays*, ed. Hubert Davis, 1967; John C. Hodges, *William Congreve the Man: a Biography from New Sources*, 1941.

**Conrad, Joseph** (1857–1924), novelist and short story writer, was born Teodor Josef Konrad Korzeniowski near Mohilow in Poland. His father, a member of a landed family and a literary personality who had translated

*Shakespeare and Victor Hugo (1802–85) into Polish, brought his family to Warsaw in 1862 to start up a literary periodical, though this was a front for his political activity against Russian rule, for which he was exiled to the Urals. His wife accompanied him with the child, but she died in 1865. Father and son were allowed to leave Russia in 1867 and, on his father's death in 1869, the boy became the ward of his uncle, and studied classics and German at St Anne High School in Cracow. When he was 16 he persuaded his guardian to let him go to sea, and served on various French ships based at Marseilles, including one involved in gun-running for the Spanish Carlist cause. Ashore, he seems to have lost money by gambling, and on one occasion attempted suicide. In 1878 he joined the British ship, *Mavis*, bound for Constantinople, and returned with it to Lowestoft, Suffolk, hardly knowing a word of English. Yet he now determined to become a British seaman. He learned English while serving on a coastal ship plying between Lowestoft and Newcastle, and then worked his way in other vessels, having adventures which later reappeared in his novels, and qualifying as third mate in 1880, mate in 1883, and master in 1886, the year he changed his name and took British citizenship. His first command lasted from January 1888 to March 1889, after which, while waiting around on shore for another posting, he had the breakfast-table cleared early one day, and began to write a novel, as he describes in *Some Reminiscences* (1912): 'The necessity which compelled me was a hidden, obscure necessity, a completely masked and unaccountable phenomenon....Till I began to write that novel I had written nothing but letters....The conception of a planned book was entirely outside my mental range.' (It would have spoilt an otherwise perfectly reasonable record to have revealed that in 1886 he wrote a story for the magazine *Tit Bits*, which was not printed.) The unfinished manuscript of his novel accompanied him on subsequent voyages, including a traumatic trip on a Congo steamer which broke his health and almost his spirit. In January 1894 he resigned from the Merchant Navy, finished his novel, which was based on his experiences in and off the Malayan Archipelago in 1887–9, and submitted it to T. Fisher Unwin, whose reader, Edward Garnett (1868–1936), recommended it for publication — it appeared as *Almayer's Folly* (1895) — and encouraged him to write more. *An Outcast of the Islands* (1896) and *The Nigger of the 'Narcissus'* (1897) were followed by several further novels, notably *Nostromo* (1904), *The Secret Agent* (1907), and *Under Western Eyes* (1911), a psychological and political study in the ironical strain which runs through most of his work, and books of short stories — 'Heart of Darkness' first appeared in *Youth and Two Other Stories* (1902) and 'The Secret Sharer' in *'Twixt Land and Sea* (1912).

Conrad married a bookseller's daughter in 1896 and they had two children. Family life in London was made more difficult by his bouts of illness, despondency, and money problems. His fortunes changed with the publication in the USA of *Chance* (1913), in which he deliberately employed his craft to appeal to a wider public with a novel, in two parts ('The Damsel' and 'The Knight'), of strange passion and remorse, with a happy ending. In *Victory* (1915) he pursued a similar theme of the redemption of a girl abused by fate, but paradoxically, now that his reputation was assured and his financial position relieved, the inspirational and innovatory vein that had distinguished his work began to fade.

Conrad was a depressive nihilist whose attempts to find an identity and to express his views on the nature of human existence, though written in a language which he only consciously began to learn when he was 21 and never spoke clearly, took the English novel out of the Victorian age and gave it new dimensions. The exotic or romantic settings, the horrors, and many of the situations were real, and as is particularly exemplified by *Lord Jim* (1900), which was originally intended as a short story, he uses techniques entirely his own to build up the story-line in such a way that complex designs and ambiguous motives are most vividly revealed. See Jocelyn Baines, *Joseph Conrad: a Critical Biography*, new edn 1986; C. B. Cox, *Joseph Conrad: the Modern Imagination*, 1974; Frederick R. Karl, *A Reader's Guide to Joseph Conrad*, 1960.

**Cowper, William** (1731–1800), poet, was born in Great Berkhamstead, Hertfordshire, son of the rector. His mother, a descendant of *Donne, died when he was six, and he was sent to a local boarding school, where he was bullied, and then to Westminster School, after which he studied law. In 1750 he fell in love with his cousin Theodora (to whom, as 'Delia', he addressed several poems), but was forbidden to marry her because of his incipient madness. In 1763, unable to face the interview for a clerkship at the House of Lords, he attempted suicide, and was confined for a time in an asylum. On his discharge, and with a pension from family and friends, he lodged with a clergyman and his wife, Morley and Mary Unwin. On Morley's death in 1767, Cowper set up house with Mary (*d*.1796) in Olney, Buckinghamshire, and would have married her but for recurring fits of madness. Here, with the local rector, John Newton (1725–1807), he wrote *Olney Hymns* (1779). *Poems* (1782) was indifferently received. In 1783 Lady Austen suggested he write a poem in blank verse about a sofa, which grew into a 5200-line paean on country life called 'The Task'. It was included, with the hilarious song 'John Gilpin', in *Poems II* (1785), which made him famous. He was a most versatile poet, who left a mass of occasional poems, of which the last, 'The Castaway', reflects the turmoil of his illnesses. His poetry was exactly right for his time in that it was direct and often raised everyday sights and activities to genuine poetic levels, while speaking also for the Methodist and Evangelical movements. His letters (see *The Letters and Prose Writings*, ed. James King and Charles Ryskamp, 5 vols 1979–86), especially those on domestic and literary matters, are as felicitously written as any in the language. See David Cecil, *The Stricken Deer*, new edn 1988 (biography).

**Crabbe, George** (1754–1832), poet, was born in Aldeburgh, Suffolk, eldest child of a salt-tax collector. A bookish boy, he went to school in Stowmarket, was apprenticed to a surgeon, worked in a warehouse while studying and, in about 1777, set up practice himself. He had in 1774 published a didactic poem, 'Inebriety', and in 1780, engaged to be married and unable to make medicine pay, he went to London to try to sell his manuscripts. Though his poem 'The Candidate', was published in the *Monthly Review*, he was almost destitute when *Burke responded to a plea for help, secured a publisher for *The Library* (1781), had the poet to stay, advised him to take holy orders, and found him a job as chaplain to the Duke of Rutland, in whose castle he finished *The Village* (1783). This anti-romantic survey of rural life ('...I paint the cot, / As truth will paint it, and as bards will not') earned him literary fame, and he married at last. He got several livings, but after *The Newspaper* (1785), a satirical poem, he published nothing until *Poems* (1807), having made periodic bonfires of much that he had written in the meantime. *The Borough* (1810) is a series of unlinked poetic sketches, one of which, 'Peter Grimes', is the source of the opera by Benjamin Britten (1913–76), and in *Tales of the Hall* (1819) two half-brothers meet after a separation and exchange experiences. Most of Crabbe's verse is in heroic couplets. He took a realistic, moral, lower-middle-class view of life, writing with compassion and wit, and using his verse form in an original way. See Lilian Haddakin, *The Poetry of Crabbe*, 1955.

**Crashaw, Richard** (*c*.1613–49), poet, was born in London, son of a Puritan clergyman, and educated at Charterhouse and Pembroke Hall, Cambridge, becoming a Fellow of Peterhouse. In 1644 he and five colleagues were dismissed for refusing to take the oath of the Solemn League and Covenant accepting uniformity of worship according to the Reformed Church. Having formally converted to Catholicism, he spent some time in Paris before becoming an attendant to Cardinal Palotta in Rome. He died in rather suspicious circumstances while on a pilgrimage to Loreto. From an early age Crashaw wrote poetry of an occasional and celebratory nature, and his first book of verse (in Latin) was published in 1634. *Steps to the Temple: Sacred Poems; with the Delights of the Muses* (1646) is in two parts, religious and secular. Crashaw has been classified as a 'metaphysical poet' because of his figurative language and extravagant comparisons. His religious verse is unusual in English literature in that it is written from a Catholic standpoint, and in his use of rhyme and rhythm, recurrent verbal motifs, and resounding climaxes, he demonstrates a keen ear for music. Most typical of his technique are 'The Flaming Heart' and other odes to St Teresa, especially those written in his favourite metre of octosyllabic couplets, and 'The Weeper' (to Mary Magdalene), while 'In the Holy Nativity of Our Lord God' is in the form of a Greek pastoral sung by shepherds and chorus. A memorable secular poem is 'Wishes to his Supposed Mistress', beginning 'Whoe'er she be — / That not impossible She'. See *Poems*, ed. L. C. Martin, new edn 1957.

**Darwin, Charles** (1809–82), naturalist, the son and grandson of a physician, was born in Shrewsbury, and educated at Shrewsbury School and Edinburgh University before transferring to Christ's College, Cambridge, to read for the Church. He became more interested in zoology, however, and in 1831 was recommended by the Professor of Botany as official geologist and naturalist (unpaid) to H. M. S. *Beagle*, which was sailing to South America and India on survey duties. The round-the-world excursion lasted five years, during which Darwin was in constant misery at sea because of sea-sickness and suffered severe hardships on land in pursuit of the objects of his research. The results were published in diary form as Volume III of Captain Robert Fitzroy's *Narrative of the Voyage* (1839). Darwin was now working on his theory of evolution through 'natural selection' of the fitter species, which he presented in 1858 with Alfred Wallace (1823–1913), who had come to similar conclusions, and published in 1859 as *On the Origin of Species by Means of Natural Selection*. Equally contentious theologically, but quite acceptable in biological terms, was *The Descent of Man* (1871), which traces human origins to the same ancestors as those of the higher apes. He also wrote various scholarly works on plants and on earthworms. His prose is a model of scientific exposition. See *Autobiography*, rev. edn ed. Nora Barlow, 1958; *Charles Darwin's Beagle Diary*, ed. R. D. Keynes, 1988; William Irvine, *Apes, Angels and Victorians*, 1955 (dual biography of Darwin and T. H. Huxley).

**Defoe, Daniel** (1660–1731), journalist and novelist, was born Foe (he added the 'De' in about 1703) in Cripplegate, London, son of a Nonconformist butcher, and was educated as a Dissenter at Stoke Newington Academy. He married in 1684, played a part in the rebellion of Monmouth in 1685, went into business as a hosiery agent, and was made bankrupt in 1692. *Essays upon Projects* (1697), written shortly after this experience, contains sound economic, social, and educational proposals, and places him among the forward thinkers of the day. Many political pamphlets followed, some in verse, including the popular satire, *The True Born Englishman* (1701). *The Shortest Way with Dissenters* (1702), however, an ironic attack on the 'high-flyers' in the Church, misfired. A warrant was issued for his arrest and, after four months in hiding, he was taken, tried, and sentenced to prison indefinitely, a heavy fine, and three consecutive days in the pillory. The last part of the ordeal was eased by the crowds who, instead of hurling bricks and ordure, garlanded the scaffold with flowers, drank his health, and bought copies of 'Hymn to the Pillory', which he had courageously composed for the occasion. Though he was released from Newgate after five months, and his fine was paid by the Crown, he had lost his decorative roof-tile business, was bankrupt again, and had a wife and six children to support. He now responded to the approach of Robert Harley (1661–1724), Secretary of State and later the Tory head of Government, to act as a secret negotiator in various ploys of state, and also to produce a journal, entirely written by himself, *A Weekly Review of the Affairs of France, Purged from the Errors and Partiality of News-Writers and Petty-Statesmen of All Sides* (more often and later known simply as the *Review*), which from 1704 to 1713 came out three times a week. This was a journalistic feat all the more extraordinary in that he was also active, and often away, on his other business (which included arrangements for the Union of the Scottish and English Parliaments), and that his comments on the various issues of the war were invariably shrewd. Though *de facto* he was no longer politically untainted and in particular had to submerge his Whig principles, he was forging a vivid and popular prose style which he was able to use to advantage and sustain in longer works, while still continuing to the end of his life indefatigably to write political, topical, and instructional tracts.

The first manifestation of Defoe the novelist was the moral adventure story, *The Life and Strange Surprizing Adventures of Robinson Crusoe, of York, Mariner* (1719), followed the same year by *The Farther Adventures of Robinson Crusoe*, and in 1720 by *Serious Reflections During the Life and Surprising Adventures of Robinson Crusoe*, all inspired by the experiences of the Scottish seaman, Alexander Selkirk (1676–1721). The genre of the desert island story had now been created. Encouraged by his success, Defoe published in 1720 two further novels of action, known by their short titles of *Memoirs of a Cavalier* and *Captain Singleton*, and then his second masterpiece, *The Fortunes and Misfortunes of the Famous Moll Flanders* (1722). The lengthy, often reproduced and titillating subtitle of this romance tends to obscure the fact that this first-person narrative of a streetwise adventuress, in the words of Professor Bonamy Dobrée in *English Literature in the Early Eighteenth Century 1700–1740* (1959), 'marks the birth of the modern novel, if...the peculiar mark of the novel as an art form distinct from other literary forms is that it shows the interplay of the individual and society'. *A Journal of the Plague Year* (1722) began as a piece of opportunist journalism in the form of a pamphlet warning the public of the dangers of the plague, which was raging in Marseilles, and became a reconstruction of the actual London epidemic of 1665, graphically and dramatically told as if by an eye-witness.

Defoe's powers of observation as well as of descriptive prose, and his energy, are also demonstrated in *A Tour thro' the Whole Island of Great Britain* (1724–7). While the original notes for this essential source book of geography and social and economic history were made years before, he undertook several visits to Scotland between 1724 and 1726 to check his impressions, and he makes some prophetic as well as perceptive comments. See James R. Sutherland, *Defoe*, new edn 1950; John R. Moore, *Defoe: Citizen of the Modern World*, 1958; Ian Bell, *Defoe's Fiction*, 1985.

**Dekker, Thomas** (1572–1632), dramatist and prose writer, was a Londoner probably of Dutch origin, whose life was punctuated by prison sentences for debt. He collaborated variously with John Ford (1586–1639), *Massinger, *Middleton, and *Webster to write a total of some sixty plays, of which 17 survive. He appears in ridiculous guise in *Jonson's play *The Poetaster*, to which he retaliated with *Satiro-Mastix, or the Untrussing of the Humorous Poet* (1602). The first two plays under Dekker's single authorship (both first performed in 1599) were *Old Fortunatus*, a pleasant poetical piece, and *The Shoemaker's Holiday*, a sound, realistic comedy whose aim is purely to entertain. There are in the latter some excellent scenes, carefully-studied characters (snobbish dignitaries, loyal craftsmen, star-crossed lovers), stock deceptions, neat comparisons and contrasts, with racy dialogue and clever rhyming exchanges. The only other play known to be entirely his own work is the second part of *The Honest Whore* (1630), an uneven Italianate drama of morality and social class. Dekker was above all a chronicler of London life at all levels. *The Wonderful Year* (1603) was the first of a series of pamphlets in which busy portraits of London provide a background to social comment and the grimmest of reports of the plague. *The Gull's Hornbook* (1609) is a satirical vade-mecum addressed to the rural gallant on how to disport himself most destructively in the city. See *Dramatic Works*, ed. Fredson Bowers, 1953–61; *The Plague Pamphlets*, ed. F. P. Wilson, 1925.

**de la Mare, Walter** (1873–1956), poet, novelist, children's writer, anthologist, and critic, was born in Charlton, Kent, sixth child of a Bank of England official, and educated at St Paul's Cathedral Choristers School. At 16 he joined the Anglo-American Oil Company, for which he worked until 1908. His first book, prophetically entitled *Songs of Childhood* (1902), under the pseudonym of Walter Ramal, was followed by a literary fantasy, *Henry Brocken* (1904), by *The Return* (1910), a stunning novel of possession, and by his first work for children, *The Three Mulla-Mulgars* (1910). The basis of all his subsequent work had now been realised, but his popular success began only with *The Listeners and Other Poems* (1912), to be confirmed by *Memoirs of a Midget* (1921), a classic incursion into microscopic fantasy. Most of his work has undertones of sadness, mystery, and danger, especially where there is a confrontation with or absorption into the other world. De la Mare's hold on reality, however, combined with his attention to detail and to precision of language and, in his poetry, with command of rhythm and rhyme, has ensured his appeal at many levels — to the child in the adult as well as to the adult in the child. *Pleasures and Speculations* (1940) contains essays on *Tennyson and *Brooke. He was made CH in 1948 and awarded the OM in 1953. See *The*

*Complete Poems*, 1969; C. Duffin, *Walter de la Mare: a Study of His Poetry*, new edn 1982; Leonard Clark, *Walter de la Mare*, 1960 (on his writing for children).

**De Quincey, Thomas** (1785–1859), prose writer and critic, was born in Manchester, son of a prosperous merchant, who died when the boy was seven. He was educated in the West Country before being sent in 1801 to Manchester Grammar School, from which he promptly ran away. With a small allowance from his mother, he wandered in Wales, and when the money was exhausted he ended up in London, subsisting on charity. In 1803 his guardians entered him for Worcester College, Oxford, where he remained intermittently for five years, but left without a degree, having been unable to face his final viva. In 1804 a well-meaning acquaintance had prescribed opium for a toothache: by 1813 he was an addict. In the meantime he had come into his inheritance and settled in the Lake District. In 1817 he married a local farmer's daughter, by whom he had eight children, and in 1821, to earn a living, he turned his talents and wide interests to writing. *Confessions of an English Opium Eater*, signed 'X. Y. Z.', appeared in the *London Magazine* in two parts in 1821, and thereafter he contributed articles to various journals, especially *Blackwood's Edinburgh Magazine* — he and his family moved to Edinburgh in 1830. Later works in which the materials of his waking dreams are superimposed on autobiography are *Suspiria de Profundis* (1845) and *The English Mail-Coach* (1849), which contains in 'The Vision of Sudden Death' and 'Dream Fugue' passages of particular graphic and poetic power. See Grevel Lindop, *The Opium Eater*, new edn 1985 (critical biography).

**Dickens, Charles** (1812–70), novelist, was born in Landport, Portsmouth, second of eight children of a Navy pay clerk. His father's postings, and inability to maintain a suitable style of living for his family, culminating in his imprisonment for debt, meant that the boy had 14 moves of home in as many years, several months' labour in Warren's Blacking Warehouse, and only two short periods of formal education. These were in Chatham when he was nine, and at Wellington House Academy, Hampstead, from 1824 to 1827, when he started as a solicitor's clerk. In 1829, having learned shorthand, he became a newspaper reporter. He applied for an audition at Covent Garden Theatre in 1832 but missed it through illness, and abandoned the idea of the stage when in 1833 his first story, 'A Dinner at Poplar Walk' (later reprinted as 'Mr Minns and his Cousin'), was published in the *Monthly Magazine*, followed by eight more in January–February 1834. Subsequent series of pseudonymous sketches appeared in various journals, and were collected and published as *Sketches by Boz* (1837). *The Posthumous Papers of the Pickwick Club, edited by 'Boz'* (1837) began serialisation in March 1836, a few days before his marriage to Catherine Hogarth (1815–79). All Dickens's novels were written and originally appeared as serials, the first of 24 instalments of *The Adventures of Oliver Twist: or, the Parish Boy's Progress* (1838) being published in *Bentley's Miscellany*, of which he was himself editor 1837–9. In May 1837, the sudden death, literally in his arms, of his wife's 17-year-old sister Mary, who had come to live with the couple soon after their wedding, proved particularly traumatic, and she became a perpetual embodiment for him of youth and innocence: the tragedy also caused the suspension for a month of his writing of *Pickwick* and of *Oliver Twist*. Early in 1838 he went to Yorkshire to investigate reports of brutality in boarding schools for unwanted boys, and on his return began *The Life and Adventures of Nicholas Nickleby* (1839), the first episode being published on 31 March 1838.

This became the established pattern of his career, an almost incessant round of writing (only halted by his death from a cerebral haemorrhage after finishing six instalments of *The Mystery of Edwin Drood*), punctuated by frequent fact-finding, publicity, and family journeys, and by miscellaneous literary works. In 1842 he and his wife spent six months in America where, amid the fêting, he gave addresses on international copyright and inspected conditions in gaols. From 1850 to 1858 he was editor of *Household Words*, where several of his novels were serialised, starting with the satirical *Hard Times* (1854), which doubled the journal's circulation even though his normal style suffered because of constrictions of space. In December 1853 he gave the first public reading of his works, for charity. This became such a welcome diversion for the public, and such a personal preoccupation, that in 1858 he started doing it regularly, for his own financial benefit — that year he toured 44 centres in Britain, and in 1867–8 a dozen American cities, in spite of continuous ill-health. His theatrical bent manifested itself also in his arrangement of and participation in amateur productions at Tavistock House, his home from 1851 to 1860, and at other places in England. For a tour in 1857 he engaged, with her mother and sister, the young actress Ellen Ternan (1839–1914), who became his mistress and the ultimate cause of his separation from his wife in 1858, after she had borne him ten children. From 1859 until his death he was owner-editor of a new journal, *All the Year Round*.

Dickens wrote two historical novels, *Barnaby Rudge* (1841) and *A Tale of Two Cities* (1859). The rest, excluding his shorter excursions into the supernatural, notably *A Christmas Carol* (1843), are stories of contemporary life, ranging from the broad fun of Mr Pickwick, the lighter comedy surrounding Nicholas Nickleby, and the black humour of *Bleak House* (1853), to the tear-jerking demise of Nell in *The Old Curiosity Shop* (1841), the darkness of *Little Dorrit* (1857), and the depth and suspense of *Great Expectations* (1862). The perennially popular *The Personal History of David Copperfield* (1850) contains elements from his own childhood and his early career in a solicitor's office and as a writer. Essentially he was a comic writer of genius and a remarkable student of character, with a highly-developed sense of drama and a perception of the exact image and most telling descriptive detail. He was less of a social reformer — being too inconsistent in his arguments — than a great novelist who used social conditions to enhance his effects. See Edgar Johnson, *Dickens: His Tragedy and Triumph*, new edn 1986 (biography); John Carey, *The Violent Effigy: a Study of Dickens' Imagination*, new edn 1979; Philip Collins (ed.), *Dickens*, 1982 (criticism).

**Disraeli, Benjamin** (1804–81), statesman and novelist, was born in London of Jewish parentage, and educated privately. When he was 13, his father, a minor literary figure with private means, was in disagreement with his synagogue and had all his children baptised. Benjamin studied law, but abandoned it for politics and literature. Between 1826, when he published anonymously the first part of *Vivian Grey*, whose cynical hero manipulates his way to political power (and disaster), and 1837 when, after several unsuccessful attempts, he was elected to Parliament, he wrote ten novels of varying genres. The most notable of these are *Contarini Fleming* (1832), 'a psychological autobiography', and *Alroy* (1833), an oriental romance with a Jewish hero. The subsequent trilogy, *Coningsby* (1844), *Sybil* (1845), and *Tancred* (1847), highlights the duties of Church and Crown, the dichotomy between rich and poor, and the differences which affect relations between Christians and Jews. When he had become a senior political figure, he returned to fiction with *Lothair* (1870), a quest novel in which the hero is torn between, and tempted by, three women and by the conflicting claims of Anglicanism, Catholicism, and Italian patriotism; and *Endymion* (1880), a reflection of his own early political career. In 1852 he served the first of three terms as Chancellor of the Exchequer, and he was Prime Minister in 1868 and again 1874–80. He was created Earl of Beaconsfield in 1876. He was the first British political novelist and the first major novelist in English who was of Jewish origin and wrote about Jewish themes. His considerable verbal and literary wit, however, was of the flamboyant English kind rather than of the more deprecatory nature usually associated with Jewish humour. See Daniel Schwarz, *Disraeli's Fiction*, 1979.

**Donne, John** (1572–1631), poet, prose writer, and cleric, was born in Bread Street, London, of a prominent Catholic family. He studied at both Oxford and Cambridge, though was prevented by his faith from taking any degree. He and his brother Henry entered Lincoln's Inn in 1592, but in 1593 Henry was arrested for harbouring a priest, and died in gaol before coming to trial. From this period come 'Satire III', an agonised expression of the doubts that led to his apostasy, and the half-bantering prose 'Paradoxes and Problems', as well, no doubt, as some of his secular songs and elegies. After two years serving with the fleet (see his poems 'The Storme' and 'The Calme'), he became in 1597 secretary to Sir Thomas Egerton, Lord Keeper of the Great Seal, and was elected to Parliament in 1601. Unfortunately for his career prospects, he had fallen in love with, and in 1601 secretly married, Egerton's 16-year-old niece, Ann, whose father had him imprisoned and dismissed from his post. A fairly miserable period followed. Donne spent much time looking for patronage or a job, writing *Biathanatos*, a treatise on suicide (not for publication); many of the 'Holy Sonnets' and other religious poems; and verses to order, including the erotic St Valentine's Day 'An Epithalamion...on the Lady Elizabeth and Count Palatine Being Married' and the highly diplomatic 'Epithalamion', for the Earl of Somerset and his 'virgin' bride, the former wife of the Earl of Essex. 'A Funerall Elegie' (for Elizabeth Drury, died 1610) and its two *Anniversaries* so pleased the girl's father that he pressed for their publication, embarrassing the poet, who did not want his praise of the subject to offend two female patrons he was courting. Definitely intended for publication was *Pseudo-Martyr* (1610), an argument in favour of Catholics taking the Oath of Allegiance to James I, a copy of which he astutely presented to the King in person. James's response was equally shrewd. He turned down all Donne's requests for political and other posts, and insisted that he enter the Church, which he did in 1615 after a terrible year in which he was ill, his wife miscarried, and two of his children died.

The King now appointed him a royal chaplain, and got him a Cambridge doctorate and several benefices. Donne also became Reader in Divinity at Lincoln's Inn in 1616, which entailed giving 50 sermons a year to an influential and intelligent congregation. In 1617 Ann died giving birth to their twelfth child. Donne's grief is apparent from the sonnet 'Since she whom I loved...', which begins as a conventional hymn to the goodness of God and then breaks down, 'But though I have found thee, and thou my thirst has fed, / A holy thirsty dropsy melts mee yett...'. In 1619 he was chaplain to Viscount Doncaster's mission of mediation between the Protestant Bohemians and the Emperor of Germany. The summit of his ambitions and the culmination of years of assiduous soliciting came in 1621 with his nomination as Dean of St Paul's Cathedral. Though he was only required to preach three times a year, he did so frequently. It was as a preacher rather than as a poet that he expected to be remembered, with some justification, in the light of his powers of imagery, rhetoric, and frequent economy of thought. The first volume of his sermons was published in 1622, and eight more before 1633. He died a few weeks after preaching his own death sermon before King Charles I at Whitehall, and having acted as model for his own effigy in St Paul's.

While many of his poems were circulated in manuscript in his lifetime, the first published edition of his poetry was in 1633, and included both secular and divine works. His apparent lack of melody and the doubts sparked off in *Dryden's *A Discourse Concerning Satire* (1693), 'He affects the metaphysics...where only nature should reign', from which came the term 'metaphysical poets', hindered his recognition. It is the very depth, allusiveness and, above all, revelation of experience that distinguish his work and influenced twentieth-century poetry, especially that of *Eliot. These qualities are to be found particularly in his poems of love, such as 'Loves Infiniteness', 'The Sunne Rising', 'A Lecture upon the Shadow', 'Elegie XIX: Going to Bed', 'Elegie XII: His Parting from Her', and the songs 'Goe, and catche a falling starre...' and 'Sweetest love, I do not goe...'. His poetry is also distinctive for the way in which conceits graphically yoke together heterogeneous elements. See *The Divine Poems*, 2nd edn 1981, and *Elegies and the Songs and Sonnets*, 1965, ed. Helen Gardner; *Selected Prose*, ed. Neil Rhodes, 1987; R. C. Bald, *John Donne: a Life*, 1970; John Carey, *John Donne: Life, Mind and Art*, 1981.

**Douglas, Gavin** (*c*.1474–1522), Scottish poet and cleric, was born at Tantallon Castle, third son of Archibald 'Bell-the-Cat', 5th Earl of Angus, and educated at St Andrews University and, probably, in Paris. He was much at the court of James IV, in whose honour he wrote an allegorical poem in courtly, Italianate style, *Palice of Honour*. After the disaster of the battle of Flodden and the death of the King (1514), Douglas's nephew, the 6th Earl, married James IV's widow, who proposed the poet unsuccessfully for the vacant archbishopric of St Andrews and then successfully as Bishop of Dunkeld, which he became in 1516. For the rest of his life he was much in demand as a promoter of causes and a dealer in political intrigue, but he was finally exiled, and died in London of the plague. His position in literary history is very properly founded on *Eneados*, his translation into Scots rhyming couplets of the twelve books of Virgil's *Aeneid*, plus a thirteenth book from an original composed in 1428 by Maphaeus Vegius, all of which he completed by 1513. It is regarded as the best translation of that epic until *Dryden's, and livelier and more in tune with its readership in that the climate, landscapes, treatment of the supernatural, and the battles and ship sequences, are rendered in terms of the contemporary Scottish experience. See *The Poetical Works of Gavin Douglas*, ed. J. Small, 1874; *Selections from Gavin Douglas*, ed. David F. C. Coldwell, 1964; P. J. Bawcutt, *Gavin Douglas: a Critical Study*, 1976.

**Doyle,** (Sir) **Arthur Conan** (1859–1930), novelist and short story writer, was born in Edinburgh of an artistic Irish Catholic family, and educated at Stonyhurst College and Edinburgh University, qualifying as a doctor in 1881, and practising in Southsea from 1882 to 1890. During the Boer War (1899–1902) he volunteered as a senior physician in the field and was knighted for his services. His first full-length work, *A Study in Scarlet*, in which the detective Sherlock Holmes is introduced, was published in

*Beeton's Christmas Annual* in 1887. A second Holmes novel, *The Sign of Four*, appeared in 1890, and stories about the private detective and his worthy henchman Dr Watson, including the longer tale *The Hound of the Baskervilles*, were published regularly in *Strand Magazine* from 1891 to 1893, at which point Doyle killed off his hero by having him fall off a precipice. Popular opinion prevailed and Holmes was miraculously resuscitated for *The Return of Sherlock Holmes* (1905). Another creation was the scientist Professor Challenger — in *The Lost World* (1912) and *The Poison Belt* (1913) — while Doyle also adapted his easy, narrative style to historical romance with *The White Company* (1891), *Sir Nigel* (1906), and the stories about the Napoleonic Brigadier Gerard. He was a vigorous campaigner for causes in which he believed — notably that of Oscar Slater, condemned to death (commuted to life imprisonment) in 1909 and finally pardoned in 1928 — and developed a strong interest in spiritualism, while retaining his love of boxing, the theme of *Rodney Stone* (1896). See *Memories and Adventures*, new edn 1989 (autobiography); Owen Dudley Edwards, *The Quest for Sherlock Holmes*, 1982.

**Dryden, John** (1631–1700), poet, dramatist, critic, and translator, was born in Aldwinckle, Northamptonshire, into a landowning Puritan household, and educated at Westminster School and Trinity College, Cambridge, after which he settled in London. His first published work was a contribution, 'Heroique Stanzas...', to a volume of three complimentary poems commemorating the death of Oliver Cromwell. He greeted the Restoration of the monarchy in 1660 in the person of Charles II with two equally effusive renderings, 'Astraea Redux' and 'To His Sacred Majesty', a demonstration of inconstancy which *Johnson justifies in *The Lives of the Poets* (1779–81), 'if he changed, he changed with the nation'. He was elected to the newly-established Royal Society in 1662, and in 1663 married a daughter of the Earl of Berkshire, Lady Frances Howard, who felt that she had wed beneath her. He now began a career as a dramatist which lasted until 1694, during which he published over thirty tragedies, tragicomedies, and comedies. In *Annus Mirabilis: the Year of Wonders* (1667), he describes in rhyming quatrains the Great Fire of London and celebrates, with some irony, the war against the Dutch and the glories of the Royal Society. In 1668, in which year he published his critical study, *Of Dramatick Poesie*, he was appointed the first Poet Laureate, and he became Historiographer Royal in 1670.

In the political upheavals and long-running personal animosities of the time he now found the perfect outlet for his talents, and in the heroic couplet the ideal medium. In *Mac Flecknoe: or a Satyr upon T. S.*, largely written in 1678 but not published until 1682, he rounded on his former friend and now political enemy, the writer Thomas Shadwell (1642–92), and silenced him and his cronies. *Absalom and Achitophel* (1681) — a second part by Nahum Tate (1652–1715), with a long insertion by Dryden, was published in 1682 — is overtly political and uses the biblical story as a parallel in order to discredit the Earl of Shaftesbury in his support of the Duke of Monmouth, illegitimate son of Charles II, against future claims on the Crown by the Catholic James, Duke of York, the King's brother. In 1682 he published *Religio Laici*, a poem in which he defends the compromise between Catholicism and Deism offered by the Anglican Church. After the accession of James II in 1685, he became a Catholic, and wrote *The Hind and the Panther* (1687), a political and religious allegory from the standpoint of Catholicism, to which he remained faithful, even though on the accession of William and Mary in 1688 he lost his official posts and his steady income. He now turned to verse translation, including the satires of Juvenal (1693) and the whole of Virgil (1697). *Fables Ancient and Modern* (1700), for which he was best known throughout the following century, contains tales from *Chaucer as well as Homer, Ovid, and Boccaccio.

Dryden was a consummate craftsman. Many of the songs and lyrics sprinkled through his plays are justly memorable, as are his odes on the deaths of John Oldham (1684), Charles II (1685), and Anne Killigrew (1686), and *A Song for St Cecilia's Day* (1687) and *Alexander's Feast* (1697), both of which were set to music. Of his many plays, the best are the tragicomedy, *Secret Love: or the Maiden Queen* (1667), and the tragedy *All for Love: or the World Well Lost* (1677), a deliberate attempt to emulate rather than copy *Shakespeare's *Antony and Cleopatra*, for which he abandoned rhyme for blank verse and, by restricting the action to events after the battle of Actium and the setting to Alexandria, succeeds in observing the classical unities of time and space. His value and significance as a critic, an art which he practised throughout his career in the form mainly of prefaces, lie in his incisive mind, his ability to appreciate different, and often divergent, literary traditions, his prose style and the general consistency of his arguments on major matters. These qualities are as apparent in his last piece, the preface to the *Fables*, as they are in his essay, *Of Dramatick Poesie*. With his command of language (which became accepted poetic diction), his wit, his technical skill, and the control which led him to perfect the heroic couplet, he founded a school of satirical verse in which his follower, and his only equal, was *Pope. See *A Selection*, ed. Keith Walker, 1987 (poetry and prose); *Of Dramatic Poesy and Other Critical Essays*, ed. George Watson, 1962; Charles E. Ward, *Life of John Dryden*, 1961; David Hopkins, *John Dryden*, 1986 (critical study).

**Dunbar, William** (*c.*1460–*c.*1520), Scottish poet, was probably born in East Lothian of the family of the Earls of Dunbar and March, and studied at St Andrews University 1473–9. By his own account, he became an itinerant Franciscan friar, renounced the calling, and was employed by James IV on diplomatic assignments abroad. In 1500 his name appears as being granted a royal pension for life, or until promoted to a benefice. He was one of the mission to London in 1501 to arrange James's marriage to Margaret, daughter of Henry VII, about which he wrote 'The Thrissill and the Rois', and he composed a celebration of Aberdeen for the Queen's visit there in 1511. His name disappears from the records after 1513, which may suggest that he got his benefice, for it is improbable that he followed the King to Flodden and participated in the disastrous defeat of the Scots at the hands of the English. In the meantime he seems to have been much around the Court, writing religious poems, satirical poems, love poems, autobiographical poems, rude poems, moral poems, and poems of admonition and petition to the King, while continually complaining about his pension, grousing about the weather and his health, and harping on about his benefice.

Not until *Burns, who was also Scottish, is there a poet whose range of themes is matched by such versatility in the use of metrical forms, nor one so confident in his art that in true Scottish fashion he can imbue it with such frankness of tone. At its best, which is often, his poetry has a plangent rhythm, enhanced by alliteration and internal as well as end-rhymes. These qualities are apparent even when he is addressing the King about his entourage ('Schir, ye have mony servitouris...') or the Queen about her wardrobe-master ('The wardraipper of Venus house...'). His revelations about court life are as colourful and comic as those about female sexuality in his alliterative satire on the epic of courtly love, 'The Twa Mariit Wemen and the Wedo', and he is not averse to ending a blessing for the practical skills of tailors and shoemakers ('Betuix twell houris and ellevin...') with a quiet dig at their honesty in business matters. There is, too, a strong imagination at work in visionary poems such as 'The Goldyn Targe' and 'The Dance of the Sevin Deidly Synnis', and an honest depth of feeling in his divine poems, especially on the Nativity, '*Rorate celi desuper...*', and the resounding hymn to the Resurrection, 'Done is a battell on the dragon black...'. While the sheer panic of 'I that in heill wes and gladness...' (known also as 'Lament for the Makaris'), with its refrain every fourth line of '*Timor mortis conturbat me*', makes it one of the most engagingly sympathetic of poems about death.

Six of Dunbar's poems were printed in 1508, and 24 (in adapted versions) by *Ramsay in *The Ever Green* (1724). The first edition proper of his works was in 1834. See *Poems*, ed. James Kinsley, new edn 1979; Tom Scott, *Dunbar: a Critical Exposition of the Poems*, new edn 1977.

**Durrell, Lawrence** (*b*.1912), poet and novelist, was born in India and educated at St Joseph's College, Darjeeling, and St Edmund's School, Canterbury. He lived in Corfu from 1934 to 1940, and was attached to the British Information Office in Cairo and Alexandria in World War II, after which he held government public relations' posts in Greece, Jugoslavia and Cyprus. His first novel was *Pied Piper of Lovers* (1935): *The Black Book: an Agon* was published subterraneously in Paris in 1938. His poetry began with *Quaint Fragment* (1931) and continued through the war years and into the 1970s. Quiet, sometimes humorous, often lyrical, and especially effective when evoking places, it is his poetry, with his three so-called 'travel books', *Prospero's Cell* (1945), about Corfu, *Reflections on a Marine Venus* (1953), about Rhodes, and *Bitter Lemons* (1957), about Cyprus, which many British critics regard as his most lasting work. Durrell's international reputation, however, is based on his 'Alexandria Quartet' of novels, *Justine* (1957), *Balthazar* (1958), *Mountolive* (1958), and *Clea* (1960), the first three of which, in the author's words, 'interlap, interweave in a purely spatial relation', while the last is a sequel in time. Multi-layered patterns of sexual involvements and intrigues, with the action and characters seen from different viewpoints, illuminate an inherently dramatic, at times romantic, plot. See *Collected Poems 1931–1974*, rev. edn 1985; G. S. Fraser, *Lawrence Durrell: a Study*, 1968; Alan W. Friedman, *Lawrence Durrell and the Alexandria Quartet*, 1970.

**Edgeworth, Maria** (1767–1849), Irish novelist, was born in Oxfordshire, daughter of the educationist and inventor Richard Lowell Edgeworth by his first wife, and educated in England before accompanying her father and his third wife to the family estate of Edgeworthstown, Co. Longford, in 1782, where she lived for the rest of her life, and where she died in the arms of her father's fourth wife. Her first published works were *The Parents' Assistant* (1795), a series of didactic and moral tales for children which by its 1800 edition had grown to six volumes, and *Practical Education* (1798), written with her father, who was until his death in 1817 a fervent supporter of her literary endeavours, and whose *Memoirs*, written by them jointly, appeared in 1820. *Castle Rackrent* (1800), published anonymously, was a literary milestone in that it was the first regional novel in English. It follows the fortunes of a family through several generations, and the speech is the English used in Ireland — all narrated by a servant. In its historical detail and spirit, it also looks forward to *Scott, who repaid Maria's visit to Abbotsford in 1823 with one to Edgeworthstown in 1825, after which they toured Ireland together, fêted wherever they went. *Tales of Fashionable Life* (1809–12) includes 'Ennui' and 'The Absentee', which present accurate impressions of Irish contemporary life for a predominantly English readership. *Harrington* (1817) and *Ormond* (1817) are novels of English society. See Elizabeth Inglis-Jones, *Great Maria: a Portrait of Maria Edgeworth*, new edn 1978.

**Eliot, George**, pseudonym of Mary Ann Evans (1819–80), novelist, was born in Astley, Warwickshire, youngest surviving child of an estate manager and his second wife, who soon after the birth moved to Griff House, Chilvers Coton. She went to boarding school at five, and left

Nantglyn School, Coventry in 1835, shortly before her mother's death, after which she took responsibility for the household. On her brother Isaac's marriage in 1841, she and her father moved to Foleshill, on the edge of Coventry, where she became closely associated with the family of the free-thinker and philosopher, Charles Bray (1811–84). In 1842 she shocked her own family by refusing to attend church, and though she resumed going, she was now an agnostic in that her faith was in humanity rather than in God. Through the Brays she got a job of translating *The Life of Jesus Critically Examined by Dr David Friedrich Strauss* which was published without her name by John Chapman (1821–94) in 1846. This study of the Gospels in the light of both orthodox and rationalist views was well received by radical thinkers. After the death of her father in 1849, she went to the Continent and then lodged in London in an uneasy relationship with Chapman, his wife, and his mistress, while working as assistant editor on the *Westminster Review*. In July 1854 Chapman published Ludwig von Feuerbach's *The Essence of Christianity* 'translated by Marian Evans'. On 20 July she and George Henry Lewes (1817–78), the writer on science and philosophy, left together for Germany. On their return they lived as man and wife, Lewes, having condoned his wife's adultery, being prevented from obtaining a divorce.

In 1856 Marian began a story, 'The Sad Fortunes of Reverend Amos Barton', which Lewes submitted to Blackwood of Edinburgh, who printed it and two further stories in *Blackwood's Edinburgh Magazine*, and published them in volume form as *Scenes of Clerical Life* by 'George Eliot' (1858). This was followed by *Adam Bede* (1859), which received excellent notices. Speculation was now rife about the identity, and sex, of the author, whose alarm that her irregular domestic arrangements would harm her literary reputation was justified in that the reception of *The Mill on the Floss* (1860), published after the truth broke, was mixed. *Silas Marner: the Weaver of Raveloe* (1861) restored her standing as the leading novelist of the day, without making her socially acceptable, but *Romola*, (1863) published by Smith, Elder, was a financial failure. With *Felix Holt, the Radical* (1866), rejected by Smith, Elder, she returned to Blackwood, who were persuaded by Lewes to publish *Middlemarch, a Study of Provincial Life* (1871–2), initially in eight volumes in instalments over a year. It was hailed as a masterpiece and made her £8000 between then and 1879. In the meantime she had been struggling with poetry, which was published as *The Spanish Gypsy* (1868) and *The Legend of Jubal and Other Poems* (1874). Her final novel was *Daniel Deronda* (1876). In 1880, two years after Lewes's death, Marian married, which led her brother to communicate with her after 23 years. Her husband was her accountant, John Cross (1840–1924), who on their honeymoon in Venice tried to commit suicide by jumping into the canal. She died a few months later and, interment in Westminster Abbey having been refused, was buried in unconsecrated ground in Highgate Cemetery.

Professor David Daiches in *A Critical History of English Literature* (new edn 1969) begins his assessment of George Eliot, 'Before [her] the English novel had been almost entirely the work of those whose primary purpose was to entertain', and concludes: 'A sage whose moral vision is most effectively communicated through realistic fiction [was] an unusual phenomenon... when George Eliot began to write. If it has been less unusual since, that is because George Eliot by her achievement in fiction permanently enlarged the scope of the novel.' She was different in that the logical development of a situation transcends mere considerations of dramatic plot. Her intellect enabled her to investigate shades of morality and to present characters which are psychologically consistent — only when dealing with children, and then not after *Silas Marner*, the last novel in which she re-explored her own childhood, does her perception falter. The dilemmas of her characters are always expounded in the context of their environment and often reflect actual experiences. See Gordon S. Haight, *George Eliot: a Biography*, new edn 1986; Joan Bennett, *George Eliot: Her Mind and Art*, rev. edn 1962; Rosemary Ashton, *George Eliot*, 1983 (introduction to her thought).

**Eliot, T(homas) S(tearns)** (1888–1965), poet, dramatist, and critic, was born in St Louis, Missouri, and educated at Smith Academy, St Louis, and Harvard University. After graduating in philosophy and logic, and then spending a year at the Sorbonne in Paris, where he read French literature, he returned to Harvard to study epistemological theory, ancient Indian languages, and metaphysics. During this time he wrote 'The Love Song of J. Alfred Prufrock', 'Preludes', 'Portrait of a Lady', and 'Rhapsody on a Windy Night', all poems of considerable significance. The outbreak of war in 1914 interrupted his further studies at Marburg University, and he transferred to Merton College, Oxford, to read Greek philosophy. After two years teaching at boys' schools, he joined the Colonial and Foreign Department of Lloyds Bank, for which he worked until 1925. His first volume of poetry, *Prufrock and Other Observations*, was published in 1917, followed by *Poems* (1919) and *Ara Vos Prec* (1920). He was now not only giving a new direction to English and American poetry, but in *The Sacred Wood: Essays on Poetry and Criticism* (1920) he offered *inter alia* a new assessment of parts of the accepted canon of English literature itself, and argued that a poet should write from a 'historical sense' of European literature from Homer onwards as well as from his own national literary tradition. His wife's illness (he had married in 1915) and other worries contributed to a temporary bout of writer's block, from which the sudden release on a Swiss holiday resulted in the creation of 'The Waste Land'. This long, beautiful, symbolic poem of disillusionment, in a form incorporating suggestions by his friend, the American poet Ezra Pound (1885–1972), he himself published in 1922 in the first issue of a new literary magazine, *The Criterion*, which he founded and edited until 1939. In 1925 he became a director and an editor of the London publisher Faber and Faber, for whom he worked for the rest of his life and built up an enviable list of modern poets. *Poems, 1909–25* (1925) brought together what had already been published, with the addition of 'The Hollow Men', and represented the end of one poetic phase and the beginning of another, more questioning one, epitomised in the stylised, Dante-esque world of *Ash Wednesday* (1930). In 1927 he took British nationality and also became a member of the Church of England — the ultimate expression of his spiritual redemption in terms of time and eternity is in the poems 'Burnt Norton' (1936), 'East Coker' (1940), 'The Dry Salvages' (1941), and 'Little Gidding' (1942), published together as *Four Quartets* (1944).

With *Sweeney Agonistes: Fragments of an Aristophanic Melodrama* (1932) he explored the potential of the modern poetic drama, about which he had written in *The Sacred Wood. Murder in the Cathedral* (1935), for its religious associations in particular, is often performed, and though the comedy, *The Cocktail Party* (1950), and the more farcical *The Confidential Clerk* (1954) were admired in their time as stage plays, he is, in contrast to *Fry, more a poet than a dramatist. A musical adaptation of his juvenile-orientated but sophisticated rhymes, *Old Possum's Book of Practical Cats* (1939), has been produced under the title of *Cats* (1981).

As a poet, Eliot makes considerable demands on his readers, and it is up to them to respond. He is regarded as the founder of modernism in poetry, of whom as early as 1932 F. R. Leavis could write in *New Bearings in English Poetry*, 'We have here ... poetry that expresses freely a modern sensibility, the ways of feeling, the modes of experience, of one fully alive in his own age'. As a poet-critic in the tradition of *Dryden, *Coleridge, and *Arnold, his influence on the understanding and appreciation of literature has been profound. He pointed the way to a more incisive interest in Elizabethan and Jacobean drama, particularly *Massinger and *Webster, and in *Donne and other Metaphysical poets. In *The Idea of a Christian Society* (1939) and *Notes Towards the Definition of Culture* (1948) he turned his attention to the criticism of modern society. He was awarded the Nobel Prize for Literature, and also the OM, in 1948. See *The Complete Poems and Plays of T. S. Eliot*, 1969; *Selected Prose of T. S. Eliot*, ed. Frank Kermode, 1975; Lyndall Gordon, *Eliot's Early Years*, 1978, and *Eliot's New Life*, 1988 (biography); Helen Gardner, *The Art of T. S. Eliot*, new edn 1968; D. E. Jones, *The Plays of T. S. Eliot*, new edn 1963.

**Evelyn, John** (1620–1706), prose writer and diarist, was born on the family estate of Wotton in Surrey, but was boarded out with his grandparents in Sussex, whose home he refused to leave to go to Eton. So he was educated locally, then at Balliol College, Oxford (without taking a degree), and subsequently studied law in London. He joined the army of

Charles I too late to participate in the defeat at Brentford in 1642, and then, perhaps prudently, returned home before he could be associated with the cause. This kind of discretion governed his life, which he dedicated to learning and public service, without ever seeking, or accepting, the outward trappings of success — he even refused a knighthood. His famous diary, which he kept from 1641 until his death, was first published as his *Memoirs* in 1818, having apparently been found the year before in a clothes basket at Wotton. It is a record of an age rather than the revelations of an individual. Events and places (he was an inveterate traveller and guide) are often described with the help of newspaper and other accounts. There are, however, graphic descriptions of the Great Fire of London in 1666 and of the freeze of 1683–4, and penetrating observations on unusual aspects of life, and on the impact of religion upon daily existence at different levels. Among the books published during his lifetime were *Fumifugium* (1662), a plea for a smokeless London, and *Sylva: or a Discourse on Forest Trees* (1664), on which he was an authority. See *The Diary*, ed. John Bowle, 1985; John Bowle, *John Evelyn and His World*, 1981.

**Farquhar, George** (1678–1707), Irish dramatist, was born in Londonderry, one of seven children of a poor Church of England cleric, and educated (initially as a sizar, a student with a maintenance grant in return for certain domestic duties) at Trinity College, Dublin. He became an actor with Dublin's Smock Theatre, but left (to go to London), having inadvertently wounded a colleague in a stage duel through not using a blunted sword. His first comedy, *Love in a Bottle* (1698), was moderately successful: *The Constant Couple* (1699) did better. Several flops followed, and Farquhar's financial position was not advanced when he discovered that the widow with two children whom he had married was penniless. He was commissioned in Lord Orrery's regiment and sent to Lichfield and Shrewsbury to drum up recruits. He drew on this experience to write *The Recruiting Officer* (1706), which was so highly thought of by a London impresario that he advanced him £16.2s.6d. Farquhar, having resigned his commission, fell ill and into financial straits again. His actor friend Robert Wilkes gave him 20 guineas as an encouragement to write *The Beaux' Stratagem* (1707). Stock situations and characters abound (though Lady Bountiful's name has since entered the language), but the dialogue has a splendid vitality, and the ultimate dénouement is not the conjoining of the lovers, Aimwell and Dorinda, but the divorce by consent (after an exchange which draws heavily on *Milton's pamphlet on divorce) of the Sullens so that the wife may marry Aimwell's companion. See *Works*, ed. S. S. Kenny, 2 vols 1988; Eric Rothstein, *George Farquhar*, 1967.

**Fielding, Henry** (1707–54), novelist, dramatist, and journalist, was born at Sharpham Park, Somerset, son of an army officer who became a lieutenant-general in 1739. He was educated at Eton, which he had barely left when he fell violently in love with an orphan heiress, whose guardian was so frightened of her suitor that he had her sent away. Fielding now threw his considerable and athletic bulk into the pleasures of London, to pay for which he started to write plays, the first being a comedy of manners, *Love in Several Masques* (1728). After a period abroad, studying law in Leyden, he resumed a dramatic career, completing in all over thirty plays, of which *Tom Thumb* (1730), subsequently reworked and presented as *The Tragedy of Tragedies* (1731), and *Pasquin* (1736), both burlesques of stage conventions, playwrights, and politicians of the time, are notable for their wit. He married in 1734 and in 1736 took a lease on the Haymarket Theatre, only to be forced out of the dramatic world by the licensing act of 1737, to the framing of which his own plays and productions had contributed. He was admitted to the Bar, and practised on the western circuit. The success of *Richardson's *Pamela* (1740), which he felt exhibited dubious morality, nettled him into producing a burlesque novel, *An Apology for the Life of Mrs Shamela Andrews* (1741). He followed this, in a less boisterous and more comic vein, with *The History of the Adventures of Joseph Andrews, and of His Friend Mr Abram Adams, Written in Imitation of the Manner of Cervantes* (1742), which as it develops ceases to be a parody and becomes, beneath the picaresque plot, an attack on affectation and hypocrisy in general. The writer of burlesque surfaces again in *The Life of Mr Jonathan Wild the Great* (1743), a skilfully presented novel based on the exploits of a criminal who was hanged in 1725, in which normal standards are upturned, and greatness is deliberately confused with goodness, and kindness with weakness.

After his wife's death, probably in 1743, Fielding returned to political journalism, which he had practised briefly before, editing the pro-government *The True Patriot* during the rebellion of 1745, and *The Jacobite's Journal* from 1747 to 1748 — see *The Jacobite's Journal and Related Writings* (1974) and *The True Patriot and Related Writings* (1987), both ed. W. B. Coley. He married his former wife's maid in 1747 (their first child was christened three months later), and from 1749 to 1753 he served energetically and with distinction as a magistrate for Westminster and Middlesex — his legal and social pamphlets of this period are in *An Enquiry into the Causes of the Late Increase of Robbers and Related Writings*, ed. Malvin R. Zirker, 1987. In *The History of Tom Jones, a Foundling* (1749) he succeeded in putting together and sustaining through one mock-heroic masterpiece all the aims he had previously expressed about structure and narrative, morals, and artistic standards. *Amelia* (1752), Fielding's own favourite, is by contrast a novel of harsh domestic incident and social comment, modelled on classical epic lines. Its lack of spark has been regarded by some critics as a reflection of the author's ill health — he suffered badly from gout. In 1754, with his wife and daughter, he sailed for the warmer weather of Portugal, as he describes with good humour and realism in *The Journal of a Voyage to Lisbon* (1755). It was his last book, and his last journey, for he died in Lisbon two months after his arrival.

In the preface to *Joseph Andrews*, Fielding describes his novel as a 'comic epic poem in prose'. In Book IX. i. of *Tom Jones* he sets out the qualifications which are 'in a pretty high degree necessary to this order of historians' (i.e. novelists). They are 1) 'genius', which he defines as 'invention and judgment'; 2) a 'good sense of learning'; 3) 'conversation' (i.e. being fully conversant) with 'the characters of men' of 'all ranks and degrees'; 4) 'Nor will the qualities I have hitherto given my historian avail him, unless he have what is generally meant by a good heart, and be capable of feeling'. While in some ways his brand of morality, whereby goodness of heart and generosity outweigh the natural proclivities of youth, may be no more admirable than that of Richardson, subsequent generations of readers have responded enthusiastically to the ingenuity of the plot of *Tom Jones*, its satire as well as mock-heroic banter, the attention to descriptive detail, the clever drawing and contrasting of characters, and the gusto of the writing. See F. Homes Dudden, *Fielding: His Life, Works and Times*, 1952; Martin C. Battestin, *Henry Fielding: a Life*, 1989.

**Fitzgerald, Edward** (1809–83), poet and translator, was born near Woodbridge, Suffolk, and educated at King Edward VI's Grammar School, Bury St Edmunds, and Trinity College, Cambridge. With a brief interval for a disastrous marriage in 1856, he lived quietly with or near his parents until their deaths, and then in various parts of East Anglia, where he could indulge in his outdoor pursuit of sailing. From his self-imposed seclusion he cultivated literary friendships by means of a voluminous, elegant, and witty correspondence — see *Letters*, ed. J. M. Cohen, 1960. The first literary work to carry his name was a translation, *Six Dramas of Calderón* (the seventeenth-century Spanish poet), published in 1853. In 1857 he came across a manuscript of epigrams by Omar Khayyám, a twelfth-century Persian astronomer. The verse form of rhyming quatrains and the poet's philosophy appealed to Fitzgerald enough to attempt a poetic translation, first published in 1859 as *The Rubáiyát of Omar Khayyám*, and reissued with variations several times during his life. His aim was to reproduce the spirit and form of Omar's work, rather than the precise meaning — the famous 'Book of Verses underneath the Bough' is in the original Persian a leg of mutton, but that would have offended his readers' poetic sensibilities. The result, in whatever version it is read, is a finely polished, rhythmical expression of Victorian hedonism, whose nostalgic melancholy appealed, and still appeals, to generations whose existence is haunted by perplexity. See Alfred M. Terhune, *The Life of Fitzgerald*, new edn 1980.

**Flecker, James Elroy** (1884–1915), poet, was born in Lewisham, London, and educated at Dean Close School, Cheltenham (of which his father was Headmaster), Uppingham School, and Trinity College, Oxford, where a contemporary remembered him as an immature youth, with a penchant for conversation and a facility for verse. In 1908 he decided to enter the Consular Service, and took a course in oriental languages at Caius College, Cambridge. He was taken ill with tuberculosis during his first assignment in Constantinople and, having served in various places in the East, gave up his career in 1913. He spent the last 18 months of his life in Switzerland on his doctors' advice. His first book of poems, *The Bridge of Fire*, was published in 1907, and was followed by three more, including *The Golden Journey to Samarkand* (1913). Initially he tended towards the classical and romantic, and practised his craft by translating classical and European models. Latterly he was attracted to the French literary movement, the Parnassians, in whose work he saw a reaction against the 'perfervid sentimentality and extravagance of some French Romantics', and whose aim was to create a statuesque and objective beauty. His best-known work is *Hassan*, published posthumously in 1922, an oriental play in verse in which the spareness of his approach serves to heighten the lushness of the setting and the drama of the situation. It was first produced in 1923, with incidental music by Frederick Delius (1862–1934). See *Collected Poems*, ed. Sir John Squire, 3rd edn 1946.

**Fletcher, John** (1579–1625), poet and dramatist, was born in Rye, Sussex, younger son of the future Dean of Peterborough who insensitively delayed the execution of Mary, Queen of Scots. He was educated at St Bene't College, Cambridge. His association with *Beaumont began in about 1606, and he is credited with having a hand in over fifty plays, including *Shakespeare's *Henry VIII* and *The Two Noble Kinsmen*. The earliest play known to be by Fletcher alone is *The Faithful Shepherdess* (*c.*1609), a tragicomedy, which he defined as a play of familiar people in situations which could result in death but do not. This particular play is a complex exposition of pastoral love both spiritual and physical, with a dash of the supernatural. Other tragicomedies include *The Humorous Lieutenant* (*c.*1619), in which an aphrodisiac taken by the wrong victim causes much farce; and *Island Princess* (*c.*1621), a more romantic drama. Sheer comedy is best represented by *The Wild Goose Chase* (*c.*1621), whose in-fighting between the sexes and witty dialogue look forward to Restoration comedy. He also wrote two tragedies of Imperial Rome, *Bonduca* (*c.*1612) and *Valentinian* (*c.*1614). Fletcher became chief playwright of the King's Men. Among his songs which have passed into literary heritage are 'Melancholy' ('Hence, all you vain delights...') and 'Hear, ye ladies'. He died of the plague, having stayed in London to have a new suit made up before going into the country. See Clifford Leech, *The John Fletcher Plays*, 1962.

**Ford, Ford Madox** (1873–1939), novelist, essayist, poet, and critic, was born Ford Hermann Hueffer in Merton, Surrey, changing his name in 1919. He was the son of the German-born music critic Francis Hueffer (1845–89) and grandson of the artist Ford Madox Brown (1821–93). His mother's sister married D. G. *Rossetti's younger brother William. He was educated at University College School. Early publications were *The Brown Owl: a Fairy Story* (1892), and studies of Ford Madox Brown (1896) and Rossetti (1902). In 1894 he eloped and went through a Catholic marriage with the 17-year-old Elsie Martindale (*d*.1949), who in 1910 successfully sued him for restitution of conjugal rights and subsequently obtained damages from a newspaper for describing the novelist Violet Hunt (1866–1942), with whom he had a stormy affair, as 'Mrs Ford Madox Hueffer'. With *Conrad, he wrote the novels *The Inheritors* (1901) and *Romance* (1903). In *The Fifth Queen* (1906), *Privy Seal* (1907), and *The Fifth Queen Crowned* (1908), about Henry VIII's fifth wife, Katharine Howard, the main characters are the historical protagonists in the conflicts of the times. *The Good Soldier: a Tale of Passion* (1915) is a novel of complex relationships. In spite of his age, he served as an officer in France during World War I, and was severely wounded and gassed. The four novels called 'Tietjen's Saga' after their principal character — *Some Do Not...* (1924), *No More Parades* (1925), *A Man Could Stand Up...* (1926), and *Last Post* (1928), which he wrote as an afterthought and later regretted — span the war years. They were published together as *Parade's End* (1950). After 1923 Ford divided his time between France and America, where he was appointed Lecturer in Comparative Literature at Olivet College, Michigan, in 1937. He was an early advocate of impressionism in fiction and poetry, and an inspirational editor. He edited *The English Review* from 1908 to 1910, and founded *the transatlantic review* in 1924. His critical works include *Portraits from Life* (1937, 1938 as *Mightier Than the Sword*), and studies of *James (1913) and Conrad (1924). See *The Bodley Head Ford Madox Ford*, Vols 1–4 (introduction by Graham Greene), 1962–3, Vol. 5 (ed. Michael Killigrew), 1971; *Collected Poems*, 1941; Arthur Mizener, *The Saddest Story: a Biography of Ford Madox Ford*, 1971.

**Forster, E(dward) M(organ)** (1879–1970), novelist, short story writer, and critic, was born in Dorset Square, London, only surviving child of an architect who died of consumption a year later. The boy's creative talents were inspired and his psychological development affected by three women: his mother, who died in 1945, his maternal grandmother, and his father's aunt, Marianne Thornton, who died in 1887, leaving him £8000 in trust and the capital when he was 25, which enabled him to travel and to write. His early childhood in a Hertfordshire country house was happy and idyllic, and included his first emotional relationship with a member of his own sex, symbolically recalled in his story 'Ansell', written in about

1903. He attended Tonbridge School as a day boy, which was the source of his lifelong antipathy towards the middle-class values he found there. At King's College, Cambridge, he had a moderate academic career, abandoned religion, but discovered comradeship and freedom of thought and expression. His subsequent continental travels, partly with his mother, confirmed his attitude to the English middle class but also inspired his first story, 'The Story of a Panic' — see *Collected Short Stories* (1947) — which was inspired by and set in and around Ravello. It was published in 1904 in the *Independent Review*, founded by some of his Cambridge contemporaries. Of the four novels he then published, *Where Angels Fear to Tread* (1905) and *A Room with a View* (1908) involve differences between the English and Italian temperaments; in *The Longest Journey* (1907), the contrast is between conventional and personal values; and in *Howards End* (1910) between the creative imagination and commercial gain. All these works are distinguished by his manipulation of his characters in their search for harmony and by his quiet, pervasive humour.

In 1913–14 he wrote a homosexual novel, *Maurice*, which was posthumously published in 1971, as were a number of stories written between 1903 and 1958 which were collected into *The Life to Come* (1972). Between visits to India in 1913 and 1921, Forster served with the Red Cross in Egypt in World War I — his *Alexandria: a History and a Guide* was published in 1922. Out of these experiences came what proved to be his last novel and final fictional statement on universal harmony and diversity, *A Passage to India* (1924), whose three parts, Mosque, Caves, Temple, symbolise respectively the Muslim, Western, and Hindu approaches to truth, rationality, and spirituality. His Clark Lectures at Cambridge in 1927 on elements of fiction from *Defoe to *Lawrence were published as *Aspects of the Novel* — new edn, ed. Oliver Stallybrass (1976) — and collections of his critical essays and reviews are *Abinger Harvest* (1936) and *Two Cheers for Democracy* (1951). In 1946 he was appointed an Honorary Fellow of King's College, where he then lived until his death, being made CH in 1953 and awarded the OM in 1969. See P. N. Furbank, *E. M. Forster: a Life*, new edn 1988; John Colmer, *E. M. Forster: the Personal Voice*, new edn 1983 (critical study).

**Fry, Christopher** (*b.* 1907), dramatist, was born in Bristol, had a Christian upbringing, and was educated at Bedford Modern School. He worked as a schoolmaster, and as an actor and producer in local 'rep', before writing his first play, *The Boy with a Cart* (about St Cuthman of Sussex), in 1939 as an experiment for a local cast of amateurs. *The Firstborn*, written in 1945 but not produced in London until 1952 in a revised version, has the plagues of Egypt as its theme and Moses as its chief character, while *Thor with Angels* (1948) was written to be performed in the Chapter House of Canterbury Cathedral, and *A Sleep of Prisoners* (1951) is set in a church. In the meantime he had shown in *A Phoenix Too Frequent* (1946), loosely based on an incident in Petronius, that his verse form could be adapted to broad comedy, and in *Venus Observed* (1950) to the modern romance of manners. *The Lady's Not for Burning* (1949), set in a stylised segment of the Middle Ages, has as its chief characters a world-weary vagabond who wishes to be hanged and a suspected witch who has no desire to be burned. The intricate arguments between them and the ornate texture of the poetry offer chances of great acting, which the play got during its initial London run — it suffers unfairly when performed by a leading couple of small experience. Fry has also successfuly translated and adapted plays by Jean Anouilh (1910–87) and Jean Giraudoux (1882–1944). See Derek Stanford, *Christopher Fry*, 1954.

**Galsworthy, John** (1867–1933), dramatist, novelist, short story writer, and poet, was born at Kingston Hill, Surrey, and educated at Harrow and New College, Oxford. On a sea voyage to complement his study of marine law, he met *Conrad, who became an influence on his ultimate choice of career and a lifelong friend. After publishing several novels under the pseudonym of John Sinjohn, Galsworthy achieved a remarkable 'double' in 1906 with his first play, *The Silver Box*, a study of the comparative justice meted out to rich and poor, and the novel, *The Man of Property*, which by the addition of two sequels, *In Chancery* (1920) and *To Let* (1921), and two linking passages, grew into *The Forsyte Saga* (1922). Only a very good novelist could have sustained the reader's interest in so many characters from a single strand of society and in the process evoke sympathy for the soulless Soames, but attempts to expand the saga further were not so felicitous — better fiction is found in his shorter stories, especially those about love. His preoccupation with the iniquities of the class system is displayed with scrupulous fairness in his plays, notably *Strife* (1909), about industrial relations, and *The Skin Game* (1920), in which landed rich confronts nouveau riche. Galsworthy refused a knighthood in 1918. He was awarded the OM in 1929, and the Nobel Prize for Literature in 1932. See *Five Plays*, 1984; *Collected Poems*, 1934; Catherine Dupré, *John Galsworthy: a Biography*, 1976; Alec Frechet, *John Galsworthy: a Reassessment*, 1982.

**Gaskell, Elizabeth** (1810–65), née Stevenson, novelist and biographer, was born in Chelsea, daughter of a civil servant. Her mother died the next year, and she was brought up by her aunt in Knutsford, Cheshire — the Cranford of her writings. After lessons at home, she spent five useful years at a girls' boarding school. When she was 21 she married William Gaskell, a Unitarian minister and classical scholar. They lived in Manchester, and had four daughters, and a son, after whose death in infancy on a family holiday in 1845 Mr Gaskell encouraged his wife to write a novel. *Mary Barton* (1848) was unusual for its time in that its background was working-class and its theme industrial relations. It impressed

*Dickens, in whose journals much of her subsequent work first appeared. *Cranford* (1853), her best-known novel, is a series of linked sketches of provincial life in which the characters are beautifully drawn. In *North and South* (1855) she returns to the industrial north, contrasting it with the manners of the rural south. She had been introduced in 1850 to Charlotte *Brontë, whose confidante she became and on whose death Mr Brontë invited her to write an authorised biography. *The Life of Charlotte Brontë* (1857) is one of the finest English literary biographies. Mrs Gaskell died suddenly at a family gathering in the country house she had bought for her husband's retirement. She left an unfinished novel, *Wives and Daughters* (1866), a perceptive, witty study of family relationships. See Winifred Gérin, *Elizabeth Gaskell*, new edn 1980.

**Gay, John** (1685–1732), poet, dramatist and librettist, was born in Barnstaple, Devon, and cared for by an uncle after being orphaned at the age of ten. He was educated at the local free grammar school and then apprenticed to a London mercer, whom he left to join the literary circle of the time. He published an anonymous poem, *Wine* (1708), then several plays and volumes of minor poetry, of which only a mock-pastoral, *The Shepherd's Week* (1714), and *Trivia: or the Art of Walking in the Streets of London* (1716), a spoof in heroic couplets, reveal much artistry. Yet such were the influence of his friends and the attention of his various patrons that *Poems* (1720) earned him a large sum which he invested, and lost, in the South Sea Company (after which he was, perhaps appropriately, appointed Lottery Commissioner). *Fables* (1727) comprises moral tales in verse in which the acerbic and often topical moral usually outweighs the tale. All his previous writing experience crystallised in *The Beggar's Opera* (1728), a musical comedy of London low life, incorporating parallels with the current political situation, with songs set to popular tunes of the day, some of which echoed contemporary classical composers. Its success is also due to the situations, characters, and lyrics — the source of the lines 'If with me you'd fondly stray / Over the hills and far away' and 'How happy I could be with either / Were t'other dear charmer away'. A sequel, *Polly* (1729), was banned from the stage but published to acclaim. See S. M. Armens, *John Gay, Social Critic*, 1954.

**Gibbon, Edward** (1737–94), historian, was born in Putney, London. A bookish but sickly child, he was educated at Westminister School (where his aunt had set up a boarding house, it is said for his benefit) and for 14 profligate months at Magdalen College, Oxford, at the end of which he became a Catholic. He was sent by his father to Lausanne for four years, where he accepted Protestantism again, learned French, studied Latin, and at his father's insistence broke off his engagement to Suzanne Curchod. His *Essai sur l'Etude de la Littérature* (1761) was translated into English in 1764, though he was never much interested in the English edition. Sitting on the Capitol in Rome in 1764, he had the idea of writing a history of the decay of the ancient city, later elaborated into *The History of the Decline and Fall of the Roman Empire* (7 vols 1776–88). He entered Parliament in 1774 and served in a minor government post 1779–82. His treatment of the rise of Christianity in the first volume of his great work caused controversy, and after the appearance of Vols II and III he returned to Lausanne, where he lived quietly for the rest of his life, corpulent from his sedentary occupation, and a dandy. His grasp of history is excellent, the arrangement and flow of his material masterly, and his prose, enlivened by touches of humour and apocalyptical detail, superb. He wrote from a standpoint within the Roman world, and his religious views are anticlerical but not necessarily anti-Christian. See Roy Porter, *Edward Gibbon*, 1988 (biography): J. W. Burrow, *Gibbon*, 1985 (introduction to his work).

**Gibbon, Lewis Grassic**, pseudonym of James Leslie Mitchell (1901–35), Scottish novelist, was born in a croft in Auchterless, Aberdeenshire, and educated at Arbuthnott Village School and Mackie Academy, Stonehaven, which he left after a year to try journalism. From 1919 to 1923 he served in the Middle East in the Royal Army Service Corps and, having on his discharge failed for five months to earn a living as a writer, enlisted as a clerk in the RAF for six years, after which he lived in Welwyn Garden City until his early death from a perforated ulcer. As J. Leslie Mitchell he wrote several anthropological works, including *Hanno, or the Future of Exploration* (1928) and *The Conquest of the Maya* (1934), and seven novels. He used the pseudonym Lewis Grassic Gibbon for a life of the Scottish explorer Mungo Park (1934) and for his Scottish novels, in which he employed a stylised form of dialogue to represent the speech of the North-East, the setting of *Sunset Song* (1932), *Cloud Howe* (1933), and *Grey Granite* (1934). Reissued in 1946 as a trilogy entitled *A Scots Quair* (new edn 1986), they reflect, through the experiences of twice-married Chris Guthrie, the contrasts and clashes of culture, language, and living conditions inherent in Scottish life, and the hypnotic intensity of the land. Rural life features strongly in two of his short stories, 'Clay' and 'Smeddum', which are as good as anything he wrote after *Sunset Song*. See Ian Campbell, *Lewis Grassic Gibbon*, 1985.

**Gissing, George** (1857–1903), novelist, was born in Wakefield and educated at a Quaker boarding school and Owens College, Manchester. A brilliant academic career was cut short when he was expelled, having been sentenced to prison for stealing in order to 'rescue' a girl of the streets, whom he later unwisely married. After suffering great hardship in England and America in search of a job, he managed to study philosophy briefly at the university in Jena, and, with the help of a legacy, wrote and paid for the publication of *Workers in the Dawn* (1880), the first of a number of novels intended to reveal the 'hideous injustice of our whole system of society'. It failed to impress the public, but through it he found employment as a tutor. He wrote 22 novels in all, which in many cases chart the unhappy progress of his life, while graphically mirroring the conditions and feelings of the lower middle class. *New Grub Street* (1891) explores the seamier aspects of the literary world of his time. Long saved-up for trips to Greece and Italy resulted in a travel book, *By the Ionian Sea* (1901, ed. Virginia *Woolf 1933), and a scholarly blockbusting novel of later Rome, *Veranilda* (1904). *The Private Papers of Henry Ryecroft* (1903), a fictitious author's journal, represents his aspirations rather than his experience. Gissing brought an academic rather than simply an imaginative approach to the novel of contemporary reality. See John Halperin, *Gissing: a Life in Books*, new edn 1987 (biography); John Sloane, *George Gissing: the Cultural Challenge*, 1989 (critical study).

**Golding,** (Sir) **William** (*b*.1911), novelist, was born in St Columb Minor, Cornwall, and educated at Marlborough Grammar School, Wiltshire (of which his father was Headmaster), and Brasenose College, Oxford. Before World War II, in which he served in the Royal Navy and commanded a rocket ship, he was an actor and stage producer, and for a year a teacher. He also published a book of verse, *Poems* (1934). His first novel, *Lord of the Flies* (1954) — the title is the meaning of the Hebrew term for Beelzebub — illustrates how internal and external pressures can cause a society to disintegrate, in this case exemplified by a group of marooned children. Though some of his novels may at first sight appear to reflect different treatments of similar themes — *The Inheritors* (1955) investigates the destruction of a primitive culture, and *Pincher Martin* (1956) is also set on a desert island; while *Free Fall* (1960) and *The Pyramid* (1967) both recall a young man's experiences on the road towards maturity — in effect each has a fresh starting point and develops along distinctive lines. His leitmotifs are broadly creation, temptation, destruction, and preservation, all of which are present in *The Spire* (1964). His distinguished maritime trilogy, *Rites of Passage* (1980), *Close Quarters* (1987), and *Fire Down Below* (1989), uses a sea voyage to Australia in Napoleonic times as the medium through which emotions and drama are fomented. He has published two volumes of essays, *The Hot Gates* (1965) and *A Moving Target* (1982). He was made CBE in 1966, awarded the Nobel Prize for Literature in 1983, and knighted in 1988. See James Gindin, *William Golding*, 1988.

**Goldsmith, Oliver** (1728–74), Irish dramatist, novelist, poet, and journalist, was born in Pallasmore, Co. Longford, fifth child of a curate who became rector of Kilkenny West. He suffered an attack of smallpox in childhood which permanently disfigured him. His father having over-stretched himself in the matter of a dowry for an elder sister, Goldsmith went to Trinity College, Dublin, as a sizar. After failing to settle to anything but riotous living, he was paid for by members of his family to read medicine at Edinburgh University, which he abandoned after two years to wander through Europe on foot, arriving in London in 1756, penniless but claiming to have acquired a medical degree on his travels. He became a journalist and in 1759 published anonymously *An Enquiry into the Present State of Polite Learning in Europe*, while writing for several journals including his own, *The Bee*, which folded after eight issues. A series of observations of the London scene in the *Public Ledger*, written as though by a Chinese and bearing the unmistakable Irish stamp of polite irony towards the English, were collected as *The Citizen of the World* (1762). He had now become a member of the circle of *Johnson, who got him to finish his philosophical poem, *The Traveller: or a Prospect of Society* (1765), the first work to carry his name, and found a publisher for *The Vicar of Wakefield: a Tale* (1766). This gentle, human story of multiple misfortunes with a mercifully happy conclusion has in the course of it the delightful poems 'When lovely woman stoops to folly' and 'An Elegy on the Death of a Mad Dog', with its famous closing line, 'The dog it was that died'. His major long poem, *The Deserted Village* (1770), reflects, in flowing couplets, nostalgia for the homeliness and innocence of rural life.

In the meantime he had turned to the stage, about which he had often expressed his views in print. *The Good Natur'd Man: a Comedy* (1768) is amusing enough but structurally uneven. The extended joke upon which the action of *She Stoops to Conquer: or the Mistakes of a Night* (1773) is founded is timeless, and the absurdity of many of the resulting situations goes unnoticed in a continuous flow of economically-presented comic set pieces and exchanges between likeable characters. Overgenerous and improvident, Goldsmith spent or gave away his earnings as he received them, and at the height of his fame was forced to indulge in hack-work, albeit in his natural literary style. He produced histories of Rome (1769, abridged by himself 1772), England (1771), and Greece (1774), as well as *An History of the Earth and Animated Nature* in eight volumes (1774). It is said that his death from a fever was hastened by overwork, debts, and his insistence on doctoring himself, and that *Burke burst into tears when he heard the news, and Sir Joshua Reynolds (1723–92) laid down his brush and painted no more that day. See *Collected Works*, ed. Arthur Friedman, 5 vols 1966; Ralph M. Wardle, *Oliver Goldsmith*, 1957 (biography); A. Swarbrick (ed.), *The Art of Oliver Goldsmith*, 1984. Also *Gray.

**Gower, John** (*c*.1330–1408), poet, was of a landed family and probably spent much of his early life in Kent, where he later invested in real estate. He was closely associated with the Court, but from 1377 until his death lived in lodgings in the Priory of St Mary Overey in Southwark. He was a friend of *Chaucer (who saddled him with the title 'moral Gower'), but latterly they appear to have fallen out. *Mirour de l'Homme* ('Mirror of Man' — its Latin title is *Speculum Meditantis*) is a long exhortation about sin, written in the late 1370s in Anglo-French, the upper-class and court language of the time. He then began *Vox Clamantis* ('The Voice of One Crying...'), a critique of corruption at all levels of society, including the clergy, written in Latin elegaics, to which he added an introductory book citing the Peasants' Revolt of 1381 as justification of his arguments. In *Confessio Amantis* ('The Lover's Confession'), written between 1386 and 1390 in English octosyllabic couplets, he takes a more relaxed tone. Too much moralising, he says, often dulls a man's wits, so 'I wolde go the middel weie / And wryte a bok between the tweie, / Somwhat of lust, somwhat of love...'. The 'love' involves analysing each of the Seven Deadly Sins in five ways, while the 'lust' (or pleasure) is in the wry dialogue between the lover and his confessor, and in the stories which the poet retells from many sources. See J. H. Fisher, *John Gower: Moral Philosopher and Friend of Chaucer*, 1964; and in C. S. Lewis, *The Allegory of Love*, 1936.

**Graves, Robert** (1895–1985), poet, novelist, translator, classicist, critic, unorthodox mythologist and biblical scholar, was born in Wimbledon, London. He was educated at Charterhouse, enlisted in the Royal Welch Fusiliers at the outbreak of World War I, and was badly wounded on the Somme. After the war he went to St John's College, Oxford, and though he did not take a degree, he was granted a B. Litt. for his thesis *Poetic Unreason and Other Studies* (1925). In *Goodbye to All That* (1929), one of the best of all autobiographies, he records his life at school, at the front, and as a struggling writer. His other most seminal prose work is *The White Goddess: a Historical Grammar of Poetic Myth* (1948, rev. edn 1966), a treatment of mythology in which he ascribes the poet's impulse to an ancient matriarchal presence, who recurs figuratively as the opponent of Christ in his novel *King Jesus* (1946). *I, Claudius* (1934) and *Claudius the God and His Wife Messalina* (1934) rank as the best historical novels of the Roman period. Graves largely rejected the poetry of his experiences in the war and immediately after, to come to stand pre-eminent as a poet of romantic and sexual love, whose skilfully honed work has an underlying tension, often heightened by supernatural elements. Among his criticism is *On Poetry: Collected Talks and Essays* (1969). After World War II he settled permanently in Majorca. He was Professor of Poetry at Oxford 1961–6. See *Collected Poems*, 1947, 1959, 1965, and 1975; *Collected Short Stories*, 1971; Martin Seymouth-Smith, *Robert Graves: His Life and Work*, new edn 1987; J. M. Cohen, *Robert Graves*, 1960 (critical study).

**Gray, Thomas** (1716–71), poet, was born in London, son of a bad-tempered scrivener, and educated, thanks to his mother, at Eton and

Peterhouse, Cambridge, though he did not take his degree in law until four years later, having in the meantime travelled in Europe with his schoolfriend *Walpole. He preferred to study rather than practise law and for most of his life lived in Cambridge, being appointed Professor of Modern History in 1768, though he never gave a lecture. Reserved and shy — he refused the Poet Laureateship in 1757 — he removed his lodgings after undergraduates had placed a tub of water under his window and raised the fire alarm. Gray, who had a pathological fear of fire, shinned down his personal rope-ladder, and into the tub! His output reflects his contemplative and fastidious nature. *Ode on a Distant Prospect of Eton College* was published anonymously in 1747. He worked on *An Elegy Wrote in a Country Churchyard* (1751) for nine years and it too was first published anonymously as a pamphlet, after the poet had refused permission for it to be printed in a magazine. Its outstanding place in eighteenth-century poetry has been magnified by its down-to-earth appeal, and its lasting popularity ensured by the familar quotations enshrined in it. *Poems by Mr Gray* (1768) included these and the mock-heroic 'Ode, on the Death of a Favourite Cat', with seven poems which illustrate his absorption with Greek, Celtic, and Norse studies. See Roger Lonsdale (ed.), *The Poems of Thomas Gray, William Collins, Oliver Goldsmith*, new edn 1976; R.W. Ketton-Cremer, *Gray: a Biography*, 1955.

**Greene, Graham** (*b.*1904), novelist, short story writer, dramatist and critic, was born in Berkhamsted, Hertfordshire, and educated at Berkhamsted School (of which his father was Headmaster) and Balliol College, Oxford. While he was at school he wrote poetry, stories (one of which was published in the *Star*), and a play, which was accepted by a dramatic society but never performed. Verses written at Oxford, by his own account mainly inspired by love for his sisters' governess, were published in various journals, in the *Oxford Outlook*, which he edited, and in book form as *Babbling April* (1925). When he became engaged to a Catholic, he decided to discover more about her beliefs and as a result was himself converted in 1926, and married the following year. After working unpaid for the *Nottingham Journal*, he joined *The Times* as a sub-editor in 1926, which he regards as having been a formative experience for a novelist. After many false starts and the rejection of a detective story, he got the idea for a new novel while in hospital recovering from an appendicectomy. He finished it and it was accepted. *The Man Within* (1929) is a historical romance, whose pursuit theme recurs in different forms in all his subsequent novels, whether the character is trying to run away from society, the police, his own conscience, or God. Emboldened by its success, he persuaded his publisher to advance him money against two further novels, whereupon he threw up his job. He relates, 'I sometimes find myself wishing that, before starting my second novel...I had found an experienced mentor.' The two novels, in much the same vein as his first, were financial failures and he later suppressed them. In debt and distress, having wasted time by writing a biography of *Rochester which his publisher rejected (it was finally published in 1974), he started a thriller. *Stamboul Train* (1932) was published only after changes were made to the printed copies under the threat of a libel action from *Priestley, whom he had never met. It was a popular success, and his reputation, and way of living, were established.

In his autobiography of these early years, *A Sort of Life* (1971), Greene writes, 'If I were to choose an epigraph for all the novels I have written, it would be from [*Browning's] "Bishop Blougram's Apology": "Our interest's in the dangerous edge of things. / The honest thief, the tender murderer.... / We watch while these in equilibrium keep / The giddy line midway".' He is himself no stranger to personal danger, as witness *Journal Without Maps* (1936), an account of a trip through Liberia. The inveterate traveller in him is reflected in the foreign and often exotic settings of many of his novels — Mexico for *The Power and the Glory* (1940), Sierra Leone (to which he went for the Foreign Office in World War II) for *The Heart of the Matter* (1948), Vietnam for *The Quiet American* (1955), Cuba for *Our Man in Havana* (1958), a leper colony in the Congo for *A Burnt-Out Case* (1961), Haiti for *The Comedians* (1966), Argentina for *The Honorary Consul* (1973). Also significant is the journalistic instinct which enables him to select situations of topical interest — this sense is further affirmed by his controversial pamphlet, *J'Accuse: the Dark Side of Nice* (1982). Violence, suspense or mere unease are always below the surface of his English novels, too, such as *England Made Me* (1935), *A Gun for Sale* (1936), and *The End of the Affair* (1951). The Catholic element in his novels, which was first evident in *Brighton Rock* (1938) and is a central concern in *The Heart of the Matter*, serves as a natural concomitant to the action rather than as an expression of a particular message.

In the introduction to *Collected Stories* (1972) he relates his surprise at realising 'that since the beginning I have really been all the time a writer of short stories', and these examples of a different approach to that which he employs as a novelist include some of his rare, and late, excursions into humour in what he calls 'comedies of the sexual life'. Of his plays, *The Living Room* (1953) treats of despair in Catholic terms, *The Potting Shed* (1957) is a drama of mystery with a spiritual solution, and *The Complaisant Lover* (1959), outwardly a comedy, has melancholic undertones. *Collected Essays* (1969) includes studies of authors, while articles he wrote for the *Spectator* are in *The Pleasure-Dome: the Collected Film Criticism 1935–40 of Graham Greene*, ed. John Russell Taylor (1972). He was made CH in 1966 and awarded the OM in 1986. See Norman Sherry, *The Life of Graham Greene: Volume One, 1904–39*, 1989; Grahame Smith, *The Achievement of Graham Greene*, 1986; John Spurling, *Graham Greene*, 1983 (critical study).

**Hardy, Thomas** (1840–1928), novelist and poet, was born in Higher Bockhampton, near Stinsford, Dorset, eldest child of a master stone-mason. He was educated at a local private school until he was 16, when he was apprenticed to a church architect in Dorchester. In 1862 he went to London to further his studies and his career, which he did while continuing to educate himself in classics and poetry. A bout of illness led him to return home in 1867 and to work for his former employer. Writing interested him passionately and, having had many poems rejected by London literary journals, he decided to try his hand at fiction. His first attempt, a combination of socialist satire and rusticity, was accepted, but the publisher's reader, who was *Meredith, advised him to withdraw it and write something with a bit more plot. The result was *Desperate Remedies* (1871), a story of murder and intrigue, whose anonymous appearance with a different publisher he himself subsidised, though he got most of his money back from sales. He used some of the country scenes from his first novel as a basis for *Under the Greenwood Tree* (1872), a rustic comedy. Yokels reappear as minor characters in *A Pair of Blue Eyes* (1873), in which he exercised his penchant for heavy romance and high drama, using as a starting point his own experience of conducting a survey of a remote Cornish church, at which he met his future wife.

In the meantime he had been invited to write a serial for *Cornhill Magazine*. The impact of his anonymous contribution, *Far from the Madding Crowd* (1874), was such that some critics attributed it to George *Eliot, which Hardy resented, though its success meant that he was now able to give up his job and to marry. *Far from the Madding Crowd* is firmly and recognisably set in what he calls by its ancient name of Wessex, and he gets exactly right the balance between the steady, ritual progress of the country year, the eruptions of passion and violence, and the courting of the magnetic and erratic Bathsheba Everdene by her patient shepherd, Gabriel Oak, who wins her on the very last page. There is even more passion, and more tragedy, in *The Return of the Native* (1878), for which, at the request of the journal which accepted it, the sub-plot was changed so as to have a happy ending, and whose main theme, though simple and controlled, depends overmuch on chance. The subtitle of *The Mayor of Casterbridge: the Life and Death of a Man of Character* (1886) only partly sums up this powerful study of a tragic hero in the Shakespearian mould. These three are the most readable of his 17 novels and volumes of short stories — see *The Short Stories of Thomas Hardy* (1928) — but the greatest fame, and controversy, were reserved for *Tess of the d'Urbervilles* (1891), even in its bowdlerised form. When *Jude the Obscure* (1896), written with rather less attention to art, got a still more critical press, he gave up fiction for good.

Hardy had continued all this time to write poetry. Now, with *Wessex Poems and Other Verses* (1898), a third of which he had composed in the

1860s, he began to publish it. He was not a great poet, but he wrote some very good short poems and ballads among the nine hundred in *Collected Poems* (1930). His style is rugged, his tone often melancholic, and his humour grim, but his choice of words is magical and his meaning is always clear. Particularly poignant is the group 'Poems of 1912–13', which he composed after his wife's death, having discovered among her papers notes about their marriage. His most ambitious work of all, *The Dynasts: a Drama of the Napoleonic Wars*, 'intended simply for mental perform-ance and not for the stage', was published in three parts 1903–8. The scope is vast and the stage directions often on a cosmic scale, but the mixture of blank verse and prose, fact and historical imagination, and humble as well as noble characters, gives a total effect of grandeur. His second marriage in 1914 proved so agreeable that he was able to dictate to his wife large chunks of the two biographies of him that were published under her name in 1928 and 1930. His final rites were typical of his creative duality. While his ashes were being carried for interment in Westminster Abbey by a squad of literary pall-bearers, his heart, which had been cut from the corpse, was being buried in Stinsford churchyard, where he had wished to lie. He was awarded the OM in 1910. See *Hardy's Poetry 1860–1928*, ed. Dennis Taylor, 1987; *Thomas Hardy: Selected Letters*, ed. Michael Millgate, 1989; Michael Millgate, *Thomas Hardy*, new edn 1985 (biography); J. I. M. Stewart, *Thomas Hardy*, 1971 (critical biography); Desmond Hawkins, *Thomas Hardy: Novelist and Poet*, 1981.

**Hartley, L(eslie) P(oles)** (1895–1972), novelist and short story writer, son of a retired solicitor who managed a prosperous brick factory, was brought up in the family home of Fletton Tower, near Peterborough, and educated at Harrow and Balliol College, Oxford, with a two-year gap for war service. From 1922 to 1939 he spent half of each year in Venice, which features in many of his stories and 17 novels, and wrote book reviews for several journals. Apart from a short novel in the manner of *James, *Simonetta Perkins* (1925), his early published works are stories of the macabre, included in *Night Fears and Other Stories* (1924) and *The Killing Bottle* (1932). His first major novel, *The Shrimp and the Anemone*, was begun in the 1920s, but he did not publish it until 1944, feeling that it might be regarded unfairly as overtly autobiographical. It reveals, with great psychological insight, the intellectual relationship between a boy and his elder sister, which is continued through *The Sixth Heaven* (1946) and *Eustace and Hilda* (1947), the title by which the trilogy is known. In *The Go-Between* (1953), the position and tribulations of a child in an adult world are further explored in an Edwardian country-house setting. In this book, too, and in *The Hireling* (1957), the apparent dangers of sexual relationships between different classes loom large. See *The Complete Short Stories of L. P. Hartley*, 1977; Anne Mulkeen, *Wild Thyme, Winter Lightning: the Symbolic Novels of L. P. Hartley*, 1974.

**Hazlitt, William** (1778–1830), essayist and critic, was born in Maidstone, Kent, son of a Unitarian minister who then moved to Ireland and America before settling in Wem, Shropshire. At 14, Hazlitt was entered for the ministry at New College, Hackney, but gave up his faith three years later. In 1798 he met *Coleridge, under whose influence he determined to be a writer, though in the meantime he studied painting, for which he had some talent. In 1804 he joined Coleridge and *Wordsworth in the Lake District, but had to leave after attempting sexual assaults on local girls. After some time in the wilderness he ventured to London, was taken up by *Lamb, and became a reporter for the *Morning Chronicle*. He was soon promoted to drama critic and book reviewer, and moved to other journals, including *The Times*. Within a few years he had enough material to publish *Characters of Shakespeare's Plays* (1817), *A View to the English Stage: or a Series of Dramatic Criticisms* (1818), and *Lectures on the English Poets* (1818). His attacks on the Romantic poets caused some offence, though he later reconsidered his judgments in *The Spirit of the Age: or Contemporary Portraits* (1825), where he develops his belief that to a critic the personality of the writer is as relevant as what he writes. Hazlitt had two broken marriages and an unfortunate love-affair, details of which he paraded in *Liber Amoris: or, the New Pygmalion* (1823). See *Complete Works*, ed. P. P. Howe, 1930–4; David Bromwich, *Hazlitt: the Mind of a Critic*, new edn 1986.

**Heaney, Seamus** (*b.*1939), Irish poet and critic, was born in Mossbawm, Co. Derry, eldest of nine children of a Catholic cattle-dealer and farmer, and educated at St Columb's College, Derry, and Queen's University, Belfast. He has lectured on poetry at Queen's University and at Harvard. The twin preoccupations of his youth, the land which gave his family their living, and the sectarian hatred afforded to Catholics in Northern Ireland — he has lived in the Irish Republic since 1972 — have influenced his choice of themes, which he has always presented with effective rhythm and without obscurity, a reflection also of his loyalty to his unbookish ancestry. He feels deeply, too, about the peat-bog caches of Ireland's ancient heritage (mud is a recurrent image in his verse), and has compared the sacrificial and penitential victims whose bodies have been unearthed (described in 'The Grauballe Man', 'Punishment', and 'Bog Queen') with those who have lost their lives in the conflicts in modern Ireland. Memories of childhood abound, as in the title poem of *Death of a Naturalist* (1966), while *The Haw Lantern* (1987) contains a sonnet sequence to the memory of his mother, who died in 1984. A critical work, *The Government of the Tongue* (1988), explores the place of poetry in the contemporary environment, while expressing his own ambivalent attitude to poetry as his chosen career. He was elected Professor of Poetry at Oxford in 1989. See *Selected Poems 1965–1975*, 1980; *Preoccupations: Selected Prose 1968–1978*, 1980; Blake Morrison, *Seamus Heaney*, 1982.

**Henryson, Robert** (*c*.1425–*c*.1500), Scottish poet, is named in \*Dunbar's 'Lament for the Makaris' (printed in 1508): 'In Dunfermelyne he [Death] hes done roune [talked] / With Maister Robert Henrisoun'. 'Maister' usually means Master of Arts, and though there is no firm evidence of his having attended St Andrews or Glasgow universities, he may have studied abroad, and he displays enough knowledge of law to have done so. Or the title may refer simply to the calling of schoolmaster, in which case he probably taught at the grammar school of Dunfermline Abbey. He, Dunbar, and \*Douglas in particular are sometimes called 'Scottish Chaucerians', and though Henryson, more than the others, owes and acknowledges a debt to Chaucer, the term is unjustified if it is meant to imply that they were merely imitators.

In *Testament of Cresseid*, Henryson employs as a starting-point Chaucer's *Troilus and Criseyde* and its metre (but with the telling, and very Scottish, addition of alliteration), and develops from the situation an original, tragic, and moving end to the story. Cresseid, used and then abandoned by Diomeid, descends to prostitution in the Greek camp, reproaches the gods for her state, and is struck with leprosy as punishment. As she sits by the roadside with her leper's cup and clapper, her former lover Troilus passes by. Something reminds him of the girl he once knew, and he throws her alms, but they do not recognise each other. Henryson's wit flows in his 'Fables', 13 morality tales, again in rhyme royal, lightly based on Aesop but set in the contemporary social climate of Scotland, in which the attributes of his animal characters are described with a refreshing pre-Romantic realism and the same attention to detail that Beatrix Potter (1866–1943) gave to her characters five hundred years later. The dialogue with which he invests them is appropriate, colloquial, and pithy. His third sustained work is *Orpheus and Eurydice*, a reworking of the classical legend as a Christian allegory. Two of his shorter poems are especially noteworthy, and enjoyable. 'The Bludy Serk' (The Bloodstained Shirt) suggests the existence already of a ballad tradition and the traditional ballad metre. 'Robene and Makyne', probably the earliest pastoral dialogue in post-Classical European poetry, has a secular, and pointed, moral. Robene is more concerned with counting his sheep than making love to Makyne. When he gets round to responding, she has had second thoughts.

Henryson's achievement was remarkable. He combined his poetic talent with a profoundly religious but compassionate nature, a ready wit, and the ability to illuminate precisely and graphically the cosmic knowledge and social background of his times. *The Morall Fabillis of Esope, Compylit in Eloquent and Ornate Scottis Meter* was first published in Edinburgh in 1570. *Testament of Cresseid* was first printed by William Thynne in his edition of *The Workes of Chaucer* (1532). See *The Poems*, ed. Denton Fox, 1987; Matthew P. MacDiarmid, *Robert Henryson*, 1982.

**Herbert, George** (1593–1633), poet, was born in Montgomery, Wales, fifth of seven sons of a member of a powerful, aristocratic family, and was educated at Westminster School and Trinity College, Cambridge, where he became a Fellow, later being appointed Public Orator of the University. Though taking orders within seven years was a condition of his college post, and he was a devout Anglican, he first settled for politics and was elected MP for Montgomery in 1624 and again in 1625. Only in 1630 did he decide on ordination, in which he may have been influenced by his and his mother's friend *Donne, and for the rest of his life he was rector of Bemerton, Wiltshire. *A Priest to the Temple or, the Country Parson His Character, and Rule of Holy Life*, first published in full in 1671, is a prose treatise on the duties and responsibilities of such a position. From Cambridge he had addressed two sonnets to his mother in which he dedicated his poetic inspiration totally to religious themes. Much of his poetry was written in his thirties and reflects primarily the spiritual struggles which haunted his earlier years. Particularly effective are 'The Collar' and 'The Pulley'. His often original and ingenious metrical forms include two early examples of concrete verse, 'The Altar' and 'Easter Wings', and his poetry is particularly distinguished by his frequent use of homely images. His poems were published in 1633 after his death from consumption as *The Temple: Sacred Poems and Private Ejaculations*. See *A Choice of George Herbert's Verse*, ed. R. S. Thomas, new edn 1988.

**Herrick, Robert** (1591–1674), poet, was born in Cheapside, London, seventh child of a goldsmith who a year later fell, or jumped, to his death from the upper floor of the house. He may have been educated at Westminster School, but at 16 he was apprenticed to his uncle, another goldsmith, from whom he got his release in 1613 to go to St John's College, Cambridge, though he took his BA and MA degrees from Trinity Hall. He was ordained in 1623, but preferred the literary life of London and the frequent company of *Jonson, before being given the living of Dean Prior in distant Devonshire by Charles I in 1629. Here he remained for the rest of his long life except for the years 1647–62, during most of which he was suspended by Parliament for his royalist affiliations. *Hesperides: or Works both Humane and Divine* (1648) — with a separate section and title-page for 'Noble Numbers: or his Pious Pieces' — includes most of his lyrics. Delicately constructed and infused with wit, they reflect some discontent with country routine, but still represent a joyous return to classical forms and themes and a celebration of romantic love and rustic life (especially fruit, cream, flowers, and revels). Much of his religious poetry is characterised by a childishness which some critics have regarded as naïveté or complacency and others as a conscious attempt to counter the Puritan preoccupation with original sin. See *Poetical Works*, ed. L. C. Martin, 1956; F. W. Moorman, *Herrick: a Biographical and Critical Study*, new edn 1924.

**Heywood, Thomas** (*c.*1570–1641), dramatist, poet, translator, and miscellaneous writer, was probably born and brought up in Lincolnshire and studied at Cambridge. By 1598 he was a playwright for the Lord Admiral's Men. In the preface to *The English Traveller* (1633) he refers to having had 'an entire hand, or at least a main finger' in 220 plays, and the bookseller Francis Kirkman (*fl.*1674) describes him as acting regularly but still writing 'a sheet every day', even if many were the backs of tavern-bills, which may explain why so few of his plays survive. His verse is rugged (*Lamb called him a 'prose Shakespeare'), but his distinction lies in exploiting the possibilities of the drama of domestic life. Thus the interest in the two parts of *Edward the Fourth* (1599) is the relationship between Jane Shore, the King's mistress, and her husband. The theme of *A Woman Killed with Kindness* (1607) is the seduction of a happily-married woman by her husband's best friend, and its development, though melodramatic, is sympathetic and catches the situation's underlying horror and confusion. *The English Traveller* is also convincing once the more complex circumstances are accepted. Other plays have classical or more romantic plots. *An Apology for Actors* (1612) is a thesis on the contemporary stage, and *Gynaeceon: Nine Books of Various History Concerning Women* (1624) an early feminist history. See Arthur M. Clark, *Thomas Heywood: Playwright and Miscellanist*, 1931, a critique of which is in T. S. Eliot, *Elizabethan Dramatists*, 1963.

**Hogg, James** (1770–1835), Scottish poet, novelist, and journalist, the 'Ettrick Shepherd', was born in Selkirkshire and had little education beyond an inheritance of Border ballads and folklore. First a cowherd and then a shepherd, he had some poems printed in Edinburgh as *Scottish Pastorals* (1801). A meeting with *Scott led to their collaborating in collecting Volume II of *Border Minstrelsy* (1803), and a second book of Hogg's verse, *The Mountain Bard* (1807), did better than the first. He earned £300 for a treatise on the diseases of sheep, but from 1810 to 1815 he preferred the literary life of Edinburgh, where for a year he published a critical journal, the *Spy*. *The Queen's Wake* (1813), a poetic sequence in honour of Mary, Queen of Scots, which includes the charming fairy kidnap poem 'Kilmeny', made his reputation and earned him a rent-free farm in Yarrow from the Duke of Buccleuch. From 1817 to 1830 he was chief contributor with 'Christopher North' (John Wilson 1785–1854) and John Gibson Lockhart (1794–1854) to *Blackwood's Edinburgh Magazine*. Three novels, *The Three Perils of Man* (1822), a folk-fantasy, *The Three Perils of Woman* (1823), an attempt at the fiction of manners, and *The Private Memoirs and Confessions of a Justified Sinner* (1824), were all condemned or ignored in his lifetime, but the last, a powerful psychological account of possession, is one of the finest novels in the Scottish tradition. See *Selected Poems and Songs*, ed. David Groves, 1987; *Selected Stories and Sketches*, ed. Douglas S. Mack, 1983.

**Holinshed, Raphael** (*d*.1580), historian, was born in Cheshire and probably educated at Cambridge, after which he is said to have taken holy orders. Early in the reign of Elizabeth I he was working in London as a translator in the printing office of Reginald Wolfe (*d*.1573), under whose direction he helped to compile the British sections of a history and geography of the world, from various sources, notably the chronicles of Jean Froissart (*c*.1333–*c*.1410), Hector Boethius (*c*.1465–1536), John Major (*c*.1470–1550), Edward Hall (*c*.1500–47), and Richard Grafton (*d.c*.1572), a manuscript on Ireland by the saint Edmund Campion (1540–81), and the voluminous notes left by John Leland (*c*.1505–52). A more modest work, comprising just the history and topography of England, Scotland, and Ireland, was finally published in 1577, and known as 'Raphael Hollingeshed's Cronycle', though there was considerable input from Richard Stanyhurst (1547–1618) on Ireland 1509–47, William Harrison (1534–93) on the description of England, John Hooker *alias* Vowell (*c*.1525–1601), and Francis Thynne (*c*.1545–1608). It was, however, much censored in obedience to the Government, as was a further edition of 1586–7. The expurgated passages were not printed until 1722, and the full text, in six volumes, in 1807–8. The chief interest in the work today is the use *Shakespeare made of it as a source for his historical plays, and also for *Macbeth, King Lear*, and part of *Cymbeline*. See Allardyce and J. Nicoll, *Holinshed's Chronicle as Used in Shakespeare's Plays*, 1927.

**Hooker, Richard** (1553/4–1600), theologian, was born and educated in Exeter before going to Corpus Christi College, Oxford, of which he became a Fellow. He took holy orders in 1581, and was then apparently tricked into marriage with the daughter of a woman who had nursed him through a 'distemper and cold'. In 1585 he was appointed Master of the Temple in London, where he preached every Sunday morning to the legal establishment. A long-running theological altercation with the afternoon preacher, the Puritan Walter Travers (*c*.1548–1635), ended with Archbishop Whitgift of Canterbury suspending Travers, and Hooker at his own request retiring to a living in Dorset, from which he was translated to Bishopsbourne, Kent, by Elizabeth I after the publication in 1595 of the first four books of *Of the Laws of Ecclesiastical Polity*. The seminal fifth book, containing the justification of the Church of England, was published in 1597, the final three being finished just before he died. His distinction is that he elucidates the confused church history of his time, explains the philosophy of the settlement forged by the Queen and Whitgift to establish a national religion, and propounds the background to the religious thought of writers such as *Donne, *Milton, *Shakespeare, and *Spenser. His use of English rather than Latin in which to write a work of scholarship was itself a landmark, were it not also that a writer of English prose could now fairly be compared with Cicero for style and effective argument. See Peter Munz, *The Place of Hooker in the History of Thought*, 1952.

**Hopkins, Gerard Manley** (1844–89), poet, was born in Stratford, Essex, eldest of nine children of a marine insurance expert with literary ability, and educated at Highgate School and Balliol College, Oxford, where he got a first in Greats. He suppressed his ambition to be a painter-poet such as D. G. *Rossetti because painting would 'put a strain on the passions which I should think it unsafe to encounter', and in 1866 he was received by *Newman into the Catholic Church, to his family's disapproval. In 1868, when he began training for priesthood in the Society of Jesus, he burned the finished copies of all his poems, resolving to write no more 'unless it were the wish of my superiors'. In 1874 he began a theology course at St Beuno's College in Wales, where he learned Welsh in order to study classical Welsh poetry. In 1875, with the encouragement of his rector, he gave vent to his exciting poetic talent by writing 'The Wreck of the Deutschland', in memory of five Franciscan nuns, exiled for their faith, who went down with the ship. Though it was rejected by the Jesuit journal, *The Month*, for its metrical 'oddities', at least he now felt free to write poetry again. After being ordained in 1877 he served the Society in various capacities but with only moderate distinction in several cities, the conditions in some of which deeply affected him. In 1884 he was appointed Professor of Greek Literature at University College, Dublin, but the spiritual and physical distance from home, expressed in the sonnet, 'To seem the stranger lies my lot ...', and doubts about his work moved him to frustration and despair, in which state he wrote several further sonnets of tragic intensity. He died of typhoid and was buried in Dublin.

None of Hopkins's poetry was published in his lifetime, but his friend *Bridges introduced some of it later into anthologies and then himself edited and published the first collected edition in 1918. Hopkins employed verbal and metrical innovations to illuminate what he called 'inscape', which is broadly his perception of the total spiritual and physical design of individual and collective manifestations of nature. He wrote in what he termed 'sprung rhythm', derived from Anglo-Saxon poetry, the stresses corresponding to the beats in a musical measure rather than to syllabic weight, and he built up a total and sometimes startling harmony by alliteration and other devices, linguistic coinages, and composite words. He stands quite outside the normal conventions of Victorian poetry, and though all critics do not agree on his ultimate poetic status, he provided much inspiration to *Auden and other poets of the 1930s, and in 'Spring and Fall' ('Margarét, áre you gríeving / Over Goldengrove unleaving? ...') wrote one of the finest lyrics in the English language. See *The Poems of Gerard Manley Hopkins*, ed. W. H. Gardner and N. H. Mackenzie, 4th edn 1967; Bernard Bergonzi, *Gerard Manley Hopkins*,

1977 (critical biography); and in F. R. Leavis, *New Bearings in English Poetry*, new edn 1972.

**Housman, A(lfred) E(dward)** (1859–1936), classicist and poet, was born in Bromsgrove, Worcestershire, and educated at Bromsgrove School and St John's College, Oxford. He took first class honours in his preliminary classical examinations, but failed his finals completely. He was passionately attached to another undergraduate, Moses Jackson, with whom he shared lodgings in London from 1882 to 1887, when Jackson married and emigrated to India. While a clerk in the Patent Office, Housman exercised his brilliant mind by publishing learned articles on classical authors and texts. He became Professor of Latin at London University in 1892, and began his monumental edition of the five books on astrology of the Latin poet Manilius (published 1912–30). He was elected Professor of Latin at Cambridge in 1910. The leading classicist of his time, his intricate attention to textual criticism was leavened by a sarcastic wit when dealing with previous editors. In 1896 he had startled the academic world by publishing a volume of lyrics, *A Shropshire Lad*. Clearly written during, or immediately after, his emotional entanglement with Jackson, heartfelt in their preoccupation with death and unrequited love, and deeply expressive in their topographical, patriotic, nostalgic, and classical allusions, they have a resounding appeal to the young and the romantic. *Last Poems* came out in 1922, and *More Poems*, edited by his brother Laurence (1865–1959), in 1936. See *Collected Poems and Selected Prose,* ed. Christopher Ricks, 1988.

**Hughes, Ted** (*b*.1930), poet, children's writer, dramatist, and critic, was born in Mytholmroyd, Yorkshire, and educated at Mexborough Grammar School and Pembroke College, Cambridge. He had a variety of jobs before his marriage to the American poet Sylvia Plath (1932–63). His first books, *The Hawk in the Rain* (1957) and *Lupercal* (1960), established him correctly as a poet of stature but incorrectly as primarily a poet of nature. The predatory personae of many of these early poems and the protagonist of *Crow: from the Life and Songs of the Crow* (1970) represent the sharp extremes that punctuate the struggles accompanying birth, life, and death. *Gaudete* (1977) is a story of the supernatural, in which a wooden changeling is substituted for an Anglican clergyman, and reflects the man's consciousness during his absence from the earth. The influence of Hughes's observation of nature and the countryside recurs in *Remains of Elmet* (1979) and *River* (1983), both with complementary photographs, and *Moortown* (1979), in which there are two mythological sequences, 'Prometheus on His Crag' and 'Adam and the Sacred Nine'. He is a thoroughly modern poet in that he is concerned with realities, and if the starkness of some of his images offends the sensitivity, then so also do the violence and brutality which appear to have become part of our normal existence. His latest volume of poetry is *Wolfwatching* (1989). He was awarded the Queen's Gold Medal for Poetry (1974) and the OBE (1977), and appointed Poet Laureate in 1984. See *Selected Poems 1957–1981*, 1982; Thomas West, *Ted Hughes*, 1985; Craig Robinson, *Ted Hughes as Shepherd of Being*, 1989.

**Hunt, (James Henry) Leigh** (1784–1859), essayist, poet, journalist, and editor, was born in Southgate, London, and educated at Christ's Hospital. A selection of his verses was printed in 1801 with the title of *Juvenilia* on the initiative of his father, an improvident and usually impoverished preacher. With his brother John (1775–1848) he established in 1808 a radical journal, the *Examiner*, but both were imprisoned for two years in 1813 for libelling the Prince Regent as a liar and 'a fat Adonis'. In prison, Hunt lived with his family and received his friends, who included *Byron and *Lamb. In 1822 he took his wife and seven children to Italy to edit the *Liberal* with Byron and *Shelley, but Shelley's death, the closure of the journal after four issues, and the understandable problems of staying with Byron, caused their return in 1825. Hunt was only a moderate poet, whose most ambitious work, *The Story of Rimini* (1816), reveals an unhappy conflict between looseness of style and loftiness of theme, and whose only memorable poems are 'Abou ben Adhem' and the rondeau 'Jenny Kissed Me'. Much of his prose suffers in comparison with that of contemporaries such as Lamb, *Hazlitt, and *De Quincey because, more than theirs, it was written as journalism, but he was a good critic, whose essay 'An Answer to the Question What is Poetry' (1844) bears rereading. His influence in encouraging, and publishing, the young *Keats and Shelley was incalculable. See *Autobiography*, ed. Edmund Blunden, 1928; Edmund Blunden, *Hunt: a Biography*, 1930.

**Huxley, Aldous** (1894–1963), novelist, short story writer, essayist, poet, critic, dramatist, and biographer, was born in Godalming, Surrey, of an illustrious literary and scientific family, and educated at Eton and Balliol College, Oxford. An eye disease contracted at school made the pursuit of science impossible, so he turned to literature, his first book, *The Burning Wheel* (1916), being followed by three further volumes of verse, before he published *Limbo* (1920), a volume of short stories. He began his career as a novelist, and also his satirical phase, with *Crome Yellow* (1921) and another biting story of post-war Britain, *Antic Hay* (1923). *Those Barren Leaves* (1925) and *Point Counter Point* (1928), in which *Lawrence appears in the sympathetic form of Mark Rampson, were written in Italy, and reflect Huxley's early preoccupation with form rather than content. This changed with *Brave New World* (1932), confirming his entry into a more sociological phase, in which the Utopian image is turned upside down and the future seen in terms of a dehumanised society — his essay *Brave New World Revisited* (1959) chillingly reconsiders his 1932 fictional prognosis. *Eyeless in Gaza* (1936), in form as well as content, heralds a final, philosophical phase, in which pacifism and mysticism are predominant influences. *Grey Eminence* (1941) is a distinguished biography of Cardinal Richelieu's adviser, Father Joseph. See *Collected Short Stories*, 1957; *Collected Essays*, 1960; John Atkins, *Aldous Huxley: a Literary Study*, 1956; C. S. Ferns, *Aldous Huxley: Novelist*, 1980.

**James I** (1394–1437), King of Scotland, poet, was born in Dunfermline. When he was eleven, he was sent for safety to France by his father, Robert III, but was captured *en route* by the English. Robert died on hearing the news, and the new King spent the next 18 years in England, where he was well educated and looked after, before being returned to his own people with a bill for £40,000 for his board and lodging. In the meantime he had married Joan Beaufort, a daughter of the Duke of Somerset. Firm but ruthless in the pursuit of necessary reforms, and merciless in dealing with his turbulent nobility and recalcitrant Highland chiefs, he was murdered by members of an aristocratic conspiracy while taking a Christmas break at the Monastery of Blackfriars in Perth. While he was in England, as a gift to his new bride or in celebration of their first meeting, James wrote *The Kingis Quair* (The King's Book) of 197 stanzas in what is appropriately known as rhyme royal, though it had been used by *Chaucer in *Troilus and Criseyde*. Reminiscent of *Lydgate, however, rather than Chaucer, it is the earliest-known Scottish poem in the courtly love vein, while endorsing the married state and reflecting an acute observation of nature and a Christian outlook. The language is significant in that it incorporates usages, words, and rhymes from the northern English dialect from which Middle Scots developed. See *The Kingis Quair*, ed. J. Norton-Smith, 1971; E. W. M. Balfour-Melville, *James I, King of Scots*, 1936.

**James, Henry** (1843–1916), novelist, short story writer, dramatist, and critic, was born in New York, son of a philosophical and theological writer of Irish parentage and younger brother of the philosopher and psychologist, William James (1842–1910). He was taken to Europe at six months and then educated at various private schools in New York, while being allowed a great deal of freedom to roam around the city and to formulate and express his thoughts. He describes his earlier years in *A Small Boy and Others* (1913) and *Notes of a Son and Brother* (1914) — see also *The Middle Years* (1917). In 1855 the family went abroad for several years, during which he acquired a lifelong taste for Europe. In 1862, shortly after suffering a mysterious back injury, he entered Harvard University to read law, but soon gave that up in favour of a less conventional career, which he heralded by getting published in 1864 what has been identified as his first story, 'A Tragedy of Errors'. During the next ten years he twice visited Europe again and wrote many stories, reviews, and articles for English and American journals. His first novel, *Watch and Ward*, appeared as a serial in 1871 (in volume form in 1878), and his first book of short stories, *A Passionate Pilgrim and Other Tales*, was published in 1875, the year he returned to Europe, determined to settle there for good. After trying Paris, he decided on London, where he first lived in lodgings off Piccadilly and then in a flat in Kensington. He acted as a dispassionate observer, rather than a participant in or even a critic of the social, political, and economic changes of the times, and made a subsidiary art of the pleasure of dining out. He never married.

James's particular distinction as a novelist is that, born and bred in what was then the New World and living in and fully appreciating the social and cultural traditions of the Old, he created a new (if not always a welcome) bridge of understanding. Further, by a judicious mixture of what he called 'drama', the presentation of a scene without any intervening interpretation, and 'picture', the reflection of the action through the consciousness of a character, he developed a new approach to his craft. For the sake of critical convenience his career is often divided into three phases. The theme of the innocent American abroad dominates the first phase, which begins with *Roderick Hudson* (1875) and culminates triumphantly with *The Portrait of a Lady* (1881). The next phase comprises novels with American settings, such as *Washington Square* (1881) and the *The Bostonians* (1886), and studies of clashes between the classes, such as *The Princess Casamassima* (1886) and *The Tragic Muse* (1890). At this point in his literary development he appears to have abandoned hope of popular acclaim, and in his subsequent novels he is more concerned with the perfection of his art form, in reworking earlier themes with increased depth, as in *The Ambassadors* (1903), and in varying the patterns of sexual relationships, as in *The Wings of the Dove* (1902) and *The Golden Bowl* (1904). His two most famous pieces of shorter fiction are 'The Aspern Papers' (1888), whose theme is the morality of disturbing the past, and the tale of supernatural possession, 'The Turn of the Screw' (1898), each of which responds to various interpretations. The moderate reception given to the novels in his middle phase led him to experiment with drama. Only two of his plays were performed, and he was jeered by the audience when he took a bow on the first night of the second, *Guy Domville* (1895). His literary criticism is another thing altogether and is seen at its best in the prefaces to the revised editions of his novels, first published in New York 1907–9, and in *Literary Criticism*, 2 vols 1985.

In 1898 he bought Lamb House in Rye, Sussex, though he had a room permanently kept for him at the Reform Club for his frequent visits to London, and in 1913 he acquired in addition a flat in Cheyne Walk, Chelsea. The outbreak of World War I came as a profound shock to him, and he demonstrated his patriotism for his adoptive country by becoming a British citizen in 1915. He was awarded the OM in the New Year Honours List in 1916, and died two months later in London. See Leon

Edel, *The Life of Henry James*, 2 vols new edn 1977; H. T. McCarthy, *Henry James: the Creative Process*, 1975; S. Gorley Putt, *Preface to Henry James*, 1986.

**Johnson, Samuel** (1709–84), essayist, critic, poet, novelist, and lexicographer, was born in Lichfield, Staffordshire, eldest son of a bookseller, and educated at Lichfield Grammar School, King Edward VI School, Stourbridge, and Pembroke College, Oxford, which he left after a year for lack of funds. As a child he suffered from scrofula and smallpox, and all his life from defective eyesight, a convulsive tic, melancholia, and general ill health. After teaching for a few years he married a widow 20 years older than he was (she died in 1752), but with money she brought him he opened a school at Ediol, which collected only three pupils, one of them David Garrick (1717–79), the actor-manager and dramatist. In 1737 he went to London to earn a living by writing. He worked for *The Gentleman's Magazine*, published *London* (1738), a poem in imitation of Juvenal, and in 1744 a biography of the poet Richard Savage (*c*.1697–1743). In 1747 he began work on his monumental *Dictionary of the English Language* (1755). Another satirical poem, *The Vanity of Human Wishes*, appeared in 1749, in which year Garrick staged his tragedy, *Irene*. Between 1750 and 1752 he edited and largely wrote a bi-weekly journal, the *Rambler*. In 1756 he published proposals for an edition of *Shakespeare with a critical preface by himself: it came out in 1765. Between 1758 and 1760 he contributed to the *Universal Chronicle* a series of essays which were later collected as *The Idler* (1761). To pay off his mother's funeral expenses, he wrote in a week *The Prince of Abissinia* (1759), an eastern romance in the form of a didactic fable, which quickly became popular — it subsequently became known as *The History of Rasselas*, after its hero.

The grant in 1762 of a permanent pension from the Crown eased his financial problems and enabled him to enjoy his position as what *Smollett called 'the great Cham of literature', which was cultivated by his biographer *Boswell, whom he first met in 1763. In 1764 he made the acquaintance of a wealthy brewer, Henry Thrale, at whose house, Streatham Park, he became an almost permanent house-guest, and with whose wife he had a relationship so close that when she remarried after her husband's death in 1781, he never forgave her. In 1773, at the age of 64, he courageously accepted Boswell's invitation to the exhausting Scottish trip which he wrote up as *A Journey to the Western Isles of Scotland* (1755). His last work was *Prefaces Biographical and Critical to the Works of the English Poets* (1779–81), reissued in 1781 as *Lives of the English Poets*. He died in London and was buried in Westminster Abbey. He was awarded the degree of LLD by Dublin in 1765, and Oxford in 1775. His fame as a conversationalist has tended to obscure his excellence as a prose writer, and though as a critic he had serious blind spots, these are so obvious to the modern reader that his insight and directness are still valid. See *Samuel Johnson: a Selection*, ed. Donald Greene, 1984; Christopher Hibbert, *The Personal History of Samuel Johnson*, 1971; John Phillips Hardy, *Samuel Johnson: a Critical Study*, 1979.

**Jonson, Ben(jamin)** (1572–1637), poet and dramatist, was probably born in London. His own account of his early life was recorded by the Scottish poet, William Drummond of Hawthornden (1585–1649), whom Jonson visited in 1619 on a walking trip to Scotland and back. His grandfather came from the Borders, 'served Henry VIII, and was a gentleman'. His father, having been imprisoned under Queen Mary and forfeited his estate, subsequently became a minister, and died a month before the poet's birth. His mother then married a bricklayer, and Jonson was 'brought up poorly, put to [Westminster] school by a friend', apprenticed as a bricklayer, 'which he could not endure', and joined the forces in Flanders, where he killed an opponent in single combat 'in the face of both the camps', before returning 'to his wonted studies' in England. In 1594 he married Anne Lewis, 'a shrew yet honest'. His poem 'On My First Daughter' commemorates the death of their child at six months. He became an actor with a strolling company, graduating to actor-writer, and was in 1597 imprisoned for his part in a lost play, *The Isle of Dogs*. His comedy *Every Man in His Humour* was performed in 1598 by the Lord Chamberlain's Men, with *Shakespeare in the cast, and in the same year he killed another actor in a duel and served a prison sentence, during which he was converted to the Catholic faith, which he upheld for 'twelve years'. *Every Man out of His Humour*, with less plot but more satire, was performed in 1599. In *Cynthia's Revels* (1600), ostensibly a masque in honour of the aged Queen Elizabeth, he satirised not only the Court but also some of his fellow-dramatists, thus initiating the 'War of the Theatres' 1600–1, to which his contribution was *Poetaster*, the opposition being *Satiro-Mastix, or the Untrussing of the Humorous Poet* of *Dekker and *Histriomastix: or the Player Whipt* of John Marston (1576–1634). *Sejanus* (1603), a Roman tragedy, failed, perhaps because the excellent classicist in him demanded too much realism, but in this it looked forward to *Volpone, or the Fox* (1606), a comedy in which the excesses of ancient Rome are transplanted to modern Venice and represented in terms of the characters' animal-symbolism as well as their 'humours', that is their psychological temperaments. In the meantime he had become writer of masques to the Court of James I, and gone to prison again for anti-Scottish observations in *Eastward Ho* (1605), written jointly with *Chapman and Marston. All the characters in *The Alchemist* (1610, published 1612), one of the finest of social comedies, are middle-class knaves, dupes, or potentially either, and the satire is harsh and uncompromising. In *Bartholomew Fair* (performed 1614), Jonson found similar vices and failings to make fun of among the working classes.

In 1616 he did what had before been done only for the dead, and published his *Workes*, comprising plays, masques, and poems (divided into 'Epigrammes' and 'The Forest'). This act of self-publicity brought him some derision, but it was significant in giving literary respectability to plays, and its success heralded the great Shakespeare folio of 1623. He wrote no further plays until *The Staple of News* (1626, published 1631), a glance at the new business of journalism. He received the honorary degree of MA from Oxford in 1619, but his life was severely ruptured by a fire in 1623 which destroyed books, notes, and manuscripts, and by a stroke in 1628. He continued cheerfully to write and study, and friends responded to his pleas, often in verse, for relief from poverty, though he fell out with the architect Inigo Jones (1573–1652) over the relative importance in royal masques of spectacle and speech, and his later plays met with poor response.

This veritable heavyweight, who scaled 'Full twentie stone; of which I lack two pound' ('Epistle to Mr Arthur Squib'), and whose appearance was dominated by 'My mountain belly, and my rockie face' ('My Picture Left in Scotland'), was not the greatest poet of his age, though some of his occasional poems and lyrics would be others' masterpieces. But he was a founder of the satirical drama, the acknowledged leader of the literary coterie of his time, and the sage of younger writers, who dubbed themselves the 'Sons of Ben'. See *Complete Critical Edition*, ed. C. H. Herford, Percy and Evelyn M. Simpson, 11 vols 1925–52 (includes biography); *The Complete Poems*, ed. George Parfitt, 1975; Rosalind Miles, *Ben Jonson: His Life and Work*, 1986; Alexander Leggatt, *Ben Jonson: His Vision and His Art*, 1981.

**Joyce, James** (1882–1941), Irish novelist, poet, and dramatist, was born in Dublin, eldest of ten children of an artistic mother and a father whose conviviality and fecklessness led to the decline of the family fortunes. He was educated at the Jesuit Belvedere College, and having decided against the priesthood, read languages at University College, Dublin, where he caused an academic stir in 1900 by having a critical article, 'Ibsen's New Drama', published in the European literary periodical, *Fortnightly Review*. After graduating in 1902 he went to Paris, ostensibly as a medical student but in reality a near-destitute writer. The death of his mother in 1904 caused his return to Dublin, where for a time he shared with the poet Oliver St John Gogarty (1878–1957) the Martello tower which features in the opening section of *Ulysses*. A casual meeting with Nora Barnacle, a barmaid, led to a formal date on 16 June 1904. In October they eloped to Zurich, and then lived in Pola and Trieste, where he worked as a teacher of English. They were married in 1931, after she had had two children, and she died in 1951. Joyce returned to Dublin only once, in 1912, by which time he had undergone virtually all the physical and emotional experiences which inspired his published works. The first was *Chamber*

*Music* (1907), a collection of 36 short lyrical poems of conventional language and metre, extraordinarily so, considering the man. A second, even slimmer volume, *Poems Penyeach* (1927), priced at a shilling and containing 13 pieces, shows some advance towards the then prevailing mode, but it was his prose which had the greater influence on modern poetry.

The couple spent World War I in straitened circumstances in Zurich. Joyce chose Dublin to represent 'the centre of paralysis' of his native country for the 15 stories in *Dubliners* (1914), which reveals, often sardonically, the squalor and frustration of the lower middle class and culminates in 'The Dead', in which a particular human predicament reflects the complexity of life itself. Like his play, *The Exiles* (1918), written in about 1914, 'The Dead' records an incident in his relationship with Nora. He had in his teens begun a vast autobiographical novel, *Stephen Hero*, a fragment of which was posthumously published in 1944. From it he extracted and recast *A Portrait of the Artist as a Young Man* (1916), in which Stephen Dedalus, who reappears in *Ulysses*, is not Joyce, but his consciousness is the means through which the author filters the relationship between the imagination and reality. *Ulysses* is in time a continuation of *A Portrait*, the whole action taking place, significantly, on 16 June 1904, and symbolically paralleling incidents and characters in the wanderings of Homer's Odysseus. It was begun in 1914, originally as a short story, and some chapters were published in 1919 in London in the *Egoist*. In the meantime, serialisation had started in the USA in the *Little Review*, but subsequent chapters were intercepted by the postal authorities and burned. In 1921 three judges upheld a complaint, and banned further publication. Joyce kept on writing, and the book was published in 1922 by a small press in Paris, where he had moved with his family in 1920. An English and American edition was printed in Dijon and distributed from Paris, but many copies were identified *en route* to their purchasers and destroyed. By 1930 eight reprints of the original edition had been sold, and the book had been translated into French, German, Czech, and Japanese. It was finally cleared for publication in the USA in 1932, and was published in Britain in 1936 without legal opposition.

Joyce received virtually no money in his lifetime from his writing, and subsisted largely on the financial assistance of patrons. His eyesight deteriorated rapidly, to the extent that for his last and, to him, most significant book he had to commit to memory whole sections and to rely on amanuenses to decipher and transcribe his notes. He worked on it for 17 years, too superstitious to reveal its title until it was finished — sections of it were published in New York 1927–30 as *Work in Progress*. Where *Ulysses* was concerned with a single day, *Finnegans Wake* (1939) is a record of a night, interpreting the mind of the sleeping H. C. Earwicker with astonishing virtuosity and invention of language. See Richard Ellmann, *James Joyce*, rev. edn 1984 (biography); Harry Levin, *James*

*Joyce: a Critical Introduction*, rev. edn 1960; Samuel L. Goldberg, *The Classical Temper: a Study of Joyce's Ulysses*, 1961.

**Kavanagh, Patrick** (1904–67), Irish poet, novelist, critic, and journalist, was born in Iniskeen, Co. Monaghan, son of a part-time cobbler and small farmer, whose trades he followed after leaving school at twelve until he moved to Dublin in 1939, where for the rest of his life he supported himself largely by journalism. In the meantime he had educated himself and written some fine lyric verse which depicted the realities of rural life (*Ploughman and Other Poems* was published in 1936), and an often hilarious early autobiography, *The Green Fool* (1938). His concern about the nature and function of literature and the responsibility of the author is demonstrated in much of his critical writing, and is further reflected in *The Great Hunger* (1942), a strong, despairing poem of the land, and *Tarry Flynn* (1948), a semi-autobiographical if in some respects fanciful novel. For three months in 1952 he published his own weekly newspaper. A lost libel action against the *Leader* in 1952, for allegedly impugning his professional reputation, was immediately followed by his going into hospital with lung cancer. He referred to his recovery from both disasters as his 'rebirth', and celebrated it by changing his tune from savagery and attempted satire on modern issues, government, art, and Irish life, to more personal themes in which innocence and comedy predominate, as in his impressive 'Canal Poems'. This return to simplicity is well illustrated in *Come Dance with Kitty Stobling and Other Poems* (1960). See *Collected Poems*, rev. edn 1973; *Collected Pruse*, 1967; Darcy O'Brien, *Patrick Kavanagh*, 1981.

**Keats, John** (1795–1821), poet, was born in Finsbury, eldest of four children of the groom at the stables of the Swan and Hoop Inn in the City of London, who had married the proprietor's daughter and in 1802 inherited the business. In 1803 the poet entered John Clarke's School, Enfield, and in 1804 his father was killed in a riding accident, whereupon his mother remarried and boarded the children out with her parents. She left her new husband in 1806, returned to the children in 1809, but died the following year. Guardians were now appointed, at the instigation of one of whom Keats was apprenticed to a surgeon. He wrote his first poems in 1814, and in February 1815 celebrated with a sonnet the release from prison of *Hunt, whom he met later and who published 'O Solitude, if I must with thee dwell...' in the *Examiner* in 1816. Keats had continued his medical studies at Guy's Hospital and was now a member of the Society of Apothecaries, but having written 'On First Looking into Chapman's Homer', been cited (with *Shelley) in an *Examiner* article 'Young Poets', and met Hunt's literary friends, he gave up medicine for poetry, much to his guardian's dismay.

In March 1817 he published *Poems*, a collection of his poetry up till then. It begins and ends with two longer poems in rhyming couplets, 'I stood tip-toe upon a little hill...', which looks forward to *Endymion*, and 'Sleep and Poetry', written after a night on Hunt's sofa, in which he expresses his ambition, 'O for ten years, that I may overwhelm / Myself in poesy; so I may do the deed / That my own soul has to itself decreed'. From April until the end of November he stayed in various places in the south of England and wrote the more than 4000 lines of his allegorical romance, *Endymion*, which was published, with its abrupt ending, in April 1818. He responded philosophically to the critical mauling it got in the *Quarterly Review*, and to an attack in *Blackwood's Edinburgh Magazine* on him and other members of the 'Cockney School' of Hunt's followers. In June he and Charles Brown (1786–1842) set off on a walking tour of the Lakes and Scotland, Keats all the time writing poetry and letters to family and friends. At Oban he developed a sore throat, which got so bad that Brown sent him back to London by boat from Inverness. On his return he found his brother Tom ill with tuberculosis, and nursed him until he died in December. In the meantime he had met and fallen in love with the 18-year-old Fanny Brawne, who shortly afterwards moved with her mother into a house in Hampstead, the other half of which was occupied by Brown and in which Keats was living too.

From January to October 1819, between bouts of depression and recurrences of throat trouble, Keats composed in various places a succession of masterpieces: 'The Eve of St Agnes', 'La Belle Dame Sans Merci', his six great odes (including 'Ode on a Grecian Urn' and 'To Autumn'), and the two parts of 'Lamia', while tinkering with 'Hyperion'. He also wrote sonnets (including 'To Sleep') which for quality and feeling matched those of *Wordsworth, as well as (with Brown) the blank-verse drama, 'Otho the Great'. Back in Hampstead at the end of the year, he became engaged to Fanny, but his health worsened, as did his finances with the appearance from America of his brother George, with whom he made a settlement which left him virtually destitute. *Lamia, Isabella, The Eve of St Agnes and Other Poems* was published in July 1820 and was very well received, but by now he had suffered two lung haemorrhages and, after being nursed by the Hunts when Brown left his half of the house, he was taken in by the Brawnes and looked after by Fanny. On medical advice, he sailed to Italy for the winter with the painter Joseph Severn (1793–1879). On 30 November he wrote from Rome his last known letter, to Brown. He died on 23 February 1821 and was buried in the Protestant cemetery. He was a little over 25. Fanny put on widow's weeds when she heard the news. (She married Louis Lindon, twelve years younger than herself in 1833, and died in 1865.) The feverish restlessness that drove Keats to poetry and, when he could no longer harness his faculties, to despair, is illustrated in his letters, as is his genius for friendship and his care for ordinary people and ordinary things. See *The Poems of John Keats*, ed. Miriam Allott, new edn 1972; *Letters of John Keats*, ed. Robert

Gittings, 1970; W. J. Bate, *John Keats*, new edn 1979 (biography); Aileen Ward, *Keats: the Making of a Poet*, rev. edn 1986.

**Kingsley, Charles** (1819–75), novelist, academic, and poet, was born at Holne Vicarage near Dartmoor, and educated at King's College, London, and Magdalene College, Cambridge, where he got a first in classics. He entered the Church and in 1844 became rector of Eversley, Hampshire, where he spent most of the rest of his life. *The Saint's Tragedy*, a drama about St Elizabeth of Hungary in a mixture of blank verse and prose, was published in 1848. *Yeast* (1848) and *Alton Locke* (1850) are novels dealing respectively with the issues of the rural and urban working class. *Westward Ho!* (1855) is social propaganda of a different kind in the form of a stirring attempt to strengthen patriotic sinews through an account of Elizabethan naval heroism. Kingsley was Professor of Modern History at Cambridge 1860–9, and in 1864 attacked *Newman in an anonymous review in *Macmillan's Magazine* which precipitated the writing of the latter's *Apologia pro Vita Sua*. *The Water Babies* (1863), with *The Heroes, or Greek Fairy Tales* (1856) his lasting work for children, is a didactic fantasy with a social purpose. In *Hereward the Wake* (1866), he records in fictional form the deeds of that legendary hero. He was appointed a canon of Westminster and a chaplain to the Queen in 1873. His enthusiasm for health and strength of body and mind led to his being regarded as a chief exponent of 'muscular Christianity', though he was also a considerable scholar and a fine prose writer, if not much of a poet. See Robert B. Martin, *The Dust of Combat: a Life of Kingsley*, 1959.

**Kipling, Rudyard** (1865–1936), short story writer, poet, novelist, and children's writer, was born in Bombay, son of a sculptor and writer. He and his younger sister were brought to England and boarded with foster-parents in Southsea from 1871 to 1877, when he went to the United Services College, Westward Ho!, Devon. He returned to India in 1882 and became a reporter on the *Civil and Military Gazette* in Lahore, where his father was now principal of the art college. He graduated to contributing sketches, stories, and verses, and in 1887 was transferred to the staff of the Allahabad *Pioneer*. *Departmental Ditties and Other Verses* and *Plain Tales from the Hills* were published in 1886 and 1888 in India, and in 1890 in England, where the initial reception was muted, though he was becoming known through paperbacks issued by the Indian railways, many of which were brought 'home'. He returned to England via America in 1889 and published his first novel, *The Light that Failed* (1890), a further volume of stories, *Life's Handicap* (1891), *Barrack-Room Ballads and Other Verses* (1892), and *The Naulahka* (1892), a novel written with the American Wolcott Balestier, whose sister he married in 1892. The couple lived in Vermont until 1896, returning to England after a quarrel with his wife's family. In the meantime he had written his classic children's stories, *The Jungle Book* (1894) and *The Second Jungle Book* (1895), and some of his finest tales, published in *Many Inventions* (1893) and *The Day's Work* (1898), and had become famous.

More children's stories followed, including *Stalky and Co.* (1899) and *Kim* (1901), also a fine novel by any standards; while *Puck of Pook's Hill* (1906) and *Rewards and Fairies* (1910) are interspersed with verses illustrating his feeling for the immutability of the English landscape, which are in contrast to his thumpingly rhythmical military ballads and patriotic songs. By 1902, when he settled in Sussex, his major literary work was done, but his activities as a public figure fiercely concerned with controversial issues and the growing threat and then the actuality of war were just beginning, though from 1915 he was hard hit by an un-diagnosed ulcer and by the death in action in that year of his only son. He was a master in the craft of prose fiction, and ordinary readers who respond enthusiastically to the poems which accurately but sympathet-ically reflect the imperialistic attitude of his age, care little for the long-running critical argument as to whether he wrote good verse or bad poetry. In 1907 he was the first English author to receive the Nobel Prize for Literature. Though regarded as the national poet of his time, he made himself unavailable for selection as Poet Laureate and three times refused the OM, on the grounds that he could serve his king and country better from the side-lines. See World's Classics editions of selected works, 1986–7; Charles Carrington, *Rudyard Kipling: His Life and Work*, new edn 1986; J. M. S. Tompkins, *The Art of Rudyard Kipling*, rev. edn 1965.

**Kyd, Thomas** (1558–94), dramatist, was born in the City of London, son of a scrivener, and educated at Merchant Taylors' School. From a letter of his to the Lord Keeper, it appears that in 1593 he had for six years been in service to a 'Lord', and that in 1591 he and *Marlowe shared a room. On 12 May 1593, while he was in prison on suspicion of inciting the populace against immigrant craftsmen, his lodgings were searched and copies found of an atheistical tract, which he claimed was Marlowe's. Kyd was later freed, having been tortured but not charged. The only play origin-ally published as his is *Cornelia* (1594), a translation from the French of a Roman tragedy by Robert Garnier (*c*.1545–1600). *Heywood in *Apology for Actors* refers to 'M. Kid, in his Spanish Tragedy', and a play of that name was in print in 1592 and frequently reissued. Francis Meres (1565–1647) in *Palladis Tamia* (1598) calls Kyd 'our best for Tragedie', and *The Spanish Tragedy*, a drama of revenge and stark retribution, though lacking the poetic inspiration of Marlowe and *Shakespeare, is as signif-icant in the development of Elizabethan tragedy as *Tamburlaine* and *Titus Andronicus*. The plot is subtler than that of *Richard III*, and the politics of dynastic marriage and the motivation of the unhappy girl Bel-imperia are presented with greater assurance than in *Romeo and*

*Juliet.* From the appearance as the play-within-a-play of a version of *The Tragedye of Soliman and Perseda* (*c*.1592), it has been surmised that Kyd was its author too, and a lost proto-Hamlet has also been attributed to him. See *The Spanish Tragedy,* ed. Philip Edwards, new edn 1977.

**Lamb, Charles** (1775–1834), essayist and critic, was born in London, son of a lawyer's clerk, and educated at Christ's Hospital. After working in South Sea House, he got a clerkship in East India House in 1792 which provided a livelihood until he retired in 1825. A family streak of insanity affected him briefly when he was 20, and his sister Mary more disastrously in 1796, when she killed their mother. His guardianship of Mary was accepted, and he cared for her, renouncing marriage, for the rest of his life. His first literary efforts were unsuccessful, and comprised some verses (though the quotability of 'The Old Familiar Faces' has ensured its survival), a novel, and a farce, *Mr H——* (1806), which he joined the first-night audience in hissing. Though only his name was on the title-page of *Tales from Shakespear* (1807), he wrote the accounts of six tragedies and Mary the 14 comedies. His major critical work, *Specimens of English Dramatic Poets who Lived about the Time of Shakespeare* (1808), contains extracts from and percipient comments on hitherto unappreciated writers; otherwise his best literary criticism is in his letters to friends. In 1820 he wrote 'The South-Sea House', the first of 67 essays in the *London Magazine* as Elia — he took a fellow-clerk's name for that essay to avoid embarrassing his brother, who was still working there. Elegant, informal, often fanciful, a collected edition was published in 1823, and *The Last Essays of Elia* (from various journals) in 1833. See David Cecil, *A Portrait of Charles Lamb*, new edn 1986.

**Langland, William** (*c*.1330–*c*.1386), poet, author of *The Vision of William Concerning Piers the Plowman*, was a younger or possibly illegitimate son of an Oxfordshire gentleman farmer. From evidence in the poem itself, he was born in the parish of Colwall, near the Malvern Hills, was educated at the expense of his father and friends (probably at Malvern Priory), and took minor orders. At some point he moved to London, where he lived with his sensually-inclined wife Kitty and their daughter Calotte, and worked as an itinerant clerical hack, saying prayers for those who contributed to his upkeep. *Piers Plowman* exists in three distinct versions: A-text (completed after 1362); B-text (a longer revision, written between 1377 and 1379); C-text (a further revision, probably finished just before the poet's death). Brimming with stirring descriptions and powerful imaginative passages, and studded with colloquialisms and humour, it is the finest alliterative poem in Middle English and has been described by Professor Nevill Coghill in *Langland: Piers Plowman* (1964) as 'the greatest Christian poem in our language'. It opens with the poet being lulled to sleep in the Malvern countryside, and continues in a series of 'visions', representing an exhaustive pilgrimage after truth, reason, and the love of God, in the face of falsehood, temptation, ignorance, and the Seven Deadly Sins graphically personified, through disputation to the ultimate vision, and beyond to salvation. See *The Vision of Piers Plowman*, ed. A.V.C. Schmidt, 1978.

**Larkin, Philip** (1922–85), poet and novelist, was born in Coventry and educated at King Henry VIII School and St John's College, Oxford. From 1955 until his death he was Librarian of the Brynmor Jones Library, University of Hull. His first book of verse, *The North Ship* (1945), had echoes of both *Auden and *Yeats, and it was not until *The Less Deceived* (1955) that his own distinctive voice emerged, now that he had been encouraged by a study of *Hardy to concentrate on projecting his own experiences and perception. In the meantime he had written two novels of youthful anguish, *Jill* (1946) and *A Girl in Winter* (1947). The appearance of some of his poems in the anthology *New Lines* (1956), ed. Robert Conquest, suggested that he was a member, if not a leader, of the Movement, a group of writers who were offering a progressive but sardonic image, but Larkin's was a personal and private, not a public, image. He was a poet of plain feeling and speaking, with shafts of humour. His technical control of rhyme, rhythm, metaphor, and adjectival phrases was painfully achieved through innumerable drafts, all coming together in such poems as 'The Whitsun Weddings', 'Church Going', 'Toads', and 'Toads Revisited'. While the predominant themes in his last complete volume, *High Windows* (1974), are perhaps predictably the ebbing of life, disaster, and death, his mastery of form is as sure in 'The Old Fools' and 'The Building' as ever. See *Philip Larkin: Collected Poems*, ed. Anthony Thwaite, 1988; Andrew Motion, *Philip Larkin*, 1982; Janice Rossen, *Philip Larkin: His Life Work*, 1989.

**Lavin, Mary** (*b*. 1912), Irish novelist and short story writer, was born in East Walpole, Massachusetts, but has lived in the Irish Republic since her childhood, being educated at Loreto Convent, Dublin, and the National University of Ireland. The inspiration which sparked off her writing of fiction was a chance meeting with an elderly woman who remarked that she had recently had tea with Virginia *Woolf. From this came her first volume of short stories, *Tales from Bective Bridge* (1942). Writing, and particularly the revelation of character through the short story, later became to her a 'passionate occupation', and the effectiveness of her mastery of this medium is enhanced by the way she selects and dramatically depicts the moment of truth when the protagonist becomes aware of the meaning or consequences inherent in a situation. She has also written two novels, *The House in Clewe Street* (1945), a study of lost adolescent innocence, and *Mary O'Grady* (1950), a family saga of the children of a Dublin suburb growing up into adulthood. She is an essentially Irish writer in that she has always remained in that country and her settings are exclusively Irish. She is in no particular Irish tradition, however, being rather one who writes out of her personal feeling and perceptive experience, investing her characters with Irishness and making them all the more convincing for being so imbued. See *Stories*, 3 vols 1974–85; Angeline A. Kelly, *Mary Lavin: Quiet Rebel − a Study of Her Short Stories*, new edn 1987.

**Lawrence, D(avid) H(erbert)** (1885–1930), novelist, short story writer, poet, travel writer, dramatist, and critic, was born in Eastwood, near Nottingham, third son of a miner and a former schoolteacher who had higher aims for her often sick child than the colliery. At 13 he won a scholarship to Nottingham High School, where he spent three years, and after a spell as a clerk and then a pupil teacher, he went to Nottingham University College, qualifying as a teacher in 1908 and taking a post in Croydon. His first published work was a prize-winning story, printed anonymously in the *Nottingham Guardian* in 1907, and shortly afterwards his early poems were appearing in the *English Review*. After the publication of his first novel, *The White Peacock* (1911), he gave up his job to concentrate on writing and on his psychological and physical wanderlust. *The Trespasser* (1912) was followed by *Sons and Lovers* (1913), in which he recreates the atmosphere and attitudes of the working-class home of his youth. He extended his range with *Love Poems and Others* (1913), *The Widowing of Mrs Holroyd: a Drama* (1914, first performed 1920), and *The Prussian Officer and Other Stories* (1914). In 1914 he married Frieda Weekley, the German wife of his former university professor, with whom he had eloped two years earlier and who was six years his senior and had three children. *The Rainbow* (1915) was successfully prosecuted for obscenity, as a result of which its successor, *Women in Love*, completed in 1916, was not published in Britain until 1921. This exacerbated his bitterness at the hounding the couple were getting for her German connections and his opposition to the war, in which he was unfit to serve. As soon as they could, they resumed their nomadic existence, fraught by continual financial worries, his chronic ill-health, and a traumatic marital relationship. They went to places in Italy, reflected in *The Lost Girl* (1920) and *Aaron's Rod* (1922), and in the travel book, *Sea and Sardinia* (1921); to Ceylon; to Australia, where he wrote and set *Kangaroo* (1923), which shows a remarkable understanding of the country and people considering his stay was brief and his human contacts minimal; and Mexico, the setting of *The Plumed Serpent* (1926). He continued to write short stories, poems, and articles, even after terminal tuberculosis had been diagnosed. The couple next returned to Italy. Here he also began to paint, only to have some of his pictures removed by the police from an exhibition in London; and he worked through three distinct versions of *Lady Chatterley's Lover*, which was privately printed in Italy in 1928, but not finally in full for public consumption until 1960, after a case for obscenity by the Director of Public Prosecutions failed at the Old Bailey. In 1930 his condition worsened, and he died in a clinic in Vence, in southern France. He was 44.

Lawrence's exceptional nervous energy, deep but circumscribed vision, powers of perception and description, and innate honesty of expression, were matched by his formidable all-round talent as a writer. In the preface to *Collected Poems* (1928) he wrote that 'many of the poems are so personal that, in their fragmentary fashion, they make up a biography of an emotional and inner life'. This is as true of the earlier poems about home and teaching as of the collection *Look! We Have Come Through!* (1917), which records his affair with Frieda and the early years of marriage, while his disillusionment with humanity in the early 1920s is reflected in the attention given instead to the natural world in *Birds, Beasts and Flowers* (1923). To his short stories he applied a technique different from that of his novels, equally artistic (when he is at his best) and original, but more objective and less revealing of his own psyche. His novels, of which *Sons and Lovers, The Rainbow,* and *Women in Love* are justly praised, and *Lady Chatterley's Lover* often underestimated because it has been publicised for the wrong reasons, are about symbolic, intellectual, and environmental, as well as human relationships. Some of his criticism is contained in *Selected Essays*, ed. Richard Aldington (1970), and his critical works include *Studies in Classical American Literature* (new edn 1971). See *The Collected Short Stories*, 3 vols new edn 1974; *Selected Poems*, ed. Keith Sagar, new edn 1986; Keith Sagar, *Life of D.H. Lawrence*, new edn 1982; F.R. Leavis, *D.H. Lawrence: Novelist*, new edn 1973; Graham Hough, *The Dark Sun: a Study of D. H. Lawrence*, new edn 1970.

**Lewis, C. Day**, pen-name of Cecil Day-Lewis (1904–72), Irish poet, critic, and novelist, was born in Ballintubber, son of a Church of Ireland minister. The family moved to England in 1905, and after the death of his mother in 1908, the boy was looked after by her sister (see his poem 'My Mother's Sister'), and educated at Sherborne School and Wadham College, Oxford. Here he mixed with left-wing poets (notably *Auden, with whom he edited *Oxford Poetry* in 1927) and expressed left-wing views (he was briefly a member of the Communist party), which coloured much of the verse he wrote between about 1928 and 1934 — his first book, *Beechen Vigil* (1925), and its successor, *Country Comets* (1928), contain no such leanings. *Overtures to Death* (1938) marks the second of several changes of direction and reflects more general concerns (graphically presented in 'The Nabara') and the beginning of his frequent use of images from his childhood (as in 'Cornet Solo', 'The Gate', and 'Last Words'). *The Georgics of Virgil* (1940) is the first of his verse translations of the complete works of that author, and by the end of World War II he had become an eminent pillar of the establishment. He delivered the Clark Lectures at Cambridge in 1946, published as *The Poetic Image* (1947), was Professor of Poetry at Oxford 1951–6, and was appointed Poet Laureate in 1968. In 1935 he published the first of an extensive series of detective novels under the pseudonym of Nicholas Blake. See *Collected Poems*, 1954; *The Buried Day*, 1960 (autobiography); Sean Day-Lewis, *C. Day-Lewis: an English Literary Life*, 1980 (biography).

**Lewis, C(live) S(taples)** (1898–1963), scholar, critic, popular theologian, and novelist, was born in Belfast, son of a solicitor, and educated at Malvern College and privately, before winning a scholarship to University College, Oxford. He served in France 1917–18, being wounded at Arras, and returned to Oxford in 1919, where he got a double-first, in Greats and then in English. He was a Fellow of Magdalen College, Oxford, from 1925 to 1954, when he became Professor of Medieval and Renaissance Literature at Cambridge, to which he commuted weekly from his Oxford home. His ultimate acceptance of Christianity in 1931, or his examination of allegory, and sometimes both together, are reflected in almost everything he wrote. *The Pilgrim's Regress: an Allegorical Apology for Christianity, Reason and Romanticism* (1933) was followed by his classic work of literary criticism, *The Allegory of Love: a Study in Medieval Tradition* (1936). His Clark Lectures at Cambridge in 1944 were reworked into *English Literature in the Sixteenth Century* (1954). He published a trilogy of extra-terrestrial novels beginning with *Out of the Silent Planet* (1938), and a series of Christian apologiae of which *The Problem of Pain* (1940) and *The Screwtape Letters* (new edn 1961) are still widely admired. With his Narnia sequence, ending with *The Last Battle* (1956), he triumphantly upheld his dictum that he was 'almost inclined to set it up as a canon that a children's story which is enjoyed only by children is a bad children's book'. See Roger Lancelyn Green and Walter Hooper, *C. S. Lewis: a Biography,* new edn 1988.

**Lewis, (Percy) Wyndham** (1882–1957), described himself in his autobiography, *Blasting and Bombardiering* (1937), as 'novelist, painter, sculptor, philosopher, draughtsman, critic, politician, journalist, pamphleteer, all rolled into one, like one of those portmanteau men of the Italian Renaissance'. He was born in his father's yacht moored off Nova Scotia, and came to England with his mother in about 1893, being educated at Rugby School and the Slade School of Art. After some years on the Continent he emerged as a leader of the Vorticist artistic and literary movement which flourished briefly between 1914 and 1920. He served at the front in World War I, latterly as an official war artist. After his first novel, *Tarr* (1918), a revealing and stylistically startling portrait of Parisian bohemian life, he embarked on an ambitious but unfinished philosophical fantasy, of which *The Childermass* (1928) was published with two further parts in 1955 as

*The Human Age*. His fascist sympathies and unprovoked attacks on his literary contemporaries did not improve his public image, but he was regarded in his time as an experimental novelist of some stature — see also *The Apes of God* (1930), *The Revenge for Love* (1937), and *Self Condemned* (1954) — and an attractive writer of incisive if uneven criticism, as in *The Lion and the Fox: the Role of Hero in the Plays of Shakespeare* (1927), *Men Without Art* (1934), and *The Writer and the Absolute* (1952). See *The Essential Wyndham Lewis*, ed. Julian Symons, 1989; Jeffrey Meyers, *The Enemy*, new edn 1982 (biography).

**Locke, John** (1632–1704), philosopher, was born in Wrington, Somerset, son of a land-steward, and educated at Westminster School and Christ Church, Oxford, where he was a life student until the privilege was withdrawn in 1684 on the orders of Charles II. He was attracted by the empiricism of *Bacon, and studied medicine, which he practised as physician to the future Lord Shaftesbury (1621–83), who introduced him to leading thinkers and politicians of the day, and gave him a post with the Board of Trade. For reasons of health or political expediency, Locke spent some of the years between 1675 and 1688 on the Continent, where he met philosophers and theologians. Back in England, and in favour, he was appointed to several government posts, and ended his days in comfortable retirement. *An Essay Concerning Human Understanding* (1690) works from a basic premise he had propounded twenty years earlier, which holds that a study of the nature of human understanding is a prerequisite of constructive thought and that knowledge derives from experience. It has become one of the most influential philosophical works in the English language. Other significant studies include *Two Treatises of Government* (1690, 1698), a series of 'Letters on Toleration' (1689, 1690, 1692), *Some Thoughts Concerning Education* (1693), and *The Reasonableness of Christianity* (1695), in which he advocated a reunion of the Catholic and Protestant Churches. See Maurice Cranston, *John Locke*, new edn 1985 (biography); John Dunn, *Locke*, 1984 (introduction to his ideas).

**Lydgate, John** (*c*.1370–1449), poet, was born in Lydgate, Suffolk, and educated at the Benedictine Abbey of Bury St Edmunds where, according to his poem, 'The Testament', he was an ill-behaved and inattentive schoolboy. After being a novice, he became a monk and was ordained priest in 1397. There is a gap in the record until 1415, when he reappears at Bury, and for several years after that he was Prior of Hatfield Broadoak, Essex. He knew London well, and spent some time in Paris in the 1420s. His significance as a poet depends not so much on the quality of his writing, which is generally mundane and muddled, but on its sheer volume. About 145,500 lines survive, providing evidence of the influence of patronage on the poetic output of the time and the effect on the preservation of literary works of the imminent establishment of the printing industry in England. His major, or longer, works, all adapted or translated from the French, include *The Hystorye, Sege and Dystruccyon of Troye* ('The Troy Book'), from Guido delle Colonne (*d.*1316), written between 1412 and 1421 at the command of Henry V when Prince of Wales; *The Siege of Thebes*; *The Pilgrimage of the Life of Man*, from Guillaume de Deguileville (*fl.*1330–58), for the Earl of Salisbury; and *The Falle of Princis*, done between 1431 and 1438 from an enlarged French version of the Italian of Boccaccio (1313–75) for the Duke of Gloucester. The best of his shorter poems, many of them celebrating public or private occasions, can be found among his religious lyrics. See *John Lydgate: Poems*, ed. John Norton-Smith, 1966.

**Lyly, John** (1553/4–1606), dramatist and prose writer, was born in the Kentish Weald of an erudite family, and educated probably at King's School, Canterbury, and at Magdalen College, Oxford. The appellation 'university wit' has been applied to him and several of his contemporaries. 'Wit' in this context means 'man of wits', such as is the hero of Lyly's didactic prose romance *Euphues: the Anatomy of Wit* (1578) and its sequel *Euphues and His England* (1580), from whom derives the term 'euphuism' for a style of writing that is ornamental but mannered and artistic, reflecting the humanistic education of its exponents. During the 1580s he taught at St Paul's choir school, which was in effect a theatrical company providing revels for the court of Queen Elizabeth in the form of performances by boys. It is in this light that his eight comedies must be seen, and his undoubted artifice judged. They range from the multifarious entertainment of *A Most Excellent Comedy of Alexander, Campaspe and Diogenes* (1584), to the elaborately- and minutely-constructed *Mother Bombie* (1594), and *The Woman in the Moon* (1597), which was probably intended also for general audiences, and is the first example of blank verse successfully being used as the medium of comedy. Lyly is the likely author of a government-sponsored tract, *Pappe with an Hatchet* (1589), supporting the bishops against a series of subterranean satirical pamphlets, and he was a Member of Parliament 1597–1601. See John Dover Wilson, *John Lyly*, new edn 1982.

**Macaulay, Thomas Babington** (1800–59), historian, critic, poet, and statesman, was born in Rothley Temple, near Leicester, son of Zachary Macaulay (1768–1838), the Scottish-born abolitionist, and brought up in the intellectual, activist atmosphere of London's Clapham Common. He was educated at Aspenden Hall, Hertfordshire, and Trinity College, Cambridge, where he won many prizes and was elected to a fellowship. He was called to the Bar in 1826, but became a celebrity through his critical and topical essays in the *Edinburgh Review*. He was elected to Parliament in 1830, but in 1834 money problems led to his accepting a seat on the Supreme Council of India. In four years there he drafted a new penal code which is the basis of Indian law, and exerted influence to make English the medium of instruction at all levels. He was in 1839 elected MP for Edinburgh, which he remained, except for five years, until 1856 — his defeat in 1847 is recalled in his poem 'Lines Written in August'. He was Secretary for War 1839–41. *The Lays of Ancient Rome* (1842), with their strong plots, redounding rhythms, and predictable rhymes, were instantly popular. The first two volumes of *The History of England from the Accession of James II*, which he intended to go up to 1830, were published in 1848. He became ill in 1852, but managed to complete and see published in 1855 two further volumes. The fifth, up to the death of William III in 1702, was finalised from his notes by his sister, and published in 1861. He popularised history by force and pace of narrative, picturesque detail (culled from voluminous and energetic research), sparkling phraseology, and graphic characterisation. Some of his portraits, though, are biased or feature contradictory attributes, and some events are distorted by selectivity of facts — he was a Whig politician as well as an historian. He could also be vindictive, as in his essay on *Boswell's life of *Johnson (1831), for which he made partial amends by his article on Johnson for *Encyclopaedia Britannica* (1856). He was created Baron Macaulay of Rothley in 1857. He died, fully dressed, sitting in his armchair in the library of his house in Kensington, and was buried in Westminster Abbey. See *Selected Writings*, ed. John Clive and Thomas Pinney, 1974; *The Letters of Thomas Babington Macaulay*, ed. Thomas Pinney, 6 vols 1974–81; Owen Dudley-Edwards, *Macaulay*, 1988.

**MacCaig, Norman** (*b*.1910), Scottish poet, was born in Edinburgh and educated at the High School of Edinburgh and Edinburgh University, where he read classics. His father was from Dumfriesshire and his mother came to Edinburgh from the Outer Hebrides at 16, speaking only Gaelic. According to MacCaig, it was a holiday in his mother's native Scalpay when he was twelve that inspired in him a sense of family and collective history and an acute awareness of sights and sounds (see especially his poems 'Drifter' and 'Return to Scalpay'). Some of his early poetry was published in anthologies of the New Apocalypse (see *Treece), and his first two volumes of verse are held to have followed that trend. *Riding Lights* (1955) heralds the work of the poet he had then become, and that and succeeding collections reveal his vivid attention to ordinary things and creatures (his nature poetry embraces pigeons, ducks, frogs, goats, and sheep), and to ordinary activities, such as walking, fishing, playing skittles, and hospital visiting, all expressed with precise language and straightforward images. He is as assured when writing about experiences in Assisi and Manhattan as he is when evoking the essential spirit of north-western Scotland. His poetry is always accessible and, even when inflected with sadness, enjoyable to read. After a lifetime as a schoolteacher, MacCaig was Reader in Poetry at Stirling University from 1972 to 1979, in which year he was awarded the OBE. See *Collected Poems*, new edn 1988; Roderick Watson (ed.), *The Poetry of Norman MacCaig*, 1989 (critical study).

**MacDiarmid, Hugh**, pseudonym of Christopher Murray Grieve (1892–1978), Scottish poet, was born in Langholm, Dumfriesshire, son of a postman, and educated at Langholm Academy before becoming a pupil-teacher, then a journalist, and serving in World War II as a Royal Army Medical Corps sergeant. His restless and controversial public life there-after belied his inherently gentle nature. He was at different times expelled from the Scottish National and Communist parties, and he laboured hard and world-wide in pursuit of his political and literary ideals. Initially he wrote poems and stories in English, published in *Annals of the Five Senses* (1923). In the meantime he was studying the etymology and development of Lowland Scots, from which he created a literary form, using words from different dialects, which was capable of expressing the experiences and aspirations of modern civilisation. His first attempts were attributed to a friend called 'Hugh M'Diarmid' and published in *Sangschaw* (1925) and *Penny Wheep* (1926), and the move-ment known as the Scottish Renaissance had been launched. His pro-found influence on Scottish letters is due also to the fact that he was a fine lyrical and philosophical poet, with a gift for rhyme, whose *A Drunk Man Looks at the Thistle* (1926) is a sustained study of national and personal introspection. See *Lucky Poet*, 1943 (autobiography); *Selected Essays*, 1969; *Complete Poems 1920–1976*, ed. Michael Grieve and W. R. Aitken, 2 vols new edn 1985; Alan Bold, *MacDiarmid*, 1988 (biography).

**Mackenzie,** (Sir) **Compton** (1883–1972), Scottish novelist, was born Edward Montague Compton in West Hartlepool of a theatrical family, and assumed the family name of Mackenzie to emphasise his Scottish ancestry. He was educated at St Paul's School and Magdalen College, Oxford. He chose writing as a career, and published a book of verse and several successful novels, including *Carnival* (1912), a melodramatic romance of the stage, and *Sinister Street* (1913), a vivid study of contempo-rary adolescence and early manhood, before serving both in action and in the secret service in World War I. His devotion to Scottish issues is reflected in his sequence of six semi-autobiographical novels published as *The Four Winds of Love* (1937–45). These cover four decades in the many-faceted life of John Ogilvie in various parts of the world according to the points of a compass, from the establishment of the Scottish National Party (of which Mackenzie was a founder member) to 1945. His later novels include the more light-hearted but nevertheless elegantly-written comedies of and satires on Scottish life, manners, and super-stitions, such as *Whisky Galore* (1947) and *Hunting the Fairies* (1949). A flamboyant but often financially-embarrassed figure, a lover of cats and a staunch supporter of friends and causes that he admired, Mackenzie was knighted in 1952. His life is faithfully and meticulously recorded in his ten-volume autobiography, *My Life and Times* (1963–71). See Andro Linklater, *Compton Mackenzie: a Life,* 1987.

**MacNeice, Louis** (1907–63), Irish poet, translator, and critic, was born in Belfast, son of a future Anglican bishop, but educated in England after the death of his mother in 1914 (see his poems 'Carrickfergus' and 'Carrick Revisited'). He went to Marlborough College and Merton College, Oxford, where he got a first in Greats and edited *Oxford Poetry* with *Auden. He also had his first book of poems published, *Blind Fireworks* (1929). He was a lecturer in classics at Birmingham University 1929–36, and lecturer in Greek at Bedford College, London 1936–9 — his verse translation *The Agamemnon of Aeschylus* (1936) is highly regarded and was successfully staged. From 1941 to 1961 he was a producer of radio features for the BBC, for whom he also wrote some outstanding documentaries and dramas — see *The Dark Tower and Other Radio Scripts* (1947). He combined a full-time career and the distractions of an unsettled family life with his creative impulse, publishing regular volumes of verse and writing critical works, including *Modern Poetry: a Personal Essay* (1938), and his 1963 Clark Lectures, *Varieties of Parable* (1965). He was an inspirational poet, who let the form and content find their own disposition, the ensuing variety of themes and moods being matched by his ear for an exact sound and his eye for a precisely remembered image. He was made CBE in 1958. See *Collected Poems,* ed. E. R. Dodds, new edn 1979; *The Strings are False,* new edn 1982 (posthumous autobiography); Edna Longley, *Louis MacNeice: a Study,* 1988.

**Malory, (Sir) Thomas** (*c.*1410–71), prose writer, was of an old Warwickshire family, came into his father's estate at Newbold Revel in about 1433, served in France at the raising of the siege of Calais in 1436, and was Member of Parliament for Warwickshire in 1445, having in the meantime been knighted. Between about 1450 and 1460, however, he was arrested and imprisoned eight times (and escaped twice) on charges including ambush and intent to murder, aggravated burglary, cattle rustling, and extortion. In 1462 he was with the Earl of Warwick's army in Northumberland, but it would appear that he was soon back in prison, where he died, having completed there in 1469 what he refers to as 'the hoole book of kyng Arthur and of his noble knyghtes of the Rounde Table', which was printed and published in 1485 by William Caxton as *Le Morte Darthur*. This was regarded as the definitive text until the discovery in 1943 in the Fellows' Library of Winchester College of a fuller contemporary manuscript version. Whether one takes the view of Eugène Vinaver — see *Malory: Works* (2nd edn, reissued in 1977) — that it comprises eight separate books or that of C. S. *Lewis that it is a conglomerate of many often unfinished or unconnected stories, this remarkable prose romance is the most comprehensive rendering of the legends of King Arthur, told in a racy, descriptive style, with complete balance of dialogue and narrative, and is a landmark, if not an oasis, in the history of English prose. See Marylyn J. Parins (ed.), *Malory*, 1988 (criticism).

**Marlowe, Christopher** (1564–93), poet and dramatist, was born in Canterbury, son of a prosperous shoemaker, and educated at King's School, Canterbury, and Corpus Christi College, Cambridge. He graduated as BA in 1584, and as MA in 1587, but only after the Privy Council had mediated with the authorities, stressing that Marlowe had in the meantime undertaken a confidential mission abroad, which almost certainly would have involved attempting to unearth potential Catholic plots against Queen Elizabeth. He was probably destined for the Church, but he preferred to pursue the literary career begun at Cambridge. In 1589 he was involved in a sword-fight in which his friend Thomas Watson killed a man but was acquitted of murder. In 1592 the constable of Shoreditch sought an injunction to bring Marlowe to justice. On 18 May 1593, a warrant was issued by the Privy Council, on the evidence of *Kyd, for his arrest for possessing heretical documents. He was never questioned. On 30 May he was killed, apparently in a tavern brawl.

Blank verse had been first used in English by *Surrey for a translation of Virgil in 1557, and was employed by the authors of the first-known English tragedy, *Gorboduc* (1561) by Thomas Sackville (1536–1608) and Thomas Norton (1532–84). Marlowe developed the form into what is basically the blank verse of *Shakespeare and *Milton. His known plays are six. *The Tragedy of Dido, Queen of Carthage* (performed in 1586, published in 1594), written with Thomas Nashe (1567–1601) while they were both at Cambridge, is based on Virgil's *Aeneid* Books I, II, and IV. The two parts of *Tamburlaine the Great* (1587/1590) tell with massive sweeps of oratory and dramatic visual action the rise to power of the fourteenth-century Tatar conqueror, Tamerlane. *The Jew of Malta* (1591/1633 with foreword by *Heywood) follows the fall to and escape from ignominy of a Jewish merchant, who wreaks awful and indiscriminate revenge, betrays the island to the Turks, is rewarded with the governorship, and himself meets an end as ingeniously violent as any in the play. *Edward II* (1592/1594) is a telescoped account of an uneasy reign and of the King's passion for his favourite, Gaveston, concentrating on the characters and achieving dramatic tension by quick and frequent changes of scene. *The Massacre at Paris* (1593/94), which exists only in a corrupt and truncated text, covers 17 years of contemporary events from the St Bartholomew massacre of the Huguenots to the deaths of the Duke of Guise and Henry III in 1589. *The Tragical History of Dr Faustus* (1594/1604, but 1616 with a better text) is a classic version of the tale of the man who sold his soul to the devil, based on the apparent exploits of a sixteenth-century itinerant German wizard called Faust. Marlowe invests the story with genuine tragic overtones, even if the middle portion of the play, representing the 24 years between Faustus's bargain and his death, tends to lapse into a series of knockabout conjuring routines. Poetry known to have been written by Marlowe comprises: a translation of some of Ovid's *Amores* and of Lucan's *Pharsalia* Book I; the famous lyric 'Come live with me and be my love'; and the first two sestiads (books) of the mythological cautionary-tale of forbidden love, *Hero and Leander,* which was completed by *Chapman.

In the course of a short and turbulent life, Marlowe earned respect among his contemporaries and a place in literary posterity. He was a fine poet, some of whose lines are not just memorable, but familiar: 'Who ever loved that loved not at first sight' (*Hero and Leander*); the amassing of wealth by means of precious stones, enclosing 'Infinite riches in a little room' (*The Jew of Malta*); 'The sweet fruition of an earthly crown' (*Tamburlaine*); 'Was this the face that launched a thousand ships?' and 'See, see where Christ's blood streams in the firmament' (*Dr Faustus*). He inherited the metre of blank verse, with its almost uniform end-stopped line, and by varying the stresses and the position of the stops forged it into something quite new and potent, so that *Jonson could acknowledge, in his lines to the memory of Shakespeare, 'Marlowe's mighty line'. He was also the first English dramatist consistently to display an understanding of dramatic action, and of conflict and suspense as essential components of drama. See *Complete Plays and Poems,* ed. E. D. Pendry and J. C. Maxwell, new edn 1983; William Urry, *Christopher Marlowe and Canterbury,* 1988 (biography); F. S. Boas, *Marlowe: a Biographical and Critical Study,* new edn 1953; Harry Levin, *The Overreacher: a Study of Marlowe,* 1952.

**Marvell, Andrew** (1621–78), poet and satirist, was born in Winstead-in-Holderness, Yorkshire, son of the vicar, who moved his family to Hull in 1624. The boy was educated at Hull Grammar School and Trinity College, Cambridge, and in 1637 verses of his in Latin and Greek were published in a volume celebrating the birth of a child to the King. In about 1639 he had a brief association with Catholicism but was recalled to Anglicanism and Cambridge by his father, who was drowned in the Humber in 1641. He travelled abroad between 1642 and 1647, during which he flexed his poetic muscles in the satire, 'Flecknoe, an English Priest at Rome'. In 1650 he wrote 'An Horatian Ode upon Cromwell's Return from Ireland', the first of several tributes to the Lord Protector, but significant in that he is equally fair to Charles I, who even when on 'the tragic scaffold', 'He nothing common did or mean / Upon that memorable scene'. From 1650 to 1652 he was tutor to the daughter of Lord Fairfax at Nun Appleton House in Yorkshire, where it is presumed he wrote most of his lyrical poems, including 'Bermudas', as well as some very pleasing examples of local and pastoral verse, such as 'Upon Appleton House', 'Upon the Hill and Grove at Bilbrough', 'The Garden', and the 'Mower' pieces. For a time in 1656, and again between 1662 and 1665, he was abroad on political or undercover business of state. In 1657, on the recommendation of *Milton, he was appointed Latin Secretary to the Council of State, and it is said that he supported Milton at the time of the Restoration in 1660. He was elected to Parliament as Member for Hull in 1659, and sat until his death. *The Last Instructions to a Painter,* written in 1667, is a standard form of attack on the licence of the Court, and less inspired than his anonymous prose satire against religious intolerance, *The Rehearsal Transpros'd* (1672). None of his early poems were published in his lifetime. *Miscellaneous Poems* (1681) was published from manuscripts found by a 'Mary Marvell', who claimed to be his wife but appears to have been his housekeeper, Mary Palmer.

Marvell's lyric themes are conventional and at first sight their treatment almost commonplace, but his intellectual capacity and command of rhythm, rhyme, phrase, and wit endow them with extraordinary quality. 'On a Drop of Dew' begins as a nature poem but expands effortlessly into an analogy of the soul. 'The Nymph Complaining for the Death of Her Faun' incorporates a whole range of additional emotions. 'To His Coy Mistress' is rightly famous for its treatment of and scholarly but delightful variations on *Herrick's exhortation to 'Gather ye rosebuds while ye may', typified by his attribution in a single phrase of both wings and chariot to Time, 'Time's wingéd chariot', and the aptness of his metaphors. In his political and satirical poems, he looks forward to and often does not suffer by comparison with *Dryden. See *The Complete Poems,* ed. Elizabeth Story Donno, 1972; Michael Craze, *Life and Lyrics of Andrew Marvell,* 1979; Robert Wilcher, *Andrew Marvell,* 1985 (critical study).

**Masefield, John** (1878–1967), poet, novelist, children's writer, and dramatist, was born in Ledbury, Herefordshire, third of six children of a country solicitor. His mother died in 1885, and he went in 1888 as a boarder to King's School, Warwick, from which he was removed after three years on the death of his father. He continued his education in the school-ship H.M.S. *Conway,* and sailed for South America as an apprentice merchant seaman in 1894, but was sent home after being ill. He returned to sea a year later, but deserted ship in New York, spending three years working in a carpet mill in Yonkers and doing other jobs, while reading English literature and starting to write. Back in England, he was for three years a bank clerk, recovered his health, met *Yeats, and published *Salt-Water Ballads* (1902) and two further volumes, containing such popular poems as 'Sea Fever' and 'Cargoes', as well as invocations of the land, such as 'Tewkesbury Road' and 'Twilight'. These poems gave him a reputation as a kind of marine *Kipling, an influence he denied. He married in 1903 and for a time worked for the *Manchester Guardian*, before increasing his range and output with some excellent adventure stories, including *Lost Endeavour* (1910) and *Jim Davis* (1911), and plays, of which *The Tragedy of Nan* (1908), a domestic tragedy set in the early nineteenth century, is praised by Professor Allardyce Nicoll in *British Drama* (4th edn 1947) for its 'unflinching realism'. The same attribute could be applied to the narrative poem, *The Everlasting Mercy* (1911), which shocked the literary world but, according to Frank Swinnerton in *The Georgian Literary Scene* (1935), 'made the general public read what he had written'. In *Dauber* (1913), written in rhyme royal, the conflict between the artist and his environment is set within a stirring narrative of the sea. Masefield served with the Red Cross in France and the Dardanelles in World War I, immediately after which he published *Reynard the Fox* (1919), a wholly admirable narrative poem about a fox-hunt which is redolent of the English countryside.

He and his wife now settled in Boars Hill, Oxford (she died in 1960), where he built a small theatre next door, and while continuing to write poetry and plays, including *The Coming of Christ* (1928), he became a noted children's author, whose fantasies *The Midnight Folk* (1927) and *The Box of Delights* (1935), and rousing costume thrillers, *Dead Ned* (1938) and *Live and Kicking Ned* (1939), are still widely read and admired. *The Nine Days Wonder* (1941) is a prose account of the retreat from Dunkirk, written without the deliberate romanticism of his equivalent work of World War I, *Gallipoli* (1916). He was appointed Poet Laureate in 1930, a post which he undertook seriously and assiduously, and was awarded the OM in 1935. See *Collected Poems*, 1929; *So Long to Learn: Chapters of an Autobiography*, 1952; *Grace Before Ploughing: Fragments of Autobiography*, 1966; Constance Babington Smith, *John Masefield: a Life*, new edn 1985; Muriel Spark, *John Masefield*, 1953 (critical study of poetry and novels); Margery Fisher, *John Masefield*, 1963 (study of his children's books).

**Massinger, Philip** (1583–1640), dramatist, was born in Salisbury, Wiltshire, son of a man of standing in the academic and political fields, and educated at St Alban Hall, Oxford, without taking his degree. He collaborated with *Dekker and *Tourneur, and regularly with *Fletcher. His own tragedies, which include *The Duke of Millaine* (c.1621) and *The Roman Actor* (1626), fall in time between those of *Shakespeare and the more decadent horrors of John Ford (1586–1639), and though there is a superficial structure, the characters fail to inspire emotion. The same lack of vitality affects his romantic tragicomedies, of which *The Bond Man: an Antient Story* (1623) and *The Maid of Honour* (printed 1632) are nevertheless interesting examples of their kind. It is with his two out-and-out comedies, *A New Way to Pay Old Debts* (c.1626) and *The City Madam*

(1632), that he emerges as worthy to stand with *Jonson, though they are nearer to the comedy of *Congreve, over forty years ahead, in their dependence on intrigue and in their memorable portraiture of hypocrisy in the forms of Sir Giles Overreach, based on a real-life villain, and Luke Frugal, the servile brother turned monster when he believes the head of the household is out of the way. Massinger died suddenly one night in his house in Southwark, and his body, accompanied by actors, was taken to the nearby church of St Saviour's and, according to one account, buried in the same grave as Fletcher. See T. A. Dunn, *Massinger: the Man and the Playwright,* 1957.

**Maugham, W(illiam) Somerset** (1874–1965), novelist, short story writer, and dramatist, was born in Paris, youngest son of the legal adviser to the British Embassy. He lived in France until at ten he was orphaned and put into the care of his uncle, vicar of Whitstable, Kent. He was educated at King's School, Canterbury, and later spent a year at Heidelberg University without taking a degree. At his own insistence, he became a medical student at St Thomas's Hospital, and managed while studying to read voraciously and to observe human life. His first novel, *Liza of Lambeth* (1897), was published in the year he qualified as MRCS LRCP, whereupon he abandoned medicine for literature and travelled in Spain. The failure of subsequent novels and the rejection of several plays almost made him reverse his decision. His first play to be performed was a one-act piece in German, *Schiffbrüchig* (1901). *A Man of Honour* was put on by the Stage Society in 1903. In 1907 *Lady Frederick*, a traditional comedy of manners, was staged at the Royal Court as a stop-gap. Within a year he had three other plays also running in the West End. He continued to write plays until 1933, in a variety of styles and moods, his cynical comedies *The Circle* (1921) and *The Constant Wife* (1927) being the most highly regarded.

In 1911, now more comfortably off, he began to write his most lasting literary work, the semi-autobiographical *Of Human Bondage* (1915), whose depressive realism did not at first appeal to a country involved in World War I. During the war he served in the Intelligence Department, his experiences being reflected later in *Ashenden: or the British Agent* (1928). In 1916 he married Syrie Wellcome, daughter of the philanthropist Thomas Barnado; they were divorced in 1927. Meanwhile he had visited the East with his secretary/companion Gerald Haxton (1892–1944), published *The Moon and Sixpence* (1919), based on the life of Paul Gauguin (1848–1903), the French post-impressionist painter, and absorbed the basic social atmosphere which he used most effectively in the many of his short stories set in that region, of which the most famous is 'Rain' (1921). In 1928 he settled in a villa in the south of France, where he wrote *Cakes and Ale* (1930), a novel in which he gently takes revenge on the English literary establishment. He spent the war years in the USA, publishing

*The Razor's Edge* (1944), which reflects his interest in Indian mysticism, and then returned to France. He founded the Somerset Maugham Award in 1947, to enable promising young British writers to travel. He was appointed CH in 1954. See *Complete Short Stories*, 3 vols 1951; *Collected Plays*, 3 vols 1952 (with author's prefaces); *The Summing Up*, 1938 (autobiographical study); *A Writer's Notebook*, new edn 1967 (extracts from journal); Robert Calder, *Willie: the Life of W. Somerset Maugham*, 1989; Klaus W. Jonas (ed.), *The World of Somerset Maugham: an Anthology*, new edn 1972 (critical essays); John Whitehead, *Maugham: a Reappraisal*, 1987.

**Meredith, George** (1828–1909), novelist and poet, was born in Portsmouth, son of the leading naval tailor. After the death of his mother in 1833 and the departure of his father to London and then Cape Town, he was brought up by aunts and educated locally and at the Moravian school at Neuwied on the Rhine, returning to be articled to a solicitor in London. He married the widowed daughter of *Peacock in 1849, but she eloped in 1858 with the artist Henry Wallis (1830–1916), who had used Meredith as the model for his famous painting of the death of *Chatterton. A second marriage in 1864 was happier. Meredith preferred to be known as a poet, but it was as a novelist that he became (with *Hardy) regarded as a grand old man of literature, without tangible financial reward, to which his tendency to play out his own misfortunes with an overwrought intensity contributed. The title poem of *Modern Love, and Poems of the English Roadside, with Poems and Ballads* (1862) is a sonnet-like sequence, recording incidents in a broken marriage. After two early prose fantasies, he published 12 novels, and his continuous experimentation with form justifies his influential status. In *The Ordeal of Richard Feverel* (1859), a runaway wife leaves a father to care for his son. A father/son relationship is also the theme of *The Adventures of Harry Richmond* (1871), while *The Egoist* (1879), intellectually his most satisfying novel, is a practical exposition of his lecture 'On the Idea of Comedy and the Uses of the Comic Spirit' (1877). His most successful novel, *Diana of the Crossways* (1885), based on a contemporary scandal, again features an erring wife. See Lionel Stevenson, *The Ordeal of George Meredith*, 1954; Ian Fletcher (ed.), *Meredith Now: Some Critical Essays*, 1971.

**Middleton, Thomas** (1580–1627), dramatist, was born in the City of London, son of a prosperous 'citizen and bricklayer', educated at The Queen's College, Oxford, without apparently taking a degree, and by 1601 is recorded as 'daily accompanying the players' in London — he married the sister of an actor shortly afterwards. He had already published *The Wisdom of Solomon Paraphrased* (1597), *Micro-Cynicon: Six Snarling Satires* (1599), and *The Ghost of Lucrece* (1600), a continuation of *Shakespeare's poem. He collaborated with *Dekker on *The Honest*

*Whore, Part I* (1604), and then wrote several comedies for boys to perform to middle-class audiences. More sophisticated dramas followed the decline of the boys' companies. In *Women Beware Women* (performed *c*.1621), a tragedy with ironic twists and two plots, Bianca, a Venetian girl married to a Florentine, finds herself out of place in whatever social station she seeks. *A Chaste Maid in Cheapside* (1613) is a comical skit on contemporary attitudes to sex and money. *A Game at Chesse* (1624), a very popular, brilliantly staged, political satire, was so topical that it was prosecuted. *The Changeling*, written with William Rowley (*c*.1585–*c*.1626) and performed in 1622, is a skilfully constructed tragedy of the effects of lust and evil, with a depth of feeling rare for the times outside Shakespeare. *The Revenger's Tragedy* (1607) has been attributed to Middleton, but following *Eliot and other critics is here regarded as by *Tourneur. See Richard H. Barker, *Thomas Middleton*, 1958.

**Milton, John** (1608–74), poet and prose writer, was born in London, eldest son of a financier and minor composer who destined him 'from a child to the pursuits of literature'. He was educated at St Paul's School and Christ's College, Cambridge, graduating as MA in 1632, having demonstrated his skill at Latin verse and also composed the considerable poems 'On the Morning of Christ's Nativity', 'L'Allegro', and 'Il Penseroso'. Until 1638 he studied on his father's estate at Horton, Buckinghamshire, accepting commissions to write, for performance with music by the court musician, the masques 'Arcades' and then *Comus* (1634), the latter for the inauguration of the Earl of Bridgewater as Lord President of Wales and containing genuine conflict within a traditional form of entertainment. The elegy 'Lycidas' was written in 1637 in memory of a former fellow-student. He cut short a study-tour of Italy and Greece in 1639 because of the impending English Civil War. He then rented a house in London and took in pupils, starting with his own nephews, while involving himself in the arguments for a reformation of the Protestant Church. To this end he wrote several notable pamphlets in support of Puritanism, including *The Reason of Church-Government* (1642), in which he also suggested his personal responsibilities as a poet. In 1642 he married Mary Powell, the 16-year-old daughter of an Oxfordshire squire. She went home after a few weeks, which may or may not have induced him to write *The Doctrine and Discipline of Divorce* (1643), advocating incompatibility as grounds for divorce. He countered reactions of censorship with *Areopagitica* (1644), an impassioned plea for the freedom of the press. He published *Poems, both English and Latin* in 1645, the year in which Mary returned to him — she died in 1652, having had three daughters who survived. A few weeks after the execution of Charles I in January 1649, Milton defended the revolution in *The Tenure of Kings and Magistrates*, and was then appointed Latin Secretary to the Council of State. He was already going blind, and by 1652 was entirely so, though he continued in public office. He recorded his feelings in the sonnet 'When I consider how my light is spent', but was more resigned to his state when he wrote 'Cyriack, this three years' day these eyes...' (1655).

In 1656 he married Katherine Woodcock, who had a daughter in 1657, but died the following year, being remembered in the sonnet, 'Methought I saw my late espouséd saint' (1658). In spite of Cromwell's death in 1658, he courageously produced further pamphlets in support of that regime, including *The Readie and Easie Way to Establish a Free Commonwealth* (1660). He was thus in deep trouble at the Restoration of Charles II in May 1660, but thanks to the intervention of his friends escaped with a brief prison sentence and was pardoned. In 1663 he married Elizabeth Minshull, the niece of a friend, and at his house in Bunhill Fields used his family and others as amanuenses to help him complete the great epic poem he had been contemplating for years and had probably begun in about 1658. *Paradise Lost* was published in 1667, and in a revised version in twelve books in 1674. It is notable less for its encompassment of the war in Heaven and projections of world history than for the representation of Satan and the graphic and sympathetic account of the Fall of Man. During the plague of 1665–6 the family moved to a cottage in Chalfont St Giles, Buckinghamshire, which still survives, but they returned in time to endure the Great Fire of 1666. He continued to write and to publish: the lesser and shorter epic, *Paradise Regain'd*, and the biblical dramatic poem, *Samson Agonistes*, together in 1671, and a new edition of his poems in 1673, as well as prose works, including *History of Britain* (1670), in the unfinished form in which he had abandoned it in 1659. He died of gout.

Doubts about the validity of the poetic influence exerted by *Paradise Lost*, as well as its portrait of God — see F. R. Leavis in *The Common Pursuit* (1952) and William Empson, *Milton's God* (rev. edn 1981), where issue is taken with C. S. *Lewis, *A Preface to Paradise Lost* (reissued 1960) — are secondary to the fact that it is the most noble poem in the language. See *The Poems of Milton*, ed. John Carey and Alastair Fowler, 1968; *John Milton: Selected Prose*, ed. C. A. Patrides, 1974; A. N. Wilson, *The Life of John Milton*, new edn 1984; E. M. W. Tillyard, *Milton*, new edn 1968 (critical biography); Lois Potter, *A Preface to Milton*, 1972; Dennis Danielson (ed.), *The Cambridge Companion to Milton*, 1989.

**Montgomerie, Alexander** (*c*.1545–*c*.1598), Scottish poet, was a son of the Laird of Hessilheid, and was through his mother distantly related to James VI of Scotland, himself no mean poet, whose teacher he became. In 1583 the King granted him a pension, chargeable against certain rents of the archbishopric of Glasgow, which led to a protracted lawsuit, and the loss of the pension. In the meantime he was active in the Catholic interest, and was imprisoned. He was further implicated in a Catholic plot in 1597, after which he disappears from the records. 'The Flyting betwixt Montgomerie and Polwart' (Sir Patrick Hume of Polwarth, master of the royal household), a spirited, coarse, highly alliterative piece of extended invective, was probably first spoken in public in about 1582. *The Cherrie and the Slae*, published in Edinburgh in 1597, is a traditional allegorical poem, but its interest is in the interpretation of the two forces as Catholicism (the sweet, refreshing cherries in the tree) and Protestantism (the bitter but more accessible sloes on the bush), in the metrical form (probably his own invention), and in the opening realistic rather than stylised scene of nature. He also wrote some neat love sonnets, of which 'To His Mistress' and 'The Tender Snow of Granis Soft and Quhyt...' are particularly delightful. Until Robert Fergusson (1750–74) and *Burns rediscovered it as a literary form, he was the last notable poet to write in Scots. See Helena M. Shire, *Alexander Montgomerie: a Selection from His Songs and Poems*, 1960; R. D. S. Jack, *Montgomerie*, 1985.

**Moore, George** (1852–1933), Irish novelist, dramatist, and critic, was born at the family seat of Moore Hall, Ballyglass, Co. Mayo, and educated at Oscott College, Birmingham. After the death of his father, and on his coming of age, he went to Paris to be a painter but, having failed to make the grade, turned to literature. His first published works were two volumes of verse in the style of Baudelaire, *Flowers of Passion* (1878) and *Pagan Poems* (1881), and *Martin Luther: a Tragedy in Five Acts* (1879). In 1880, the money from his Irish rents having dried up, he went to London, where he wrote two novels whose social realism verges on the naturalistic — *A Modern Lover* (1883), later rewritten as *Lewis Seymour and Some Women* (1917), and *A Mummer's Wife* (1885), the prissy attitude to which on the part of the circulating libraries moved him to issue a trenchant pamphlet, *Literature at Nurse* (1885). His ambivalent feelings towards the Irish surfaced in *A Drama in Muslin* (1886), in which the plight of the tenants is contrasted with the frivolities, and domestic realities, of the well-to-do. After several further novels which he later suppressed, he produced *Esther Waters* (1894), a striking English novel which concentrates on the seduced serving girl and her subsequent struggles, against a background of the racing world which Moore knew well. In 1900, disillusioned with England, he moved to Dublin and joined *Yeats in managing the Irish Literary Theatre and in generating a new Irish literature, with bizarre results as far as their collaboration was concerned in the play *Diarmuid and Grania* (1901), which was written by Moore in French, translated into English, then into Irish, then back again into English, and finally polished by Yeats. More lasting manifestations of this Irish phase are the deliberate harshness and directness of the stories in *The Untilled Field* (1903) and the melodic line he created for *The Lake* (1905).

Moore returned to London in 1911, and settled in Ebury Street, from which distance he published three mischievous autobiographical exposés of the Irish literary renaissance and Irish Catholicism, under the general title of *Hail and Farewell* (1911–14, new edn, ed. Richard Allen Cave, 1985). Always concerned with improving what he had written, he developed an idea in his play about St Paul, *The Apostle* (1911), into the novel, *The Brook Kerith* (1916), for which he adopted a rationalistic stance, rewriting the New Testament story as though Jesus was secretly taken from the cross and saved by Joseph. It succeeds because he did not set out to shock and he had first journeyed through Palestine to absorb the atmosphere of the terrain. Held in equal regard is *Heloïse and Abelard* (1921), in which the famous lovers stand out from a canvas of dreamlike settings, crowded with colourful medieval characters. He was a respected critic, some of his essays being collected in *Impressions and Opinions* (1891) and *Avowals* (1924, privately published 1918). To recapture the essence of meetings which make up *Conversations in Ebury Street* (1924), he dictated it to a secretary. *Modern Painting* (1893) was instrumental in extending the reputation of the French Impressionists. See *Confessions of a Young Man*, 1888, and *Memoirs of My Dead Life*, 1906 (autobiography); Joseph Hone, *The Life of George Moore*, 1936; Richard Allen Cave, *A Study of the Novels of George Moore*, 1978; and in Virginia Woolf, *The Death of the Moth*, 1942.

**Moore, Thomas** (1779–1852), Irish poet and biographer, was born in Dublin of Catholic parents (his father was a grocer), and educated at Trinity College, Dublin. He read for the Bar in London, where his fine voice and musical ability made him a welcome guest of the aristocracy. *Odes of Anacreon* (1800), a metrical translation done at college, was followed by the pseudonymous but only faintly improper *The Poetical Works of the Late Thomas Little, Esq* (1801). In 1803 he was appointed Admiralty Registrar in Bermuda, but in 1804 he left the post to a deputy, travelled in America, and returned to London, where he published *Epistles, Odes and Other Poems* (1806). *Irish Melodies*, with 'symphonies and accompaniments', appeared in instalments from 1807 to 1834 and confirmed his reputation as a lyricist and Irish national bard. *Lalla Rookh* (1817), verse tales with linking prose, was a fully-researched attempt to satisfy the vogue for the oriental but, while it was popular throughout Europe, only the songs have lasted. In 1818 his Bermuda deputy decamped with the official funds. Moore was declared bankrupt, and spent several years abroad. His versatility as a writer is demonstrated also by the satirical verse collection, *The Fudge Family in Paris* (1818), a novel of the Irish situation, *The Memoirs of Captain Rock* (1824), and perceptive lives of *Sheridan (1825) and of his friend *Byron (1830). See *The Journals of Thomas Moore 1818–1841*, ed. Peter Quennell, 1964; *The Letters of Thomas Moore*, ed. Wilfred S. Dowden, 2 vols 1964; Terence de Vere White, *Tom Moore, the Irish Poet*, 1977.

**More,** (Sir) **Thomas** (1478–1535), prose writer and statesman, was born in the City of London, son of a judge, and educated at Canterbury Hall, Oxford. He was called to the Bar but chose to spend four years in retreat, from which he emerged to resume a brilliant legal career, to enter Parliament, and to marry. He was knighted by Henry VIII in 1521 and held several posts of state, the last, which he accepted reluctantly, being Lord Chancellor. He resigned in 1532, unable to accept the King's divorce. When Henry appointed himself head of the English Church in 1534, More twice refused to accept his supremacy over the Pope, and was beheaded. He was canonised in 1935. *Utopia*, one of the finest statements of humanism, partly written while on a diplomatic mission to Flanders, was published in Latin in 1516, and translated into English by Ralph Robynson (1551). The ideal, but in some respects idyllic, state is contrasted with English social, corporate, and religious life in the early sixteenth century seen by an imaginary traveller. *History of Richard the Thirde*, written in English and Latin in about 1513, became via the chronicles of Grafton and Hall (see *Holinshed) the source of *Shakespeare's *Richard III*. While awaiting execution, More wrote the moving *A Dialogue of Comfort against Tribulacion* (1553). His friendship with the Dutch humanist, Erasmus (1466–1536), whom he first met in 1497, led to a correspondence between them which upholds the Renaissance ideal of immortality through the preservation of personal letters. His son-in-law, William Roper (1496–1578), wrote *The Mirrour of Vertue: or the Life of More* (1625). See R. W. Chambers, *Thomas More*, new edn 1982; Anthony Kenny, *Thomas More*, 1983 (introduction to his philosophy).

**Morris, William** (1834–96), poet, prose writer, book designer, and craftsman, was born in the London suburb of Walthamstow, son of a city businessman, and educated at Marlborough College and Exeter College, Oxford. He gave up the idea of the Church, was articled to an architect, and then became a professional painter on the advice of D. G. *Rossetti, with whom and others he formed an interior decorating firm. In 1859 he married Jane Burden, a much painted pre-Raphaelite model. His enthusiasm for the freedom of the craftsman from the constrictions of capitalism and the dangers of mass-production was instrumental in his founding the Socialist League in 1884, and in 1890 he set up the Kelmscott Press to produce fine books. *The Defence of Guenevere and Other Poems* (1858) revealed a flair for romantic narrative verse in easy rhythm and rhyme, especially in the title-poem, a striking treatment of scenes from *Malory, and 'The Haystack in the Floods'. *The Life and Death of Jason* (1867) and *Sigurd the Volsung* (1877) are verse retellings of classical and Norse myth, but in *The Earthly Paradise* (1868–70) he used *Chaucer's storytelling framework effectively to combine Greek, Germanic, Norse, and Celtic folklore. *A Dream of John Ball* (1888) and *News from Nowhere* (1890) are prose romances in which his socialist doctrines are interwoven with forward and backward time-slips. He also wrote historical novels based on north European legend, of which *The House of the Wolfings* (1889) is a good example. See Philip Henderson, *William Morris: His Life, Work and Friends*, new edn 1986; Peter Stansky, *William Morris*, 1983 (introduction to his ideas).

**Muir, Edwin** (1887–1959), Scottish poet, novelist, critic, and translator, was born in Deerness, Orkney, son of a farmer, and attended Kirkwall Grammar School irregularly. When he was 14, the family was evicted and moved to Glasgow; within five years both parents and two brothers were dead. After working as a clerk, he married in 1919 a Scottish academic and teacher, Willa Anderson, with whom he settled in London. A near-breakdown was averted by psychoanalysis, and a European tour made possible by the publication in the USA of *We Moderns* (1918), a collection of aphorisms under the pseudonym of Edward More. On their return he published *First Poems* (1925), and three novels. His income came from reviews and critical articles — see P. H. Butter (ed.), *The Truth of Imagination: a Collection of Reviews and Essays by Edwin Muir* (1988) — and from translating European literature (notably Kafka) with his wife. He was British Council Director in Prague 1945–8 and Rome 1949–50, and Warden of Newbattle Abbey College 1950–5. Much of his best poetry was written after he was fifty. Unsensational, reflective, plainly stated, it often reaches back to his childhood and beyond into history, and forward to a time when confusion and destruction will have been exorcised. He advocated a Scottish national literature in English, which caused him to fall out with his friend *MacDiarmid. He was made CBE in 1953. See *Collected Poems*, rev. edn 1963; *An Autobiography*, new edn 1987; P. H. Butter, *Edwin Muir, Man and Poet*, 1966.

**Murdoch, Iris** (*b.* 1919), novelist, philosopher, and dramatist, was born in Dublin and educated at Badminton School, Bristol, and Somerville College, Oxford. She was an assistant principal in the Treasury 1942–4, and an administrative officer with the UN Relief and Rehabilitation Administration 1944–6. She was a Fellow of St Anne's College, Oxford, and University lecturer in philosophy 1948–63. Her first novel, *Under the Net* (1954), established her as a writer with a distinctive style and purpose, the philosophical implications and symbolism being submerged (except for those who wish to uncover them) in an entertaining and comic, but often complicated and grotesque, plot with many incidents, in which the characters are motivated by chance or contingency as well as by their search for love, knowledge, and freedom. Among her subsequent novels, which embrace a wide variety of settings, *The Sandcastle* (1957), *The Bell* (1958), and *A Severed Head* (1961) are particularly notable, and after a slight falling-off the vein of inventiveness was rediscovered in *The Nice and the Good* (1968), *The Sea, the Sea* (1978), and *Nuns and Soldiers*

(1980). *The Three Arrows, and The Servants and the Snow* (1973) contains the two plays she has written apart from adaptations of her own novels — also published, with *The Black Prince*, in *Three Plays* (1989). Among her other works are *Sartre: Romantic Realist* (1953); a collection of essays, *The Sovereignty of Good* (1971); *A Year of the Birds: Poems* (1978); and *Acastos: Two Platonic Dialogues* (new edn 1987). She was created DBE in 1987. See Richard Todd, *Iris Murdoch*, 1984.

**Newman, John Henry** (1801–90), theologian, was born in the City of London, eldest child of a banker, and educated at a private school in Ealing and at Trinity College, Oxford. He was elected a Fellow of Oriel College in 1822, was ordained in 1824, and was vicar of the University church of St Mary's 1828–43 — see *Newman's University Sermons* (1970). His disillusionment with the Church of England is charted precisely and persuasively (and when demolishing his antagonist, with irony) in *Apologia pro Vita Sua* (1864), which began as a response to *Kingsley, and became a literary and spiritual prose classic. He became a Catholic in 1845, founded the Oratory in Birmingham in 1848, and in 1879 was created Cardinal of San Giorgio in Velabro. The last of his numerous theological works was *Grammar of Assent* (1870), an examination of belief. In the early 1830s he had contributed over a hundred sacred poems, including 'Pillar of the Cloud' (better known as the hymn 'Lead, Kindly Light') to the *British Magazine*, which were reprinted, with others by members of the Oxford Movement, as *Lyra Apostolica* (1834). He returned to poetry later, when ill and envisaging death, to write *The Dream of Gerontius* (1866), a journey of the soul, later made into an oratorio by Edward Elgar (1857–1934). He also wrote two anonymous novels, *Loss and Gain: the Story of a Convert* (1848) and *Callista: a Sketch of the Third Century* (1856). See Ian Ker, *John Henry Newman*, 1989 (biography); Owen Chadwick, *Newman*, 1983 (introduction to his thought).

**Newton, (Sir) Isaac** (1642–1727), philosopher, mathematician, and physicist, was born at Woolsthorpe, Lincolnshire, posthumous son of a minor landowner, and educated at Grantham Grammar School and, as a sizar, at Trinity College, Cambridge. He was elected a Fellow of the College in 1667, Lucasian Professor of Mathematics in 1671, and in 1672 a Fellow of the Royal Society, of which he was President from 1703 until his death. He propounded the laws of gravity, on which he had been working since 1665, in a series of University lectures in 1684 under the title of 'De Motu Corporum' (On the Movement of Bodies), which formed the first part of his great treatise, *Philosophiae Naturalis Principia Mathematica* (1687), translated into English by Andrew Motte in 1729. Newton's other major scientific works are *Opticks* (1704) and *Arithmetica Universalis* (1707), but he also published several writings on theological subjects. He twice represented the University in Parliament, and was Master of the Mint from 1699. He was knighted in 1705. At times a sick and frequently a bitter and quarrelsome man, his contribution to English literature lies less in the manner in which he wrote (which was often in Latin), than in his ability to reconcile advanced scientific discoveries with Christian beliefs, and in his exposition of his Newtonian philosophy, which had a profound influence on the Enlightenment, and is reflected in the work of such poets as *Pope and *Thomson. See Richard Westfall, *Never at Rest: a Biography of Isaac Newton*, new edn 1983; John Fauvel, and others (eds), *Let Newton Be!: a New Perspective on His Life and Works*, new edn 1989.

**O'Casey, Sean** (1880–1964), Irish dramatist, was born John Casey in Dublin, youngest of 13 children of poor Protestant parents, of whom five survived. Because of a disease of the eyes, he had little schooling, and appears to have taught himself to read, while living with his mother and remaining brother in a tenement after his father's death when he was six. He worked as a casual labourer from the age of 14, educating himself from books he bought, borrowed, and sometimes stole, and revelling particularly in the language and stagecraft of *Shakespeare and other Elizabethan dramatists. In about 1910 he was caught up in the Irish political scene, and at various times joined the Gaelic League, the Irish Socialist Party, the recently-formed Irish Transport and General Workers Union, and the Irish Citizen Army, though he did not participate in the 1916 Rising. By this time he was writing plays. After four rejections, *The Shadow of a Gunman* was put on at the Abbey Theatre in 1923 (its author was working as a cement-mixer at the time), and *Juno and the Paycock* ran for two weeks the following year, the first Abbey play ever to do so. The political turbulence and violence of the times and the language and atmosphere of the tenements had been brought resoundingly to the stage, and female characters represented as more heroic than the men. With £25 royalties in his pocket, O'Casey became a full-time writer. Enraged patriots rioted in response to his off-hand treatment of the 1916 Easter Rising in *The Plough and the Stars* (1926), and when six weeks later he was invited to London to receive the Hawthornden Prize for *Juno and the Paycock*, he decided to stay in England. His self-imposed exile became complete when in 1928 his anti-war play about a disabled footballer, *The Silver Tassie*, with its symbolic second act, was rejected by the Abbey, though it was produced in London in 1929 and has since received critical acceptance.

From 1938 O'Casey lived in Devon, and continued to experiment with expressionism. *Purple Dust*, published in 1940 but not performed in England until 1945, is an Irish fantasy, played out between two English plutocrats, Stoke and Poges, their mistresses, and sundry builder's mates. The semi-autobiographical *Red Roses for Me*, produced in 1946, has a stylised Dublin setting. At this time he was also writing the six autobiographies which begin with *I Knock at the Door* (1939) and conclude with *Sunset and Evening Star* (1954) — reissued together as *Autobiographies* (1963) — of which the early volumes at least, before the querulousness obtrudes, are outstanding works of prose as well as graphic reconstructions of the life of an extraordinary man. He was a playwright with a gift of rich language, whom J. C. Trewin describes in his introduction to *Three More Plays* (1965) as 'an Elizabethan out of time'. He married Eileen Reynolds, an actress, in 1927 — see her biography of him, *Sean* (1971). See Gary O'Connor, *Sean O'Casey: a Life*, new edn 1989; James Simmons, *Sean O'Casey*, 1983 (critical study); and in Raymond Williams, *Drama from Ibsen to Brecht*, new edn 1973.

**O'Connor, Frank**, pseudonym of Michael O'Donovan (1903–66), Irish short story writer, critic, and poet, was born in Cork of a poor family and left school at twelve. He was imprisoned during the Civil War (1922–3) for his Republican activities, which are reflected in his first volume of stories, *Guests of the Nation* (1931). For the next twenty years he was prominent in Irish literary life, contributing reviews and articles to the *Irish Statesman* and *The Bell*, and being a director of the Abbey Theatre 1935–9, besides publishing short stories, two novels, *Three Old Brothers and Other Poems* (1936), *The Big Fellow* (1937), a biography of Michael Collins, and *The Fountain of Magic* (1939), a collection of translations from Irish poetry. He lived in the USA during the 1950s. His admirably crafted stories are fine examples of the narrative art, in which human experience, especially that of young people, is explicitly revealed. His literary criticism is incisive and straightforwardly expressed, and includes *The Lonely Voice: a Study of the Short Story* (1963) and *The Backward Look: a Survey of Irish Literature* (1967). His contribution to the rediscovery, in translation, of traditional Irish literature can be seen in his *Kings, Lords and Commons: an Anthology from the Irish* (1959). See *The Stories of Frank O'Connor*, 1952; *An Only Child*, 1962, and *My Father's Son*, 1968 (autobiography, published together 1988); Maurice Wohlgelernter, *Frank O'Connor: an Introduction*, 1977.

**O'Faolain, Sean** (*b*.1900), Irish short story writer, novelist, critic, and biographer, was born John Whelan in Cork, and educated locally and at University College, Cork, changing his name to its Irish equivalent while serving with the IRA. He then continued his university education at Cork and Harvard, and was a teacher, before returning permanently to Dublin to write. The contents of his first book, *Midsummer Night Madness and Other Stories* (1932), were largely experimental in form and style, and elusively romantic, but subsequent collections contain more compassion and humour, while evoking exactly an atmosphere of place or setting, and covering a broad canvas of situations inherent in the contemporary climate of Ireland. His three novels, *A Nest of Simple Folk* (1933), *Bird*

*Alone* (1936), and *Come Back to Erin* (1940), enabled him to develop in each case a single character in revolt against a central orthodoxy. Among his biographies are *De Valera* (1939), and *Newman's Way: the Odyssey of John Henry Newman* (1952). His most effective criticism is in *The Short Story* (1948) and *The Vanishing Hero: Studies in Novelists of the Twenties* (1956). As founder editor of *The Bell* 1940–6, he encouraged young, and older, Irish writers to express themselves freely, and gave them, and contemporary Irish letters, a firmer stepping-stone in the mainstream of modern literary thought and values. See *Selected Stories of Sean O'Faolain*, 1978; *Vive Moi!*, 1964 (autobiography); Paul A. Doyle, *Sean O'Faolain*, 1968.

**O'Flaherty, Liam** (1896–1984), Irish novelist and short story writer, was born in Inishmore in the Aran Islands, and educated at Blackrock College and, for a year, at University College, Dublin, after which he joined the Irish Guards in 1915 and served at the front. In 1921, at the head of a group of dockers, he seized the Rotunda in Dublin for the Communists, and he was an active Republican during the Civil War. His first two published novels, *Thy Neighbour's Wife* (1923) and *The Black Soul* (1924), have backgrounds of Aran and the cultural contrasts that exist even within a small community. He returned there with *Skerrett* (1932), which charts the progress of a reforming schoolmaster to revolutionary and ultimately to self-destruction, and *Famine* (1937), in which he uses folklore and history vividly to recreate the dispersal of the community in the 1840s. From 1927 almost until his death he was constantly on the move, and his own restlessness is reflected in the pursuit of self-discovery on the part of the main characters in his novels, and in several autobiographical works — *Two Years* (1930), *I Went to Russia* (1931), and *Shame the Devil* (1934). The best of his many short stories are those in which he records with pity but also humour the harsh realities of the vanished Aran life style. In these stories in particular, but also in his work as a whole, the speech patterns and oral traditions of the Gaelic civilisation are near the surface. See *Short Stories*, new edn 1986; A. A. Kelly, *Liam O'Flaherty the Storyteller*, 1976.

**Orwell, George**, pseudonym of Eric Blair (1903–50), novelist, essayist, and critic, was born in Bihar, India, son of a peripatetic agent in the Opium Department of the Indian government. In 1904 his mother brought him and his elder sister back to England, where they settled in Henley-on-Thames. At eight, he was sent away to a boarding school on the Sussex coast, recorded in an autobiographical sketch, 'Such, Such Were the Joys' (a quotation from *Blake), probably written in 1940 but for reasons of libel not published until 1968. The outbreak of war in 1914 inspired his first published work, a poem 'Awake! Young Men of England', in the *Henley and South Oxfordshire Standard*. In 1917 he took up the scholarship he had won to Eton, and after five years there, instead of following his contemporaries to Oxford, for which he would have needed a scholarship, he joined the Indian Imperial Police, and served in Burma. In 1927, on his first home leave, he resigned. It was not just that he wanted to write and had grown to hate the idea of the Empire, but he objected to doing the work that imperialism involved. He now needed to establish a new identity as well as to seek a different social environment. He spent some time visiting the poor in London's East End, and then took a room in a working-class district of Paris, where he did menial jobs, gave English lessons, and tried to get his work published. Finally, having had pneumonia, he had to return home to his parents in Suffolk when his money ran out. He now completed an account of his recent experiences which, after two rejections, was accepted by Victor Gollancz (1893–1967) and published as *Down and Out in Paris and London* (1933) by 'George Orwell' — the surname is a river in Suffolk. During the next few years he did some teaching and reviewing, worked in a bookshop, and published three novels, of which the first, *Burmese Days* (1934), based on his military life, came out first in New York because of libel fears in Britain.

Early in 1936 Gollancz commissioned him to write a book about the conditions of the unemployed in the north of England. He spent several months on the research, then moved into a Hertfordshire cottage, which he reopened as the village store. The account of his investigations, *The Road to Wigan Pier*, appeared in 1937. In the second half of the book, he took a revolutionary socialist stance which opposed Marxism and embarrassed members of the Left Book Club, of which it was a choice. When it was published, he was in Spain, fighting on the Republican side in the Civil War. From this experience and his analysis of the politico-historical background he wrote *Homage to Catalonia* (1938). After an illness, he wrote (in Morocco) a further novel, *Coming Up for Air* (1939), in which nostalgia for the Henley of his childhood is mixed with social philosophy presented through the persona of an insurance salesman. Unfit for service in World War II, he earned money from journalism, worked for the BBC, and was literary editor of *Tribune* 1943–5. His anti-revolutionist political satire, *Animal Farm*, was published in 1945, after the death of his wife, Eileen O'Shaughnessy. With their two-year-old adopted son, he settled in Jura, off the west coast of Scotland, in 1946, and between bouts of tuberculosis wrote his last novel, the frightening forecast of totalitarianism, *Nineteen Eighty-Four* (1949). He died in a London hospital, three months after marrying Sonia Brownell.

His critical essays include studies of *Dickens, *Kipling, *Wells, *Yeats, and *Swift ('Politics and Literature: an Examination of *Gulliver's Travels*'), as well as of boys' comics, pornography, and obscenity. In 'Why I Write' (1946) he expounds his personal history and philosophy as an author. The penetrating essay, *The Lion and the Unicorn: Socialism and* *the English Genius*, was originally published as a pamphlet in 1941. In the end he was no nearer resolving the discrepancies within the various branches and shades of socialism than he had been at the beginning, but he succeeded in illuminating the enigmas for those who want to perceive them and to accompany him on his journeys towards a revelation. See *Collected Essays, Journalism and Letters of George Orwell,* ed. Sonia Orwell and Ian Angus, 4 vols new edn 1970; Bernard Crick, *George Orwell: a Life*, new edn 1982; Peter Stansky and William Abrahams, *Orwell: the Transformation*, new edn 1981 (critical biography of the years 1933–6); Raymond Williams, *Orwell*, rev. edn 1984 (introduction to his work and thought); George Woodcock, *The Crystal Spirit*, new edn 1984 (critical study).

**Osborne, John** (*b.*1929), dramatist, was born in Fulham, London, educated in Devon, and worked as a journalist and actor before writing plays. *Look Back in Anger* (1956) revolutionised attitudes to the theatre in that its hero, Jimmy Porter, spoke for and was of an educated working-class generation which had become disaffected, like many other young people, by middle-class values and ineffective government. Osborne became the focus of a literary movement known as the Angry Young Men (\*Amis was another), and the term 'kitchen-sink drama' was applied to the style of realistic working-class family conflict typified by *Look Back in Anger*, and reflected also in the plays of Shelagh Delaney (*b.*1939) and some of those of \*Wesker. *The Entertainer* (1957) starred Laurence Olivier as a pathetic relic of the old music hall. *Luther* (1961) presents the founder of Protestantism, with fair historical accuracy and with dramatic intensity, as yet another articulate opponent of established order. *Inadmissible Evidence* (1964) is an experiment in style and form and, in later plays including *The Hotel in Amsterdam* (1968) and *A Sense of Detachment* (1972), Osborne has employed a variety of stage techniques to enforce his characters' controversial statements, which are often delivered as though they were monologues. See *A Better Class of Person: an Autobiography 1929–56*, 1981; Ronald Hayman, *John Osborne*, 3rd edn 1976; Martin Banham, *Osborne*, 1969.

**Owen, Wilfred** (1893–1918), poet, was born in Oswestry, Shropshire, on the border with Wales (both his parents were probably of Welsh origin), and educated in Birkenhead, where his father was a stationmaster, and at Shrewsbury Technical College. He failed to get to university, and responding to the training of his deeply religious mother, worked unpaid in the parish of Dunsden, near Reading. In 1913 he became an English teacher in Bordeaux, where he began to write verse. He enlisted in 1915, and was commissioned in the Manchester Regiment in January 1917 and posted to France. In June he was sent home with shell shock to Craiglockhart Hospital, where he met and was encouraged by \*Sassoon. He returned to the front in September 1918, won an MC, and was killed near Ors on 4 November. He is regarded as the finest poet of World War I, but he is a war poet only in that all his best verse was written under its influence. His distinction lies in his choice of language and the way he used it in different metrical forms, with assonance and alliteration, as well as rhyme, para-rhyme, and half-rhyme, to heighten the horror and compassion of his view, as in the last verse of 'Exposure' (completed September 1918): 'To-night, this frost will fasten on the mud and us, / Shrivelling many hands, puckering foreheads crisp. / The burying-party, picks and shovels in shaking grasp, / Pause over half-known faces. All their eyes are ice, / But nothing happens.' See *The Poems of Wilfred Owen*, ed. Jon Stallworthy, 1985; Jon Stallworthy, *Wilfred Owen; a Biography*, new edn 1988.

**Paine, Thomas** (1737–1809), radical journalist, was born in Thetford, son of a Quaker corset-maker, and educated at Thetford Grammar School. He had a variety of jobs — corset-maker, seaman in a privateer, tobacco-nist, schoolmaster, and exciseman. He was dismissed from the last of these in 1774 after being commissioned to write a pamphlet agitating for better pay and conditions for excisemen. He went to America and there published *Common Sense* (1776), advocating independence from Britain, and a series of pamphlets under the general title of *The Crisis*. After being rewarded with a number of posts of state, he returned to England in 1787, and wrote *Rights of Man: Being an Answer to Mr Burke's Attack on the French Revolution* (1791–2) in two parts, in the second of which he took a broader view and proposed several far-reaching reforms. He was forced, however, to take refuge in France, where he was first elected to the National Assembly and then imprisoned for eleven months for proposing that Louis XVI should be given asylum in America. Eventually, disgruntled with French politics, he returned to America in 1802, having in the meantime published *The Age of Reason* (1794–5), a treatise on Deism, the anti-Christian aspects of which offended even his most fervent American supporters. He died in New York. In contrast to *Burke's easy eloquence and close argument, Paine's style is rather that of a crusading journalist, plainer and more resounding. See Alfred O. Aldridge, *Man of Reason: the Life of Paine*, 1960; Mark Philp, *Paine*, 1989 (introduction to his thought).

**Patmore, Coventry** (1823–96), poet and critic, was born in Woodford, Essex, and educated privately without any thought to a career, though his journalist father was unable to support him at university. *Poems* (1844) contained several narrative works which impressed members of the Pre-Raphaelites. In 1846 his father's speculations failed, and he got a post in the printed book department of the British Museum, feeling sufficiently comfortable in 1847 to marry, a union which inspired two sequences of narrative poems extolling married love in a Victorian upper-middle-class milieu — *The Betrothal* (1854) and *The Espousals* (1856), published together as *The Angel in the House*. Some of the main characters recur in two futher verse novels, *Faithful for Ever* (1860) and its sequel, *The Victories of Love* (1863). His wife died in 1862, after having six children, and in 1864 he married again and became a Catholic. After the death of his second wife, he married his children's governess. In *The Unknown Eros and Other Odes* (1877), a tendency towards mystical eroticism becomes religious eroticism, though there are a number of poems, notably 'Departure' and 'The Toys', in which he records without symbolism normal human reactions to domestic crises, the emotion being enhanced by the metrical form he devised for his odes, longer and very short lines being supported by an irregular rhyme scheme. Though he admired the work of *Tennyson, and *Browning and *Ruskin were close friends, his criticism and reviews, collected in *Principle in Art* (1889) and *Religio Poetae* (1893), suffer from an inability to appreciate fully anyone's work but his own. See J. C. Reid, *The Mind and Art of Coventry Patmore*, new edn 1978.

**Peacock, Thomas Love** (1785–1866), novelist and poet, was born in Weymouth, Dorset, son of a London glass merchant, who died in 1788. The boy and his mother went to live in Surrey with her father, Captain Love. He was educated privately until he was 13, after which he followed his own disposition. He had published four books of verse when in 1812 he met *Shelley and became a close friend and member of his circle, handling Shelley's affairs when he left England in 1818, and being joint-executor with *Byron on his death. 1818 was the year, too, in which *Nightmare Abbey* appeared, the third of his famous strain of satirical conversation pieces lightly veiled as novels — following *Headlong Hall* (1816, anonymously) and *Melincourt* (1817) — and he found at last a congenial job with the East India Company, in which he became an expert on steam navigation, retiring in 1856. In 1819, remembering a girl he had met on a trip to Wales in 1811 but had had no contact with since, he wrote and proposed. She accepted, and thus he was to become *Meredith's father-in-law. He wrote two further satirical novels, *Crotchet Castle* (1831) and *Gryll Grange* (1861), and two amusing historical romances. He was only a minor poet, but a fine versifier. *The Four Ages of Poetry* (1820), an ironical detraction of the Romantics, prompted Shelley's *Defence of Poetry*. *Memoirs of Percy Bysshe Shelley* (1858–62) contains a vivid recreation of the poet. See *The Complete Peacock*, ed. David Garnett, new edn with foreword by Lord Blake 1989; Carl Dawson, *His Fine Wit: a Study of T. L. Peacock*, 1970.

**Pepys, Samuel** (1633–1703), diarist, was born in the City of London, son of a tailor, and educated at St Paul's School and Magdalene College, Cambridge. He came of a modest family, but a cousin, Edward Montagu (later

Lord Sandwich), gave him a post in his household, through which, and by his own abilities, he rose to positions of great influence in the country, including Treasurer to Tangier 1665–79, Secretary to the Admiralty 1673–9, Member of Parliament for Harwich 1685–9, King's Secretary for Naval Affairs 1684–9, and President of the Royal Society 1684–6. His diary runs from 1 January 1660 (the year of the Restoration of Charles II) to 31 May 1669, when he discontinued it because of eye-strain, from which he recovered. Written largely in shorthand, it was first deciphered in 1825, but was not published in full until edited by Robert Latham and William Matthews (11 vols, 1970–83). It complements *Evelyn's diary in that it is a very personal (and frank) narrative, written up from rough notes but always within a few days of the events, and not revised. Racy and colloquial, it is the richest possible record not just of a tumultuous age, an exciting society, and the minutiae of private and public life, but of a brilliant and likable man's activities and interests and his enjoyment of them. His lively but long-suffering wife, daughter of a Huguenot refugee, whom he married in 1655 when she was 15, died in 1669. He never remarried. See Richard Ollard, *Samuel Pepys: a Biography*, 1984.

**Pinter, Harold** (*b*.1930), dramatist, poet, and screenwriter, was born in London, son of a Jewish tailor, and educated at Hackney Downs Grammar School, before becoming an actor. Of his first play, a one-acter produced at Bristol University in 1957 as *The Room*, he says: 'I went into a room one day and saw a couple of people in it.... I started off with the picture and let them carry on from there.' His first full-length play to be performed, *The Birthday Party* (1958), established his distinctive, if idiosyncratic style, whereby he develops an initial situation in a charged atmosphere through dialogue whose inconsequence and apparent illogicality are nearer to real colloquial conversation than had been usual in the modern theatre except in the plays of *Beckett and Bertolt Brecht (1898–1956). Pinter's settings, though, are realistic. *The Caretaker* (1960) is set in a broken-down flat: three shorter plays, *The Collection* (1962), *The Dwarfs* (1963), and *The Lover* (1963), all first performed on television, have multiple sets representing middle-class homes. In *The Homecoming* (1965), a bizarre household plays out its sexual and general frustrations and fantasies. *Landscape* and *Silence*, first staged as a double-bill in 1969, are more experimental still, and static. In *Old Times* (1971) and *No Man's Land* (1975), the action as well as the dialogue are discontinuous. *Mountain Language* (1989) is a 20-minute play expressing the agony of political imprisonment. See *Collected Poems and Prose*, 2nd rev. edn 1986; Ronald Hayman, *Harold Pinter*, 1980; Guido Almansi and Simon Henderson, *Harold Pinter*, 1983.

**Pope, Alexander** (1688–1744), poet, critic, and translator, was born in London, son of a linen-merchant who soon afterwards, respecting the new law forbidding Catholics to live within ten miles of London, rented a house in Hammersmith and in 1700 bought Whitehall House, Binfield, by Windsor Forest. The boy had a little schooling in London and Twyford, from which he was removed after lampooning the head, but was prevented by his faith from going to university. At 15, he went to London at his own request to learn French and Italian which, with his Latin and Greek, enabled him to read even more widely, though by this time Pott's disease had set in, permanently stunting his growth and giving him severe curvature of the spine. In his teens he frequented Will's Coffee House, haunt of the London literary set, and in 1707 Jacob Tonson (c.1656–1736) offered to publish some of his poetry — the four 'Pastorals' appeared in Tonson's *Poetical Miscellanies, Part VI* (1709). In *An Essay on Criticism* (1711) Pope put into sparkling heroic couplets the general views of the time on critical taste and methodology. *Windsor-Forest* (1713) starts out as a traditional pastoral, though made all the more effective in that Pope knew and loved the setting, but praise of the retired life is extended to incorporate a splendid vision of universal peace following the Treaty of Utrecht in 1713. In 1712 a first version had appeared of *The Rape of the Lock*, inspired by an upper-class prank in which Arabella Fermor lost one of the delectable curls at the back of her neck to an admirer. A second version was published in 1714, enlarged from two cantos to five by the addition of supernatural 'machinery', notably the guardian sylphs, one of whom gets too close at the critical moment: 'Fate urg'd the sheers, and cut the Sylph in twain / (But airy substance soon unites again)...'. This mock-heroic masterpiece also succeeded in calming tempers frayed by the original incident.

Pope now announced his plan to translate Homer's *Iliad*, for which he relied heavily on earlier translations. The first four books were published in 1715, two days before a rival version by Thomas Tickell (1686–1740), and the rest followed at intervals until 1720. *The Works of Alexander Pope* was published in 1717. For the next ten years he concentrated on Homer, with the official assistance of two friends in the translation of the *Odyssey* (1725–6), and on his edition of *Shakespeare's Works* (1725). His tedious but occasionally misplaced labour to restore the texts of the plays makes him the first genuine Shakespearean scholar, but his failings were pilloried by Lewis Theobald (1688–1744), a more serious and pedantic editor, who was preparing his own edition. Pope was now living in Twickenham with his widowed mother (she died, much to his grief, in 1733) and here his friend *Swift encouraged him to write a satirical poem which appeared anonymously as *The Dunciad* (1728), with Theobald as the chief butt. *The Dunciad Variorum* (1729) is supplied with spoof footnotes and other critical apparatus, while in the final version (1743), the Poet Laureate Colley Cibber (1671–1757) appears as 'hero'. Pope published his philosophical poem, *An Essay on Man* (1733–4), anonymously, hoping thus to avoid malicious criticism — the device succeeded and he was soon glad to acknowledge the work as his. *Imitations of Horace* appeared from 1734 to 1739, and when published together in the complete works of 1751, ed. William Warburton (1698–1779), were prefaced with *Epistle to Dr Arbuthnot* (1735), a lively apologia for the profession of satirist. By devious means, because it was not etiquette to do so, he succeeded in 1735 in publishing edited versions of some of his private correspondence, which though selective, are still revealing about his mental process.

As a man, this diminutive (4′ 6″), twisted creature was loved by some and hated and feared by many — he revenged himself on the notorious publisher Edmund Curll (1675–1747) by dosing his wine with a particularly violent emetic. He could be a bitter versifier, but he was also a very great poet, whose correctness of style was a model for succeeding generations, and of whom *Cowper could write in 1781, 'Then Pope, as harmony itself exact, / In verse well disciplin'd, complete, compact, / Gave virtue and morality a grace…' (*Table Talk*, 646–9). See Maynard Mack, *Alexander Pope: a Life*, new edn 1988; Bonamy Dobrée, *Alexander Pope*, 1951 (critical biography); Geoffrey Tillotson, *On the Poetry of Pope*, new edn 1950.

**Powell, Anthony** (*b*.1905), novelist and critic, was born in London and educated at Eton and Balliol College, Oxford. His first novel, *Afternoon Men* (1931), hovers between satire and sheer comedy, and introduces the social milieu (upper-middle- and upper-class/artistic and professional) which he dissects in his works. His fifth, *What's Become of Waring?* (1939), following a hunt for the person of a mysterious author, is the most timeless of his pre-war novels. After World War II, in which he served with distinction in the Intelligence Corps, he recharged his creative impulse with his study of the antiquary, *John Aubrey and His Friends* (1948), and then embarked consciously on a sequence of novels (at first six but then twelve) in which ideas could be connected and characters thoroughly developed. These appeared under the overall title of *The Music of Time* (the reference is to Poussin's painting, 'A Dance to the Music of Time'), beginning with *A Question of Upbringing* (1951) and ending with *Hearing Secret Harmonies* (1975), and have a chronological framework corresponding to Powell's own experiences and times. Compared with his pre-war novels, the style is more relaxed, and the dialogue, though still sharp, less elusive. The characters and the interplay between them contribute the basis of the blend of the comic and the tragic which is Powell's hallmark. He was made CBE in 1956, and CH in 1988. See *To Keep the Ball Rolling*, 1976–82 (memoirs); Robert K. Morris, *The Novels of Anthony Powell*, 1968.

**Priestley, J(ohn) B(oynton)** (1894–1984), novelist, dramatist, essayist, literary and social critic, was born in Bradford, Yorkshire, son of a schoolmaster, and educated locally, after which he worked for a wool merchant while preparing to be an author. He was blown up while serving in the trenches as a subaltern in World War I, after which he went to Trinity Hall, Cambridge, before settling in London with wife and child, and £50 capital. After several books of essays and literary criticism, he published in 1927 two apprentice novels, *Adam in Moonshine* and *Benighted*. *The Good Companions* (1929), the adventures of a touring theatre company, established his reputation as a novelist, which was confirmed with *Angel Pavement* (1930), a saga of lower life in London. Later novels have settings as varied, and include *Festival at Farbridge* (1951) and *The Image Men* (1968). His equally long career as a successful dramatist began with *Dangerous Corner* (1932) — also in *Three Time Plays* (1947) — and included *An Inspector Calls* (1947) and *The Linden Tree* (1948), an understanding assessment of post-war moods of young and old. *Literature and Western Man* (1960) is less a historical survey than a critique of the current situation. Of many collections of essays, *Thoughts in the Wilderness* (1957) has proved most influential. His Sunday broadcasts after the nine o'clock news during World War II were enlightening and moving — those made during the worst times were published as *Postscripts* (1940). He was awarded the OM in 1977. See *Margin Released*, 1962 (literary reminiscences); Vincent Brome, *J. B. Priestley*, 1988 (biography); David Hughes, *J. B. Priestley: an Informal Study*, 1958.

**Pritchett,** (Sir) **V(ictor) S(awdon)** (*b.*1900), short story writer, novelist, travel writer, and critic, was born in Ipswich, Suffolk, and educated at Alleyn's School, Dulwich, which he was forced to leave at 16 to work in the leather trade. After four years, he went to Paris, where he became a photographer's assistant. He was correspondent of the *Christian Science Monitor* in Ireland and Spain from 1923 to 1926, when he became a freelance reviewer in London, especially for the *New Statesman*, of which he was appointed a director in 1946. His first book, *Marching Spain* (1928), records his travels in that country, which has remained a chief interest. The best of his five novels is held to be *Mr Beluncle* (1951), a comedy of characterisation in which a man's compulsive fantasy takes over his life. His finest work is in his short stories, the first collection of which was *The Spanish Virgin and Other Stories* (1930). In an interview in 1988, Pritchett described himself as a craftsman, not an aesthete, preferring 'the plotless story where there's plenty of action, plenty of drama, but much of it internal'. His critical works include *The Living Novel* (1946) and *George Meredith and English Comedy* (1970), the subject of his Clark Lectures at Cambridge the previous year, and he has written biographies of Balzac (1973), Turgenev (1977), and Chekhov (1988). He was knighted in 1975. See *Collected Stories*, new edn 1984; *A Cab at the Door: Childhood and Youth 1900–1920*, 1968, and *Midnight Oil*, 1971 (autobiography, published together 1986).

**Radcliffe, Ann** (1764–1823), née Ward, novelist and poet, was born in London, daughter of a tradesman who through his and his wife's family had connections in artistic and court circles. When she was 23 she married William Radcliffe, who later became editor of the *English Chronicle*. After a short novel, *The Castles of Athlin and Dunbayne* (1789), she published *A Sicilian Romance* (1790), which *Scott regarded as the first English poetical novel, followed by *The Romance of the Forest* (1791), which quickly went through several editions, was dramatised by John Boaden (*d*.1839), and translated into French and Italian. Her reputation in modern times rests on *The Mysteries of Udolpho, a Romance Interspersed with Some Pieces of Poetry* (1794), for which her publisher paid the then unprecedented sum of £500 for the first edition. The 'poetry' is puerile, but the novel itself is one of the most famous examples of the Gothic genre, and all the more impressive in that even the most bizarre manifestations have rational explanations. Such was its success that she received £800 for *The Italian, or the Confessional of the Black Penitents* (1797), a romance of the Inquisition, after which she wrote a travel book about her carriage trip through Holland and Germany, and then retired from the literary scene so successfully that in 1816 an anonymous compiler, thinking she was dead, published a book of her verses, with the addition of some of his own. See Aline Grant, *Ann Radcliffe*, 1951.

**Ralegh, (Sir) Walter** (1554–1618), poet, prose writer, man of war, and adventurer, was born in Hayes Barton, Devonshire, a younger son of a country gentleman, and spent a year or so at Oriel College, Oxford, before fighting in Europe and Ireland as a volunteer to the Protestant cause. By 1580 he had become a favourite of Queen Elizabeth, in whose honour he composed several poems (addressed to 'Cynthia'), and on whose behalf he harried the Spaniards and discovered and colonised Virginia. He was knighted on his return. His plain, racy account of the naval action in which the *Revenge* went down, and on which *Tennyson based his ballad 'The Revenge', was published anonymously in 1591. The next year he fell out of favour because of his affair with a maid-of-honour, whom he later married, but his status revived with his exploration of Guiana, of which he published in 1596 a basically accurate description. Accused in 1603 of conspiracy against James I (VI of Scotland), he was sentenced to death but was instead imprisoned for life in the Tower of London, where he wrote *The History of the World* (1614), a well-written and well-arranged account, broken off in the third century AD. He was released in 1616 to find a gold-mine in Guiana. The expedition was a disaster, and on his return the original sentence of beheading was carried out, which he awaited calmly, writing verses. There was no authenticated edition of his poetry until that edited by John Hannah in 1845. See *Poems*, ed. Agnes M. C. Latham, rev. edn 1951; Philip Edwards, *Sir Walter Ralegh*, 1953; Walter Oakeshott, *The Queen and the Poet*, 1960.

**Ramsay, Allan** (1684–1758), Scottish poet, dramatist, and anthologist, was born in Leadhills, Lanarkshire, son of a factor who died shortly afterwards. His mother married a local farmer, who educated him at the parish school and in 1700 apprenticed him to an Edinburgh wig-maker. He became a master wig-maker and was elected a city burgess in 1710. In 1724 he finally abandoned the wig trade for the book trade and in 1725 founded the first circulating library in Britain. In *Poems* (1721) he had brought together a variety of verse forms, including the epistle and what he termed the 'standard habbie' (a six-line rhyming stanza ending with a short punch line), using both English and Scots, which had ceased to be a poetic medium since James VI's court moved to London in 1603. He further revived interest in Scottish literature with *The Ever Green* (1724), an anthology of early poetry, and several collections of ballads and songs, *The Tea-Table Miscellany* (1724–37). His verse play *The Gentle Shepherd* (1725), which has good songs and excellent characterisation, was the first notable Scottish drama for almost two hundred years. In 1736 he established the first regular theatre in Edinburgh, which the Licensing Act (1737) soon forced him to close. A genuine pastoral and satirical poet, he created an atmosphere in which Robert Fergusson (1750–74) could write in Scots and from which *Burns took his inspiration. See *Selected Poems*, ed. H. Harvey Wood, 1946; Burns Martin, *Allan Ramsay: a Study of His Life and Works*, new edn 1973.

**Reade, Charles** (1814–84), novelist and dramatist, was born at Ipsden House, Oxfordshire, youngest of eleven children of a country gentleman, and educated privately and at Magdalen College, Oxford, where in spite of only a third class degree in Greats, he was elected to a fellowship and subsequently became Vice-President. He was called to the Bar in 1843, but instead chose to write. The Theatres Act (1843) paved the way for the opening of many new theatres (subject only to their obtaining a licence) and for the staging of original plays, as a result of which the melodrama could now take on a more literary aspect. Reade's most successful play was the comedy *Masks and Faces* (1852), written with Tom Taylor (1817–80), which he then turned into the novel *Peg Woffington* (1853). Some of the research he had put into *Gold* (1853) was utilised in the novel *It is Never Too Late to Mend* (1856), exposing prison conditions and the treatment of criminals, which he turned into another play in 1865. Further crusading novels were *Hard Cash* (1863), revealing the iniquities of private lunatic asylums, and *Put Yourself in His Place* (1870), on dubious trades-union practices. His passion for research led, too, to the novel for which he is universally remembered, *The Cloister and the Hearth* (1861), an extraordinary panorama of medieval European life and customs, based on a study by Erasmus and expanded from a short story, 'A Good Fight', which appeared in the journal *Once a Week* in 1859. See Malcolm Elwin, *Charles Reade: a Biography*, 1931.

**Richardson, Samuel** (1689–1761), novelist and printer, was born in Derbyshire, one of nine children of a craftsman carpenter. Though intended for university and the Church, he does not appear to have had a particularly good education (his understanding of Latin and Greek was poor), though he was early on commissioned independently by three young ladies to write love letters for them. When family financial difficulties threatened, he was apprenticed at 17 to a London printer, and in 1719 opened his own business, first in Fleet Street and then in Salisbury Court, where he became the official printer of the *Journals* of the House of Commons. In 1739 two booksellers invited him to write a handbook of model letters covering various situations to help 'country readers' compose their own. *Letters Written to and for Particular Friends on the Most Important Occasions* duly appeared in 1741, but in the meantime the initial idea had further blossomed into a full-blown novel, *Pamela: or Virtue Rewarded* (1740), which he wrote largely at his country house, North End in Hammersmith, in the three months November 1739 to January 1740. It was significant in that its 15-year-old heroine, who successfully defends her virginity throughout, is a serving-girl; and the device of letters written shortly after the events they describe gives an immediacy to each episode and heightens the tension, as does the enormous detail with which the situations are embellished. The book's success, which coincided with the beginnings of the circulating libraries, can be judged from the fact that someone immediately brought out a spurious *Pamela in High Life*, which induced Richardson to add a less impressive continuation, incorporated in the second edition of 1741. It also inspired *Fielding to enter the field of comic fiction. *Clarissa* (1748) has a similar theme but a tragic end, and is more successful as a novel in that there are four correspondents, supplementing each other's accounts and extending the book's range. *The History of Sir Charles Grandison* (1754) has a more complex but equally sensational love interest with, on this occasion, a hero who vacillates most honourably between the attractive Harriet Byron and an Italian inamorata of his past. Jane *Austen was so impressed by it that she dramatised episodes for family performance.

Richardson was a moralist who specialised in divided minds and in females in psychological as well as sometimes physical distress. In 1755 he published *A Collection of the Moral and the Instructive Sentiments... Contained in the Histories of Pamela, Clarissa, and Sir Charles Grandison*. He was a considerable artist in both his crafts. In 1754 he was elected Master of the Stationers' Company, and in 1760 he bought a half-share in the business of law printer to the King. He died of apoplexy. He was married twice, each wife bearing him six children, of whom only four daughters survived him. See T. C. Duncan Eaves and Ben D. Kimpel, *Samuel Richardson: a Biography*, 1971; Mark Kinkead-Weekes, *Samuel Richardson: Dramatic Novelist*, 1973; Jocelyn Harris, *Samuel Richardson*, 1987 (critical study).

**Rochester, (John Wilmot), 2nd Earl of** (1647–80), poet, was born in Ditchley, Oxfordshire, son of a Cavalier general, to whose title he succeeded in 1658. He was educated at Burford Grammar School and Wadham College, Oxford, after which he travelled in Europe. In 1664 he appeared at the court of Charles II, where his wit, looks, and dissipation earned him a reputation, and his outspokenness several periods of exclusion from the royal presence. He was converted on his death-bed by Gilbert Burnet (1643–1715), who wrote *Some Passages of the Life and Death of the Right Honourable Earl of Rochester* (1680). As it was to be with *Burns, Rochester's early death, his amorous exploits (in 1665 he abducted the heiress Elizabeth Mallet, for which he was sent to the Tower of London for three weeks — he married her in 1667 and had four children by her and one by the actress Mrs Barry), and the obscenity of some of his verse, overshadowed his gift for lyrical and satirical poetry. His work has the ring of truth, as in the song 'My Dear Mistress Has a Heart...', at times a tenderness ('A Song of a Young Lady to Her Ancient Lover') or a philosophical tone ('Upon Nothing', 'Plain Dealing's Downfall'), which recurs throughout *A Satyr against Mankind Written by a Person of Honour* (1679), a study of the human condition as well as of contemporary society. See *The Complete Poems*, ed. David M. Vieth, new edn 1975; Vivian de Sola Pinto, *Enthusiast in Wit: a Portrait of John Wilmot Earl of Rochester*, rev. edn 1962 of *Rochester*, 1935.

**Rossetti, Christina** (1830–94), poet, sister of D. G. *Rossetti, was born in London, youngest of four children of an immigrant Italian academic, and educated at home by her mother, her strict religious upbringing being in line with the Anglicanism of the Oxford Movement. She was ill for most of her teens, and remained at the various family homes, caring for her father until his death in 1854, her mother until she died in 1886, and then two aunts. She never married, though on religious grounds she broke off one engagement and rejected a proposal from a man with whom she was in love. She contributed seven poems to the Pre-Raphaelite journal, *The Germ*, in 1850. Helped by her brother, she published *Goblin Market and Other Poems* (1862), whose narrative title poem is a parable of love and death in the Pre-Raphaelite ethos. With *The Prince's Progress and Other Poems* (1866), it gained her a reputation among the literary élite, which her shyness made it difficult for her to enjoy. Through a prolonged period of family sorrows she continued to write, both poetry — including *Sing Song: a Nursery Rhyme Book* (1872) and *A Pageant and Other Poems* (1881) — and devotional prose. The conflict between her intellectual background and religious inclination, the depths of feeling she experienced in her personal life, and her technical brilliance in conventional verse forms, notably the sonnet, rondeau, and ballad, give her a distinctive, and sensuous, poetic voice. See Georgina Battiscombe, *Christina Rossetti*, 1981.

**Rossetti, Dante Gabriel** (1828–82), poet and painter, was born in London and educated at King's College School and the Royal Academy. With several other artists he founded the Pre-Raphaelite Brotherhood, which aimed to recapture the essence, colour, and detail of pre-Renaissance art. Their journal, *The Germ*, in which some of his poems appeared, lasted four issues. A passionate friendship with his model Elizabeth Siddal was finally consummated when she married him in 1860, but she died of a drug overdose two years later — in 1870 he retrieved from her coffin the poems he had buried with her. His other great love was Jane, wife of *Morris, who appeared unperturbed by the relationship. (Warmth and sex were for many years provided by Fanny Cornforth.) Rossetti never recovered from a breakdown in 1872, becoming a virtual recluse in his house in Cheyne Walk, Chelsea. The reception in some circles of his verse translations, *The Early Italian Poets 1100–1300* (1861), reissued as *Dante and His Circle* (1874), led him to publish *Poems* (1870). It included the 50 'House of Life' sonnets which (with the exception of 'Nuptial Sleep', criticised for over-sensuousness) were repeated in sequence in *Ballads and Sonnets* (1881), 'The Blessed Damozel', which particularly symbolises the Pre-Raphaelite mood, the contemporary but romanticised 'Jenny', and the ballad-like 'Troy Town' and 'Sister Helen'. His poetry tries partly to reflect his artistic aims in a literary form, and partly to reconcile the body, the spirit, and love. See Oswald Doughty, *A Victorian Romantic: Dante Gabriel Rossetti*, new edn 1960; Joan Rees, *Modes of Self-Expression: the Poetry of Dante Gabriel Rossetti*, 1981.

**Ruskin, John** (1819–1900), prose writer, art critic, and social philosopher, was born in London, only child of a wealthy wine merchant, and educated by his mother and by tutors until he went to Christ Church, Oxford, where at the third attempt he won the Newdigate Prize for poetry. *Modern Painters* (1843–60) began as a vindication of J. M. W. Turner (1775–1851) and became an artistic and spiritual guide to the history of Europe, which he knew from frequent tours with his parents. *The Seven Lamps of Architecture* (1849) offended architects but brought reason and eloquence to bear on the relationship between virtue and art, which he elaborated in *The Stones of Venice* (1851–3). He was one of the founders of the Working Men's College in 1854. This was the start of a phase of social and political awareness, exemplified by *Unto This Last: Four Essays on the First Principles of Political Economy* (1862 — the essays were originally published in *Cornhill Magazine* in 1860), which was regarded as absurd in its time, and *Sesame and Lilies* (1865), on the position of women in society. In 1870 he became the first Slade Professor of Fine Art at Oxford. His classic and urbane fairy tale, *The King of the Golden River* (1851), was written in 1841 for the little girl who was his unfortunate partner from 1848 to 1854 in an unconsummated marriage — she later married the painter, John Everett Millais (1829–96). Latterly the mental instability which had affected Ruskin's life became periodic insanity. See *Praeterita*, new edn 1978 (autobiography); Peter Quennell, *John Ruskin, the Portrait of a Prophet*, 1949; George Landow, *Ruskin*, 1985 (introduction to his theories).

**Russell, George William** (1867–1935), Irish poet, painter, editor, economist, and journalist, who wrote under the pseudonym of Æ (a contraction of æon), was born in Lurgan, Co. Armagh, and educated at Rathmines School, Dublin, and the Metropolitan School of Art, where he met *Yeats, who especially awakened in him a sense of mystic communication with an idealistic Celtic past. *Homeward: Songs by the Way* (1894) promised more by way of poetic vision than he later achieved, but in addition to painting he had other means of expressing his interest in the development of modern Irish literature and his concern for the Irish political scene. In 1897 he gave up his job as a draper's clerk to work for the Irish Agricultural Organisation Society, whose journal, the *Irish Homestead,* he edited from 1906 to 1923, when it amalgamated with the *Irish Statesman,* of which he was editor until 1930. His play *Deirdre* was performed in 1902, and he was associated with the Irish National Theatre Society and the United Arts Club, while his support of the Irish Literary Society led to his compiling *New Songs* (1904), which included the work of some of the younger writers whose talents he had spotted. His political writing is best seen in *The National Being* (1916), and his imaginative prose in *The Interpreters* (1922). See *Collected Works*, ed. Henry Summerfield, 3 vols 1978–84; Henry Summerfield, *That Myriad-Minded Man: a Biography of G. W. Russell — 'Æ'*, 1975.

**Sassoon, Siegfried** (1886–1967), poet and prose writer, was born in Weirleigh, Kent, of Jewish origin. His father left home when the boy was seven and died in 1895. He was educated at Marlborough College and Clare College, Cambridge, which he left without a degree to indulge his passions for cricket, hunting, and verse. In 1915 he was commissioned in the Royal Welch Fusiliers and served in France, where he won the MC, was recommended for a VC, and was severely wounded in 1917. While convalescing in England he wrote and made public a searing attack on the conduct of the war, was pronounced to be suffering from shell-shock, and was returned to the front in 1918, where he was wounded in the head. In the meantime his graphic, brutal, but compassionate war poems, published in *The Old Huntsman* (1917) and *Counter-Attack* (1918), had established him as a considerable war poet, an identity which belied his subsequent development as a writer of satirical, reflective, and spiritual poetry and of evocative prose. *Memoirs of a Fox-Hunting Man* (1928) perfectly epitomises a whole social ethos and was the first of three volumes of fictionalised experience which were published together as *The Complete Memoirs of George Sherston* (1937), whose steps he retraced in his autobiographies, *The Old Century and Seven More Years* (1938), *The Weald of Youth* (1942), and *Siegfried's Journey* (1945). He was made CBE in 1951. See *Collected Poems 1908–56*, new edn 1984; Michael Thorpe, *Siegfried Sassoon: a Critical Study*, 1966.

**Scott,** (Sir) **Walter** (1771–1832), Scottish novelist, short story writer, poet, historian, folklorist, dramatist, editor, and critic, was born in Edinburgh's insanitary Old Town, ninth child of a solicitor. He was permanently lame from infantile paralysis contracted as a baby. After some years recuperating in the Borders and in Bath, he rejoined his family, now in the New Town, and between bouts of further illness went to the High School of Edinburgh and Edinburgh University, becoming apprentice in his father's firm in 1786, and being called to the Scottish Bar in 1792. He married a girl of French birth in 1797, and was in 1799 appointed Sheriff-Depute of Selkirkshire, where he completed his collection of oral ballads, published as *Minstrelsy of the Scottish Border* (1802–3). He now turned to composing his own historical ballad-epics, *The Lay of the Last Minstrel* (1805), *Marmion: a Tale of Flodden Field* (1808), and *The Lady of the Lake* (1810). From 1806 to 1812 he was a clerk of the Court of Session, while at the same time involving himself financially with the Edinburgh publishing and printing company of Ballantyne. He had a town house in North Castle Street and a country seat at Abbotsford, Melrose, which over the years he extended into the Gothic mansion which can be visited today. In 1813, while searching there in an old desk for some fishing-tackle, he found part of a novel which he had abandoned in 1805. When he had finished it, *Waverley: or 'Tis Sixty Years Since* (1814) became the first of a long line of enormously popular historical novels which included *Guy Mannering* (1815), *Rob Roy* (1817), *The Heart of Midlothian* (1818), and *Redgauntlet* (1824), known collectively as the 'Waverley Novels'. They were all published anonymously, possibly because he felt them beneath him as an official of the law, but probably because he did not want to seem to be leading so many lives. The secret was publicly revealed at a dinner in 1827, by which time he had much enjoyed being the cause of what was a mystery to all except close friends and perceptive critics.

He was largely responsible for the rediscovery in Edinburgh Castle in 1818 of the Scottish crown jewels, lost for 111 years, and in 1819 he received a baronetcy from the hand of George IV, whose visit to Edinburgh in 1822 the now 'Sir' Walter Scott brilliantly stage-managed. His business affairs had been in trouble as far back as 1813, and when in 1826 the general economic depression caused the collapse of his partners, he was declared bankrupt. Though already suffering from recurring illness, he refused his friends' help in settling with his creditors, declaring proudly — according to Lord Cockburn's reminiscences, *Memorials of His Time* (1856) — "'No! this right hand shall work it all off!'" The events of that year, including the death of his wife four months later, and of the rest of his life, during which he drove himself to write wide-ranging works, including *The Fair Maid of Perth* (1828), three series of *Tales of a Grandfather* (1828–30), and *Letters on Demonology and Witchcraft* (1831), are recorded in *The Journal of Sir Walter Scott 1825–32* (1890). In 1830 he had the first of a series of cerebral haemorrhages. The Government put a frigate at his disposal for the winter of 1831–2, but he had to be rushed back from Naples to Abbotsford, where he died. His trustees had then paid off eleven shillings in the pound of his original debts of over £100,000.

As a very successful Romantic poet who wrote in English on Scottish themes, Scott spread Scottish culture far and wide. He was a worthy founder of the historical novel in that he was fair to both sides in a conflict, and he represented historical characters and events with intelligence and insight, while having an eye for comedy and the effective representation of Scottish speech. He was also an originator of the genre of the short story, of which he wrote several particularly powerful tragic and supernatural examples — see *The Two Drovers and Other Stories*, ed. Graham Tulloch, 1987. In all this he was instrumental in propagating, for better or for worse, the romantic view of Highland history which still popularly pertains today. He edited the works of *Dryden (1808) and *Swift (1814). His daughter Sophia married John Gibson Lockhart (1794–1854), whose admirable biography of Scott was published in 1837–8. See Edgar Johnson, *Sir Walter Scott: the Great Unknown*, 1970 (biography); Robin Mayhead, *Walter Scott*, 1973 (critical study); David Brown, *Sir Walter Scott and the Historical Imagination*, 1979.

**Shakespeare, William** (1564–1616), dramatist and poet, elder son of a glover, was baptised in Stratford-upon-Avon Parish Church on 26 April 1564. A bond was issued on 28 November 1582 for his marriage to Anne Hathaway, eight years his senior. Their daughter Susanna was baptised on 26 May 1583, and twins on 2 February 1585. That is virtually all that is known about his early life, though almost certainly he attended the local grammar school. In 1592 he is spitefully alluded to in a pamphlet by Robert Greene (1558–92), *A Groats-worth of Wit Bought with a Million of Repentance*, as 'an upstart crow beautified with our feathers'. After the plague of 1592–4 had disrupted the London theatrical scene, he surfaces as a member of the Lord Chamberlain's Men, becoming a partner in the establishment of the new Globe Theatre in 1599. The company became the King's Men in 1603, and in 1610 he retired to his Stratford house of New Place, a considerable property which he had bought in 1597.

During the plague epidemic he had written, and published, his two narrative poems, *Venus and Adonis* (1593) and *Lucrece* (1594), both dedicated to the young Earl of Southampton (1573–1624). Francis Meres (1565–1647) refers to both poems in *Palladis Tamia* (1598), and also to the circulation by Shakespeare of 'his sugred Sonnets among his private friends'. These were published, mysteriously dedicated to a 'Mr W. H.', by an adventurous bookseller in 1609, without their author's permission. There are 153 sonnets, No 126 being merely twelve lines of rhymed verse. They appear to be addressed to an unknown young man who is the poet's favoured friend and is being urged to marry, to a rival poet who has ingratiated himself with the young man, and to the poet's mistress (the famous Dark Lady), who between times has been having an affair with the poet's friend. Their quality varies, but Nos 18, 87, 89, 97, 98, 116, 130, 144, and 146 in particular are among the finest of their kind. The intensity which burns through the sequence suggests firmly that it is autobiographical, which would seem to be confirmed by the fact that it was never reissued in the poet's lifetime.

Shakespeare cared little about the publication of his plays. What are known, from their format, as the Quartos are largely pirated editions written down during a performance — the first recorded one is of *Titus Andronicus* (1594). The First Folio edition, ed. John Heminge and Henry Condell, was published in 1623. Internal and external evidence, including the dates of quartos, suggests that among his earlier plays, written between about 1587 and 1592, are *The Comedy of Errors* and *Richard III*. At about the same time as *Venus and Adonis* and *Lucrece*, he produced the lyrical comedy *A Midsummer Night's Dream*, the tragedy *Romeo and Juliet*, and the play which hovers in between, *The Merchant of Venice*. From 1596 to 1599 was his age of history, with *Richard II*, the two parts of *Henry IV*, and *Henry V*, followed by the high fantasies, *Much Ado About Nothing, As You Like It*, and *Twelfth Night or What You Will*. The effect on the progression of Shakespeare's dramatic art of the committal to the Tower of his erstwhile patron Southampton, after Essex's rebellion in 1601, was probably greater than that of the accession of James I two years later, and it is to this period that the 'dark comedies' or 'bitter comedies' belong, *All's Well That Ends Well, Troilus and Cressida*, and *Measure for Measure*. His even darker phase, of the great tragedies, had already begun in 1599 with *Julius Caesar*, in which the character of Brutus presages that of Hamlet. The source of the play of *Hamlet*, which dates from about 1601, is a tale of revenge from Norse folklore, but in Shakespeare's hands it becomes a penetrating study of man's attitude to and ambiguous relationship with life and death. In *Othello, Macbeth, King Lear, Timon of Athens, Coriolanus,* and *Antony and Cleopatra*, he poured out his messages of poetic pessimism, depicting in turn each of the major vices — jealousy, lust for power, vanity, ingratitude (also cruelty), pride, and sexuality. To his final period belong the fairy-tales (and some of his sweetest poetry) of *The Winter's Tale* and *The Tempest*, both performed in 1611. Probably the last play in which he had a hand (\*Fletcher is the most likely collaborator) literally brought the house down, as an errant cannon in *Henry VIII* demolished the Globe in 1613 on the play's third or fourth performance. See *The Complete Works: Anno-tated Edition*, ed. Samuel Schoenbaum and Stanley Wells, 1988; Samuel Schoenbaum, *William Shakespeare: a Compact Documentary Life*, 2nd edn 1987; C. T. Onions, *A Shakespeare Glossary*, 3rd edn 1986; and critical studies by Harley Granville-Barker, G. B. Harrison, John Dover Wilson, F. E. Halliday, E. M. W. Tillyard, and G. Wilson Knight in particular.

**Shaw, George Bernard** (1856–1950), Irish dramatist, novelist, essayist, and critic, was born in Dublin of Protestant parents. His father's drinking habits barred the family from genteel society, and when Shaw was 16 his headstrong but musical mother left for London, taking his two sisters with her. After four years at Wesley School, he became a clerk in a firm of land agents in 1871, being quickly promoted to cashier when the incumbent of that post decamped with some rents. He appeared in print in 1875 in *Public Opinion,* with a letter acutely analysing the effect of the American evangelists, Dwight Moody and Ira Sankey. In 1876 he threw up his job and moved to London, where he lived with his mother, and wrote five novels, of which the last, *An Unsocial Socialist,* was the first to be published (1884 as a serial, 1887 as a book), and the first, *Immaturity,* was not published until 1930. After reading Karl Marx (1818–83) in French, he became an active socialist, forced himself to be an accomplished public speaker, and became an executive council member of the Fabian Society, for whom he edited *Fabian Essays in Socialism* (1889). He was a book reviewer for the *Pall Mall Gazette* 1885–8, music critic for the *Star* (as 'Corno di Bassetto') 1888–90 and for the *World* 1890–4. From this experience derived two admirable critical works, *The Quintessence of Ibsenism* (1891) and *The Perfect Wagnerite* (1898).

In response to the challenge to the modern theatre offered by Henrik Ibsen (1828–1906), he resuscitated and rewrote a play he had begun in 1885 with William Archer (1856–1924). *Widowers' Houses* (performed 1892) was a new kind of play in that different sides of a social problem are presented and argued out upon the stage. *Mrs Warren's Profession* (written in 1893 but banned from public performance until 1926) has a similar intention. At the start, Shaw's future as a dramatist seemed no more profitable than it had been as a novelist, though *The Devil's Disciple,* an historical drama based on the exploits of General Burgoyne (1723–92), was financially successful when it was staged in New York in 1897. His prestige was enhanced, however, by his work as dramatic critic of the *Saturday Review* 1895–8, as was his political and economic experience by service as a local government councillor for Saint Pancras 1897–1903. In 1898 he broke new ground when he published *Plays Pleasant and Unpleasant,* including *Mrs Warren's Profession, Arms and the Man,* and *Candida* (first of a line of plays with remarkable heroines). He was convinced that plays should be read in the same way as novels, and he provided explicit and graphic stage directions and also prefaces, which are rather postscripts, or treatises on the play's theme. *Three Plays for Puritans* (1901) includes *Caesar and Cleopatra,* an enjoyable if imaginary representation of the famous historical romance. From now on his plays were regularly produced as well as read, and he particularly demonstrated the breadth of his social awareness and the control of his medium and of dialectics, as well as his sense of comedy, in *Man and Superman* (published 1903), *Major Barbara* (1907), *The Doctor's Dilemma* (1911), *Androcles and the Lion* (1916), *Pygmalion* (1916), and *Saint Joan* (1924). *Back to Methuselah* (1921), his 'metabiological pentateuch', is in effect five plays spanning a philosophical existence from the Garden of Eden to 'as far as thought can reach'. His most notable prose works of the inter-war period are *The Intelligent Woman's Guide to Socialism and Capitalism* (1928) and *The Adventures of a Black Girl in Her Search for God* (1932).

In 1898 overwork had caused him to collapse. An acquaintance, the Irish-born heiress Charlotte Payne-Townshend, went to his mother's house to nurse him and was so horrified by his living conditions that she insisted on removing him to the country. To avoid scandal, he proposed marriage, and was accepted. After her death in 1943, he lived on at the house in Ayot St Lawrence, Hertfordshire, which he had bought in 1906. He was a prolific letter-writer, whose correspondence with Ellen Terry was published in 1931, with Mrs Patrick Campbell in 1952, and with Harley Granville-Barker in 1956. He was awarded the Nobel Prize for Literature in 1925. See *The Bodley Head Collected Plays with Their Prefaces,* 7 vols 1970–5; St John Ervine, *Shaw: His Life, Works and Friends,* 1956; Michael Holroyd, *Bernard Shaw: the Search for Love 1856–1898,* 1988, and *Bernard Shaw: the Pursuit of Power 1898–1918,* 1989; Desmond MacCarthy, *Shaw: the Plays,* new edn 1973: R. J. Kaufmann (ed.), *G. B. Shaw: a Collection of Critical Essays,* 1965.

**Shelley, Percy Bysshe** (1792–1822), poet and essayist, was born at Field Place, Horsham, Sussex, eldest son of a Member of Parliament who succeeded to his father's baronetcy in 1815. He was educated at Sion House Academy, Isleworth, and Eton. By the time he left school he had published *Zastrozzi: a Romance* (1810), and was making arrangements for a second, and had written with his sister Elizabeth *Original Poetry by Victor and Cazire* (1810). In 1810 he went up to University College, Oxford, where he became a close friend of Thomas Jefferson Hogg (1792–1862), his future biographer. Between them they concocted and in February 1811 distributed an anonymous pamphlet, *The Necessity of Atheism*. Shelley made no attempt to conceal his authorship, and the pair were expelled for refusing to answer questions. That summer Shelley rescued Harriet Westbrook, a pretty 16-year-old school friend of his sisters, from what he saw as the tyranny of her family by eloping with her to Edinburgh, where they went through a form of marriage. The union was not a success, but while they were living together he wrote *Queen Mab: a Philosophical Poem with Notes*, which was published privately in 1813, and in subsequent unauthorised editions became a Chartist handbook. In 1814 he fell for Mary, 16-year-old daughter of the Radical thinker William Godwin (1756–1836) and Mary Wollstonecraft (1759–1797), and went off with her to Switzerland, accompanied by her even younger sister, Jane (or Claire) Clairmont. The title poem of *Alastor: or the Spirit of Solitude, and Other Poems* (1816) was written when he was back in England and reflects his depression at being hounded by creditors and by the unfortunate Harriet, by whom he now had two children, and being cast out even by the apostle of free love, Godwin, who still expected Shelley's financial support, especially after the death of the poet's grandfather in 1815 gave him a regular income. In 1816 the trio returned to Lake Geneva, where *Byron joined them, and Mary began to write *Frankenstein* (1818). A pregnant Harriet was found drowned in October, whereupon Shelley and Mary married. He now wrote a romantic epic in Spenserian metre in support of revolution, *Laon and Cythna* (1817), which was suppressed and reissued in a bowdlerised form in 1818 as *The Revolt of Islam*.

In 1818 the Shelleys took their two children to Italy, where the death of the daughter inspired the beautiful 'Lines Written Among the Euganean Hills', whose assurance is a measure of the artistic confidence which enabled him to complete *Prometheus Unbound* (1820), an idealistic, allegorical drama with much soaring poetry. *The Cenci* (1819), a melodramatic verse play composed for the theatre but regarded at the time as too strong to be staged, was written after the death of their son — later that year Mary had a further boy, who survived. The incomparable 'Ode to the West Wind' belongs to this period too. They moved permanently to the region of Pisa in 1820, where they were joined by several devotees. The discovery of a gorgeous Italian girl, Emilia Viviani, holed up in a nearby convent while her mother had an affair, rekindled Shelley's knight-errant aspirations, which he embodied in *Epipsychidion* (1821). Less Platonic was his admiration for Jane, common-law wife of Edward Williams (she had been abandoned by her army officer husband), to whom he wrote several lyrics in 1822. Early in July, he and Williams sailed his new boat to Leghorn to meet *Hunt. On the return journey the boat capsized in a squall, and they were both drowned. The bodies were later washed ashore, where in deference to the quarantine laws they were burned, in the presence of Byron and Edward Trelawny (1792–1881), who described the scene in *Records of Shelley, Byron and the Author* (1878). Mary died in 1851, having in the meantime edited Shelley's *Poetical Works* (1839).

In the light of the charisma attached to Shelley's rebellious nature, moral nonconformity, continuous questing after a personal religion,

Neo-Platonism of language and thought, and his youth (he was not yet 30 when he died), some critical hostility is perhaps inevitable. He had an extraordinary command of form and metre, and an intellectual capacity which belied his unfinished education. He produced many political pamphlets and essays, of which 'A Philosophical View of Reform' (1820) and 'A Defence of Poetry' (1821) are particularly notable. See *The Complete Poetical Works*, ed. Thomas Hutchinson, new edn 1971; Richard Holmes, *Shelley: the Pursuit*, new edn 1987 (biography); Donald H. Reiman, *Percy Bysshe Shelley*, 1969 (critical study); Earl R. Wasserman, *Shelley: a Critical Reading*, 1971.

**Sheridan, Richard Brinsley** (1751–1816), Irish dramatist and English politician, was born in Dublin, second son of Thomas Sheridan, actor-manager of the Theatre Royal, and Frances Chamberlaine. A theatre riot in 1754 caused the parents to leave Ireland, the boy joining them in England in 1759. In spite of Thomas's success as an elocutionist and Frances's with her novel, *The Memoirs of Miss Sidney Bidulph* (1761), and a comedy, *The Discovery* (1763), the couple had to take refuge from creditors in France in 1764, leaving Sheridan as a boarder at Harrow. Frances died in 1766, and in 1770 Thomas, back in England and in funds, took his son to Bath, where Sheridan was so struck by a young singer, Elizabeth Linley, that he accompanied her, and a chaperon, to France to get her away from sexual harassment by an importunate suitor. On their return, having gone through an invalid form of marriage, they were separated, though he had to fight two duels with one of her suitors. They were properly married in 1773, and Sheridan, having given up his law studies, wrote a play to earn some money at the suggestion of the manager of Covent Garden Theatre. *The Rivals,* which drew on his personal life, was withdrawn in January 1775 after two disastrous performances, but was put on again ten days later in a cleaned-up and tightened form, and was a hit, the characters of Sir Anthony Absolute and Mrs Malaprop passing into English dramatic heritage. A short farce, *St Patrick's Day,* was followed by a comic opera, *The Duenna* (1775), which with *The Rivals* moved *Johnson to observe that Sheridan 'has written the two best comedies of his age'. In 1776 he borrowed heavily to become principal manager of Drury Lane Theatre, for which he wrote an adaptation of *Vanbrugh's *The Relapse, A Trip to Scarborough* (1777); his masterpiece of anti-sentiment, *The School for Scandal* (1777); and *The Critic* (1779).

In 1780 he was elected to Parliament, representing Stafford, Westminster, and Ilchester between then and 1812, for most of the time a prominent and eloquent member of the opposition, though he served in office three times, as Treasurer of the Navy and Privy Councillor 1806–7, and as an adviser to and spokesman for the Prince of Wales. Apart from *Pizarro* (1799), a hastily composed adaptation of a German drama which contradicted his own tenet not to mix politics and the theatre, he wrote no more for the stage, but he maintained his association with Drury Lane until 1809, when he watched with equanimity its destruction by fire, replying to a friend who remarked on this, 'A man may surely be allowed to take a glass of wine by his own fire-side'. He was a chronic alcoholic, whose policy of 'borrow and fear not' contributed to his ending his life in the most wretched circumstances. *The School for Scandal,* written when he was 25, is the most glittering of English comedies, which restores rather than disturbs its audience's faith in human nature. See *Plays,* ed. Cecil Price, 1975; James Morwood, *The Life and Works of Richard Brinsley Sheridan,* 1985.

**Sidney,** (Sir) **Philip** (1554–86), poet, prose writer, and critic, was born at Penshurst Place, Kent, of a famous titled family, though for the whole of his life his means were modest and his knighthood in 1583 was not for merit but for reasons of protocol, so that he could stand as proxy at a court ceremony. He was educated at Shrewsbury School and Christ Church, Oxford, without taking a degree — he did not return after the plague had closed the University in 1571. Between 1572 and 1575 he travelled on the Continent and met prominent intellectuals, after which he spent some months with his father, who was Lord Deputy of Ireland. Like so many, he fell in and out of favour with Queen Elizabeth, his only appointment for the present, in spite of the efforts of his uncle, the Earl of Leicester, being as an ambassador to the courts of the Emperor Rudolph and William of Orange in 1577. His strong literary interests led to a close friendship with *Spenser, who dedicated *The Shepheardes Calender* to him in 1579. In about 1580, while staying with his sister, now Countess of Pembroke, during a period of unemployment, he began for her amusement a romance, which he never finished, but which was published in 1590 in a truncated edition as *The Countess of Pembrokes Arcadia*, and more fully and with revisions in 1593. For this he combined the Menippean form of prose interspersed with verse used in *Arcadia* (1501) by the Italian Jacopo Sannazoro (1458–1530) with the kind of action in the prose epic *Aethiopica* of the fourth-century Greek writer Heliodorus, from a version translated from Latin by Thomas Underdowne (*fl.*1566–87) in 1569. At about this time, too, he wrote his critical essay on the current state of English poetry, published in 1595 both as *The Defence of Poesie* and as *The Apologie for Poetrie.* He was elected to Parliament for his father's former constituency of Kent in 1581, the year in which Penelope Devereux, to whom he had once been engaged, married Lord Rich. He now addressed to her the first considerable English sonnet sequence, comprising 108 sonnets and several songs, published in 1591 as *Astrophel and Stella.* He was himself married to Frances Walsingham in 1583, and in 1585 was appointed Governor of Flushing, to pursue, under Leicester, the Dutch war against Spain. After one brilliant military exploit, he was mortally wounded by a bullet in the attack on Zutphen, handing the bottle of water which he had been brought to a dying soldier with the immortal words, 'Thy necessity is yet greater than mine.'

The Defence of Poesie is the most considerable work of English criticism, at least until *Dryden. In Arcadia he experimented with, stretched, and embellished the new literary medium of English prose. About Astrophel and Stella, C. S. *Lewis observes in English Literature in the Sixteenth Century (1954): 'Considered historically... and in relation to his predecessors, Sidney is one of our most important poets.' See Albert C. Hamilton, Sir Philip Sidney: a Study of His Life and Works, 1977; John Buxton, Sir Philip Sidney and the English Renaissance, 3rd edn 1987.

**Sitwell, Edith** (1887–1964), poet, anthologist, biographer, and critic, elder sister of Sir Osbert *Sitwell and of the poet and art critic Sacheverell Sitwell (1897–1988), was born in Scarborough and brought up at the family seat of Renishaw Hall, Derbyshire, where her early taste for literature and music and her striking but unconventional looks clashed with her parents' interests and ideals. She found no outlet for her talents until she left home in 1914 and published a volume of poetry, The Mother (1915). As a counterblast to what she saw as the reflectively rural nature of contributions to the collections, Georgian Poetry (see *Brooke), she edited annually from 1916 to 1921 Wheels, in each issue of which there appeared poems by all three Sitwell siblings, and in 1919 seven by *Owen. Her penchant for abstract phraseology and effects created by unusual vocal and tonic rhythms was widely publicised by the public performance in 1923 of her poem-sequence, Façade, set to music by William Walton (1902–83). The verbal virtuosity stayed with her, but her subsequent poetry is equally concerned with symbolic contrasts, as in the long poem Gold Coast Customs (1929), in Street Songs (1942), and in Green Song (1944). Her critical and historical works include Alexander Pope (1930), Aspects of Modern Poetry (1934), The English Eccentrics (1933), and The Queens and the Hive (1962). She was made DBE in 1954. See Selected Poems, 1965; Victoria Glendinning, Edith Sitwell: a Unicorn among Lions, 1981 (biography); Maurice Bowra, Edith Sitwell, new edn 1982.

**Sitwell, Sir Osbert, 5th Baronet** (1892–1969), poet, novelist, and prose writer, was born in London and educated at Eton. Having deliberately failed his entrance to military staff college, he was still persuaded to enter the army in 1911, and served in France in World War I as an officer in the Grenadier Guards, from which he resigned in 1919. In the same year he published The Winstonburg Line, three satirical, pacifist poems. His satiric vein persisted in a further volume of verse, Argonaut and Juggernaut (1919); in three novels, Before the Bombardment (1926), The Man Who Lost Himself (1929), and Miracle on Sinai (1933); and in his first book of short stories, Triple Fugue (1924). Satire is tempered with com-

passion in *Dumb-Animal and Other Stories* (1930), and three verse portraits, *England Reclaimed: a Book of Eclogues* (1927), *Wrack at Tides-
head* (1952), and *On the Continent* (1958). His travel books, notably
*Winters of Content* (1932) and *Escape with Me* (1939), are a judicious
blend of description and art appreciation. His master-work, however, is
his autobiographical pageant of characters, observations, and experiences, published between 1944 and 1950 under the titles of *Left Hand,
Right Hand!*, *The Scarlet Tree*, *Great Morning!*, *Laughter in the Next
Room*, *Noble Essences*; with a postscript, *Tales My Father Taught Me*
(1962). He succeeded to his father's title in 1943, and was made CBE in
1956. See *Collected Short Stories*, 1974; John Pearson, *Façades: Edith,
Osbert and Sacheverell Sitwell*, 1978.

**Skelton, John** (*c.*1460–1529), poet, went to Oxford and Cambridge universities, to both of which he was official poet. He took holy orders in
1498, when tutor to the future Henry VIII. From about 1502 to 1511 he was
rector of Diss, Norfolk, where if we are to believe the jest-book, *Merie
Tales Newly Imprinted and Made by Master Skelton* (1567), he had a fairly
wild time and kept a mistress, by whom he had a child. Back at Court, he
was appointed Henry's poet laureate. His earliest work had been translations from the Latin, after which he wrote *The Bowge of Courte* (Court
Rations), a satirical poem in the form and metre of a dream allegory. Of
the same period is *Magnificence*, a morality drama performed before
Henry VII at Woodstock. Skeltonic verse has no consistent rhythm or
line structure, only an irregularly imposed rhyme, and in this jerky form
he composed *Philip Sparrow*, a dirge for a pet bird which C. S. *Lewis in
*English Literature in the Sixteenth Century* (1954) called 'our first great
poem of childhood', and *The Tunning of Elinor Rumming*, a somewhat
coarse exposé of life in an alehouse presided over by a female publican
whose real-life counterpart was in 1525 charged with over-pricing and
with serving sub-standard measures. He used rhyme royal for *Speak,
Parrot*, but reverted to Skeltonics for *Colin Clout* and *Why Come Ye Not
to Court*, all of which so lampooned Cardinal Wolsey that the poet had to
seek sanctuary, from which he emerged to make amends by dedicating to
the prelate the poem known as *The Garland of Laurel* (1523), ostensibly
an allegorical review of medieval poetry, but finishing with seven delightful lyrics addressed to various ladies of his acquaintance. See Ian A.
Gordon, *John Skelton, Poet Laureate*, 1943.

**Smart, Christopher** (1722–71), poet, was born in Shipbourne, Kent, son
of a steward to the Vane estates, and educated at Durham School and,
thanks to an annuity from the Duchess of Cleveland, at Pembroke Hall,
Cambridge, of which he became a Fellow. In 1749 debts, drink, and
restlessness took him to London, where he lived as a journalistic hack. In
spite of also publishing *Poems on Several Occasions* (1752) and *The*

*Hilliad* (1753), a satire on a medical quack, and five times winning the Seatonian Prize at Cambridge for religious verse, his financial state was such that he is said in 1775 to have signed a 99-year lease on his exclusive services to the periodical the *Universal Visiter*. He developed symptoms of religious mania and was confined to various asylums between 1756 and 1763, during which he wrote *Jubilate Agno*, a rich amalgam of personal thoughts and devotions, in which occurs the minutely observed portrait of his cat ('For I will consider my Cat Jeoffry...'). *A Song to David* (1763), one of the most outstanding religious lyrical poems in the language, contains 86 rhyming stanzas, intricately arranged and crammed with strange and romantic images, joyfully rising and falling to a triumphant climax. The rest of his life was one of continuous publication of translations, psalms, religious lyrics, and hymns, but in April 1770 he was committed as a debtor to the King's Bench prison, where he died. See A. Sherbo, *Christopher Smart, Scholar of the University*, 1967.

**Smith, Iain Crichton** (*b*.1928), Scottish poet, novelist, and short story writer, who writes also in Gaelic as Iain Mac a'Ghobhainn, was born in the Isle of Lewis and educated at the Nicolson Institute, Stornoway, and Aberdeen University. He taught English at Oban High School from 1955 to 1977. While his bilingualism has not elicited any dichotomy in his work — he has translated into English the poetry of Duncan Ban MacIntyre (1724–1812) and Sorley MacLean (*b*.1911) as well as his own short stories and verse — it has highlighted the conflicts between the Calvinistic discipline of the Free Kirk and the comparative freedom of the life of his youth — reflected in the titles of his early collections of verse, *Thistles and Roses* (1961) and *The Law and the Grace* (1965) — and between the ancient Gaelic culture and the baseless culture of modern Scotland. In his first novel, *Consider the Lilies* (1968), an elderly woman experiences the traumas of the Clearances in the nineteenth century, and he frequently returns to the portrayal of old age in his fiction and verse, notably in the poem 'Old Woman'. *The Last Summer* (1969) and *My Last Duchess* (1971) are in essence autobiographical novels. The telling spareness in his capturing of images and situations is as effectively demonstrated in his stories as it is in his verse, especially in *The Hermit and Other Stories* (1977) and *Murdo and Other Stories* (1981). He was awarded the OBE in 1980. See *Selected Poems 1955–1980*, 1981; *A Life*, 1986 (verse autobiography).

**Smollett, Tobias** (1721–71), Scottish novelist, was born on his grandfather's estate in the Vale of Leven, Dunbartonshire, and educated at Dumbarton Grammar School and Glasgow University, where he acquired a medical qualification. In 1740 he set out for London to find a producer for his verse tragedy, *The Regicide, or James I of Scotland*. When he failed to do so, he signed on as a ship's surgeon for the chaotic

expedition against the Spanish in the West Indies. He was subsequently
stationed in Jamaica, where he found his future bride, the creole daughter of an English planter. He returned to England in 1744, having
resigned his commission. An outspokenness towards his patients mil-
itated against his establishing a profitable practice but gave him an entrée
to journalism, which he exercised with two fairly ferocious Juvenalian
satires, *Advice* (1746) and *Reproof* (1747), and other unmemorable topical verses. Then, as it were out of the blue, he produced an anonymous
novel, *Roderick Random* (1748), a semi-autobiographical account, told
with vivid detail, of a much put-upon Scot who joins the Navy, serves in
the West Indies, and finally retrieves his lost fortunes. So good was it that
it was thought to be the work of *Fielding, under whose name it was
translated into French. Smollett responded in 1749 by resuscitating *The
Regicide* and publishing it as 'by the author of *Roderick Random*'. Even
after the success of *The Adventures of Peregrine Pickle* (1751), for which
he had visited Paris in pursuit of first-hand material for its hero's Grand
Tour, money problems still loomed. Having obtained a medical degree
from Aberdeen University, he tried to set up practice in Bath, but the
nearest he ever got to medical fame, before devoting himself entirely to
literature, was to assist Dr William Smellie (1697–1763), the celebrated
obstetrician, with the revision of his *Treatise on Midwifery* (1752).

Typically, his next two novels, *The Adventures of Ferdinand, Count
Fathom* (1753), an early terror story, and *The Adventures of Sir Launcelot
Greaves* (1762), with a latter-day Don Quixote as hero, failed because of
his wish to experiment. He had meanwhile translated the original *Don
Quixote* of Miguel de Cervantes (1547–1616), and other continental
works. He also wrote a disconcertingly monitory travel guide, *Travels
through France and Italy* (1766), which moved *Sterne to dub him 'Smel-
fungus', and *A Complete History of England to 1748* (1757–8). He was
editor of the *Critical Review* 1756–63, *British Magazine* 1760–7, and *The
Briton* 1762–3. His last novel, *The Expedition of Humphry Clinker* (1771),
in which a party of travellers wander through England and Scotland
(revisited by him in 1766), is in letter form, with ever-changing points of
view, frequent but forgivable prejudices, and superb humour and narrative timing. He spent his last few years abroad for his health, and died in
Livorno. See Lewis M. Knapp, *Tobias Smollett: Doctor of Men and
Manners*, 1949; Paul Gabriel Bouce, *The Novels of Tobias Smollett*, 1976.

**Spark, Muriel** (*b.* 1918), novelist, short story writer, and poet, was born in
Edinburgh of a Jewish father (her mother was English), and educated at
James Gillespie's School for Girls, Edinburgh. During a brief marriage
she lived in southern Africa, returning to Britain in 1944. She was
General Secretary of the Poetry Society and editor of *Poetry Review*
1947–9. At this time she was writing critical and biographical works and
poetry — see *Collected Poems* (1967) — but she turned to fiction after

winning the *Observer* short story competition in 1951. She became a Catholic in 1954, which superimposed an intellectual pattern on the conflicting elements of her upbringing and earlier years. Her first novel, *The Comforters* (1957), established her motif of the social or cultural misfit, or the loner in a society of misfits, which recurs especially in *The Ballad of Peckham Rye* (1960), *The Driver's Seat* (1970), *Loitering with Intent* (1981), and *A Far Cry from Kensington* (1988). And in her most widely-publicised novel, *The Prime of Miss Jean Brodie* (1961), a strong-willed but obtusely arrogant schoolmistress is the architect of her own destruction. Muriel Spark's dialogue has the precision of a poet and the wit of a skilled satirist, while her eye for the bizarre and her skill as a short story writer — see *Collected Stories* (1967) — enable her to crystallise a character, a situation, or a complete milieu in a few paragraphs, or even words. She was awarded the OBE in 1967. See Peter Kemp, *Muriel Spark*, 1974; Alan Bold, *Muriel Spark*, 1986.

**Spender,** (Sir) **Stephen** (*b*.1909), poet, critic, editor, and translator, was born in London and educated at University College School and University College, Oxford, where he was a friend of *MacNeice and approved of by *Auden. From 1930 to 1933 he spent half the year in Germany, where he was caught up in the political and social unrest of the times, which along with his personal uneasiness is reflected in *Poems* (1933) and in the critical work, *The Destructive Element: a Study of Modern Writers and Beliefs* (1935). With the experience also of the Spanish Civil War (1936–9) — expressed in *The Still Centre* (1939) — he is regarded primarily as a poet of the 1930s, to which many of his best-known and most memorable poems belong, such as 'A Stop Watch and an Ordnance Map', 'The Express', 'Two Armies', 'An Elementary School Classroom', and 'The Pylons'. From this latter poem derives the name of the Pylon school of poets whose work was concerned with modern industrial development. He was founder-editor with Cyril Connolly (1903–74) of the literary magazine *Horizon* 1934–41, and co-editor of *Encounter* 1953–66, in which many new authors were brought to public notice, and contemporary literary controversies were aired. As translator as well as poet, he has enabled the work especially of Federico García Lorca (1898–1936) and Rainer Maria Rilke (1875–1926) to be read in English. He was knighted in 1983. See *Collected Poems 1928–1985*, new edn 1989; *World Within World*, new edn 1977, and *The Thirties and After*, 1978 (memoirs); *Journals 1939–1983*, ed. John Goldsmith, 1985.

**Spenser, Edmund** (1552–99), poet, was born in London and educated at Merchant Taylor's School from its foundation in 1561 until 1569, when he went to Pembroke Hall, Cambridge, as a sizar, graduating as MA in 1576. A contemporary was Gabriel Harvey (*c*.1549–1630), who became professor of rhetoric in 1574 and introduced him to the Earl of Leicester and to

*Sidney, to whom Spenser dedicated *The Shepheardes Calender* (1579). This series of twelve monthly eclogues, in which the poet appears as Colin Clout, represents a return to pastoral verse and to the language of *Chaucer and contradicts the correspondence between Spenser and Harvey published in 1580 (*Three Proper and Witty Familiar Letters* and *Two Other Very Commendable Letters*), in which among observations about earthquakes is an exploration of the use of Latin and Greek metres for English poetry. Spenser had married Machabyas Childe in 1579, by whom he had two children, and in 1580 he went to Ireland as secretary to the new governor, Lord Grey. His administrative career flourished, and he collected various posts and sinecures after Grey's departure, being in 1590 formally assigned the estate and castle of Kilcolman, Co. Cork.

He had begun writing *The Faerie Queen* in 1580, but it was not until 1589, on a visit to London, that he found a publisher for the first three books, which appeared under his own name in 1590, with a dedication to Queen Elizabeth, who responded by awarding him a pension for life of £50 a year. The same publisher, William Ponsonbie (c.1546–1604), 'dwelling in Paules Churchyard at the figure of the Bishops head', issued in 1591 *Daphnaïda: an Elegie upon Douglas Howard* (daughter of Lord Howard), and *Complaints,* a collection of splendid longer poems (including 'The Ruines of Time', 'Virgil's Gnat', and 'Mother Hubberds Tale') which had to be withdrawn as two of them contained unkind allusions to the Lord Treasurer, Lord Burleigh. *Colin Clouts Come Home Again* (1595) was written in 1591 and is prefaced by a letter to *Ralegh, who had sponsored his London visit. This autobiographical eclogue rehearses the excursion, describes the Court, and concludes with an appreciation of a return to a pastoral existence and to the poet's love, Rosalind. Machabyas must have died some years earlier, for Rosalind was an English girl, Elizabeth Boyle, who had settled in Ireland with her brother. The couple were married in 1594. Spenser records his courtship in a sonnet sequence, *Amoretti* (1595), published with 'Epithalamion', a gorgeous wedding hymn which is as unusual in the striking range of its musical verse, its detail, and its wit, as it is in the fact that it is the bridegroom's own gift to his bride. By contrast, *Prothalamion* (1596), written for the 'double marriage' of Lady Elizabeth and Lady Katherine Somerset, is merely a great poem. *The Second Part of the Faerie Queen,* books IV to VI, was also published in 1596, and completes all we have of the planned twelve books, apart from 'Two Cantos of Mutabilitie', presumed to belong to one of the further books and included in the edition of 1609. In 1596 he had also written *A View of the Present State of Ireland,* advocating even tougher measures against terrorists in particular (he also proposed that all Irish poets should be put to death). It was circulated, but publication was shelved pending 'further authority'. In September 1598 Spenser was appointed High Sheriff of Cork, but the following month the rebel patriot, the Earl of Tyrone, having previously routed the

English army near Armagh, invaded Munster. The province erupted, and Kilcolman was razed. Spenser escaped with his family, and was sent to London with despatches for the Government. He was taken ill shortly after his arrival, died on 13 January, and was buried in Westminster Abbey.

Whether Spenser wrote more than we have of *The Faerie Queen* is not known, but the scheme of the complete work and the incident which precipitates the action of the first book are described in the author's letter to Ralegh dated 23 January 1589. The effect of this epic dream romance, which also has myriad allegorical depths, is heightened by the stanza form he invented for it: eight iambic pentameters rhyming *ababbcbc*, followed by a triumphant Alexandrine rhyming *c*. See *The Poetical Works*, ed. J. C. Smith and E. de Selincourt, new edn 1970; W. L. Renwick, *Edmund Spenser: an Essay on Renaissance Poetry*, new edn 1965; Graham Hough, *A Preface to the Faerie Queen*, 1962; C. S. Lewis, *Spenser's Images of Life*, ed. Alastair Fowler, 1967.

**Steele,** (Sir) **Richard** (1672–1729), essayist and dramatist, was born in Dublin, son of an attorney, and educated at Charterhouse and Merton College, Oxford, which he left suddenly without taking a degree to join the Guards. Erratic as well as extravagant, he published *The Christian Hero* (1701), a treatise advocating sound Christian behaviour, and in the same year produced the first of three comedies of sentiment (*The Funeral: Or, Grief A-la-mode, The Lying Lover: Or, The Ladies Friendship*, and *The Tender Husband: Or, the Accomplished Fools*), none of which was successful. A brief marriage to an elderly heiress was followed by a more permanent one to Mary Scurlock, whom he had met at his first wife's funeral. In 1709 he founded the thrice-weekly periodical the *Tatler* which, with *Addison's continuing help, was succeeded by the *Spectator*. He was elected to Parliament in 1713, expelled in 1714 for seditious libel, but returned to grace in 1715, when he was appointed Inspector of the Royal Stables and Commissioner for Drury Lane Theatre, and knighted. His last comedy, *The Conscious Lovers*, staged in 1722, takes a more realistic and romantic view of marriage than had been usual in Restoration drama. He had more charm and humour than Addison, and was a more dedicated political journalist, but it was their combined talents and shrewd awareness of their public that brought them lasting acclaim. See *The Tatler*, ed. Donald F. Bond, 3 vols 1987; Willard Connely, *Sir Richard Steele*, 1934.

**Stephens, James** (1882–1950), Irish poet and novelist, was born in Dublin. At an early age he was placed in an orphanage, where he got a firm grounding in Protestantism but little other education, and from which he ran away, living rough and depending on people's kindness. It was probably his tiny stature which enabled him to empathise particularly with the fairies and other small beings of Irish mythology, just as, by his own account, he used as a child to squat beside a dog or a cat, or even a bush, and practise projecting himself into it. His first volume of verse, *Insurrections* (1909), was more concerned with highlighting the conditions of the Dublin poor, but latterly his poetry became more mystical in outlook, matching the surer development of his prose. He was a protégé of *Russell, who recommended the publication of his novel of urban idealism, *The Charwoman's Daughter* (1912). His most lasting work is *The Crock of Gold* (1912), a philosophical fairy tale with modern implications. His sense of comedy is more evident in *Deirdre* (1923) and in *In the Land of Youth* (1924), in which he attempts to reconcile heroic Irish mythology with simple rural delights. He was registrar of the Irish National Portrait Gallery from 1915 to 1924, after which he divided his time between Paris and London, where he became an outstanding broadcaster of his own, idiosyncratic scripts, published as *James, Seamus and Jacques* (1964). See *Collected Poems*, 1954; Hilary Pyle, *James Stephens: His Work and an Account of His Life*, 1965.

**Sterne, Laurence** (1713–68), novelist, was born in Clonmel, Ireland, son of an English army officer whose family followed him around, though the boy was settled in a school in Halifax from 1723 until his father's death in 1731. In 1733 a cousin offered to support him at Jesus College, Cambridge, from which he graduated as BA in 1736, taking holy orders in 1738. From then until 1759 he lived the life of an eccentric Yorkshire country parson. He was frequently ill with consumption, and his wife, whom he had married in 1741 on learning that she had bequeathed him her property, proved as much a trial to him as he clearly was to her. A dispute among the clergy of York Minster suggested to him the plot of a comic novel, *A Political Romance*, which was regarded as so unsuitable for publication that it did not appear until 1769, after which it was often reprinted as *The History of a Good Warm Watch Coat*. The success it achieved among his friends, to whom it had been privately circulated in 1759, determined him to become a novelist, and he wrote the first two books of *The Life and Opinions of Tristram Shandy, Gentleman* which, having been turned down by the London publishing firm of Dodsley, he had printed in York at a friend's expense. The reaction of the international literary world was phenomenal. Sterne moved to London to capitalise on his new reputation, and an embarrassed Dodsley was only too pleased to reissue the first two books (1760), to commission the author to supply a further volume every year for the rest of his life, and to publish a collected edition of his sermons as *The Sermons of Mr Yorick* (7 vols 1760–9). In spite of recurrent illness, Sterne plunged enthusiastically into fashionable life in London and France, while keeping to his contract for *Tristram Shandy* (the ninth book was published in 1767) and writing *A Sentimental Journey through France and Italy* (1768), though Italy remained unvisited by the whimsical traveller. During the spring of 1767 he indulged in an energetic but platonic affair with Eliza Draper, a 23-year-old charmer, until she sailed to join her husband in India. For her he wrote *The Journal to Eliza,* discovered in 1851.

'Digressions, incontestably, are the sunshine,' wrote Sterne in *Tristram Shandy* (I, 22), but along with his quirkish typographical devices and punctuation, and non sequiturs which are rather associations of ideas on the principles of *Locke, they are integral to a unique construction by a comic genius and in part anticipate the stream of consciousness technique. By the time he came to write *A Sentimental Journey,* more feeling and decorum had set in, but even if he did intend to complete the odyssey, the present conclusion is sheer perfection. See *The Life and Opinions of Tristram Shandy, Gentleman,* ed. Ian Campbell Ross, 1983; *A Sentimental Journey through France and Italy with Mr Yorick* with *The Journal to Eliza* and *A Political Romance,* ed. Ian Jack, 1984; Arthur H. Cash, *Laurence Sterne: Early and Middle Years,* 1975, and *Later Years,* 1986; and in Virginia Woolf, *Collected Essays,* vol. I 1966, and vol. III 1967.

**Stevenson, Robert Louis** (1850–94), Scottish novelist, short story writer, poet, essayist, and travel writer, was born in Edinburgh, only child of Thomas Stevenson of the famous family of lighthouse engineers, and Margaret Balfour, a minister's daughter. Constant illness disrupted his education, of which the years 1861–3 were spent at Edinburgh Academy. His first published work, paid for by his father, was a novel of the last days of the Covenanters, *The Pentland Rising* (1866). The following year he went to Edinburgh University to read engineering, but on explaining to his father in 1871 that he wanted to make writing his career, he was persuaded at least to study law for the time being, and qualified as an advocate in 1875. Meanwhile he had shocked his parents by expressing agnostic sympathies. A meeting with W. E. Henley (1849–1903) resulted in their writing together four poor plays, but also gave him an entrée to outlets for reviews and essays, of which he made several collections, the first being *Virginibus Puerisque* (1881). Foreign expeditions, by unusual means, for his health gave him the material for *Inland Voyage* (1878) and *Travels with a Donkey in the Cévennes* (1879). In 1879 he went to California to persuade a woman he had met in France, Fanny Osbourne, ten years his senior and just divorced, to marry him. Back in Europe and still travelling, he completed his first full-length novel, *Treasure Island* (1883), published initially in *Young Folks' Magazine* and particularly memorable for its subtle narrative technique. In *Kidnapped* (1886), its sequel *Catriona* (1893), and *The Master of Ballantrae* (1889), he is concerned with personal conflicts and Scottish history and topography as well as adventure. Conflict in the form of a dual personality is the theme of *The Strange Case of Dr Jekyll and Mr Hyde* (1886). *Not I and Other Poems*

(1881) had contained several poems expressing the anguish of youth. *A Child's Garden of Verses* (1885) is a nostalgic recapitulation of the pleasures and fantasies of childhood. On the whole, however, his poetry is mild stuff beside the supernatural short stories 'Thrawn Janet' (1881) and 'Markheim' (1886), which were published in *The Merry Men and Other Tales* (1887).

In 1887 he and his wife sailed for America and chartered a racing schooner to take them to the South Seas in a final search for a congenial climate for him. They found it in Samoa, where they built a house on the estate of Vailima. Here he wrote with his stepson, Lloyd Osbourne, two tales of violent adventure, *The Wrecker* (1892) and *The Ebb-Tide* (1894). He also completed nine chapters of *Weir of Hermiston*, which for depth of character, insight into a father–son relationship such as he had himself experienced, and power of style, exceeds anything else he wrote. His significance to English literature lies more in what he promised to achieve than in what he wrote during his short life; in terms of Scottish literature, however, he was in several ways a true successor to *Scott. See Jenni Calder, *RLS: a Life Study*, 1980; Robert Kiely, *Robert Louis Stevenson and the Fiction of Adventure*, 1964; J. R. Hammond, *A Robert Louis Stevenson Companion: a Guide to the Novels, Essays and Short Stories*, 1984.

**Stoppard, Tom** (*b*.1937), dramatist, was born in Zlin, Czechoslovakia, taken by his parents to Singapore just before World War II, and then sent with his mother to India to avoid the Japanese invasion, in which his father died. After the war, his mother married an Englishman, whose name he took. He was educated at Pocklington School, Yorkshire, and worked as a newspaper journalist in Bristol from 1954 to 1960, when he went freelance to write for the theatre, though his first published works were short stories in *Stories by New Writers* (1964) and a comic novel, *Lord Malquist and Mr Moon* (1966). His first play, *A Walk on the Water*, was produced on television in 1964, and in a revised form on the London stage in 1968 as *Enter a Free Man*. The central theme of *Rosencrantz and Guildenstern are Dead* (first staged in Edinburgh in 1966), as of many of his plays, is the powerlessness of man in the face of fate and external forces, in this case seen through the eyes of two of *Shakespeare's minor characters. In *Jumpers* (1972), regarded as his best play, the predicament of the moral philosopher in a pragmatic world is highlighted by the invasion of his privacy by public events on a vast television screen. *Professional Foul* (1978), written for television, is a philosophical drama of human rights set in Czechoslovakia. Stoppard uses theatrical and technical devices as well as verbal gymnastics to amuse, and startle, his audience, and what may sometimes appear derivative is intentional parody. See Ronald Hayman, *Tom Stoppard*, 3rd edn 1979; Anthony Jenkins, *The Theatre of Tom Stoppard*, 2nd edn 1989.

**Strachey, Lytton** (1880–1932), critic and biographer, was born at Stowey House, Clapham Common, London, son of General Sir Richard Strachey and his second wife, and educated at Leamington College, Liverpool University (for two distressing years), and Trinity College, Cambridge. He wrote regular articles for the *Spectator* and other literary journals, and was a prominent member of the Bloomsbury Group (see Virginia *Woolf). His first and, to some, his most balanced book was *Landmarks in French Literature* (1912). At the time of World War I, during which he was a conscientious objector, he devised a technique of biography demonstrated in *Eminent Victorians* (1918), in which he aimed by elegant prose and judicious selection and presentation of detail to reveal illustrious figures as less virtuous than they had seemed hitherto. Though heavily criticised, the book made his reputation. His attempt to repeat the formula in *Queen Victoria* (1921) foundered in that he could not dent the heroic mould of his subject, but resulted in a fairer exposition. *Elizabeth and Essex* (1928) contains more speculation but is even more readable. From 1916 he lived in close relationship with the painter Dora Carrington (1893–1932) and, after her marriage in 1921, with her husband too. She committed suicide after Strachey's death from cancer. While unable to bring much understanding of psychology to his biographical studies, he invented a literary form which, for better or for worse, led to the fictionalised biography. *The Shorter Strachey* (1980), selected and introduced by Michael Holroyd and Paul Levy, comprises 30 of his essays. See Michael Holroyd, *Lytton Strachey: a Biography*, new edn 1987.

**Suckling, (Sir) John** (1609–41), poet and dramatist, was born in Twickenham, Middlesex, eldest son of a wealthy statesman, and was educated privately and at Trinity College, Cambridge, after which he served in military capacities and studied on the Continent, being knighted on his return in 1630. The foremost wit and poet of the court of Charles I, he was also a notorious gambler (and possibly the inventor of the game of cribbage), a formidable opponent in the bowling alley, a philanderer, and an enthusiastic but inglorious soldier, who fled to France after participating in a royalist army plot to rescue the Earl of Strafford from jail, and probably committed suicide there. That he was an effective writer in prose is shown by his political thesis in the form of a letter to 'Mr Henry German' (Henry Jermyn), 'In the Beginning of Parliament 1640', and his tract on Socinianism addressed to the Earl of Dorset, *An Account of Religion by Reason*, written in 1637 but not published until 1646. He wrote four unremarkable plays, of which *Aglaura* (1638) has alternative tragic and tragicomic fifth acts. His literary reputation rests on his comic verse, notably 'A Ballade Upon a Wedding', and his lyrics, largely unpolished but particularly delightful for their inventiveness of language. His famous song, 'Why so pale and wan, fond lover, / Prithee, why so pale?', occurs in *Aglaura*, IV. ii. See *The Works of John Suckling: the*

*Non-Dramatic Works*, ed. Thomas Clayton, 1971; *The Works of John Suckling: the Plays*, ed. L. A. Beaurline, 1971.

**Surrey, Earl of** (*c.*1517–47), poet, was born Henry Howard, probably at Kenninghall, Norfolk, and was given his courtesy title when his father became Duke of Norfolk in 1524. He was well educated at home, and in 1529 became companion to Henry VIII's illegitimate son, the Duke of Richmond. He married Frances Vere, daughter of the Earl of Oxford, in 1532. His professional life comprised military service in England and France (his ability was questionable, but not his bravery) and court favour (he was elected Knight of the Garter in 1541), interspersed with bouts of violence and law-breaking (he was twice imprisoned), and he was finally beheaded for treason. His distinction is in his being an innovative and technically skilful poet, who owed much to the inspiration of *Wyatt, with whom he shares the credit for introducing into English the Petrarchan sonnet, in which medium his themes are love, friendship, and chivalry. There are two revealing poems of polite complaint about his incarceration, one from Windsor, and the other a satire against the citizens of London for misinterpreting his 'protest', which took the form of breaking their windows. He also translated Books II and IV of Virgil's *Aeneid,* described by their first printer (*c.*1554) as 'drawne into a straunge metre', being the first example of English blank verse. Other poems were first published in *Songes and Sonettes by Surrey and Other* (1557), edited by Richard Tottel (*c.*1530–94) — 'Tottel's Miscellany'. See *Poems*, ed. Emrys Jones, 1964.

**Surtees, Robert Smith** (1803–64), novelist, was born at Hamsterley Hall, Co. Durham (to which he succeeded on his father's death in 1838), and educated at Durham Grammar School and for a career in the law, which he abandoned in 1831 to become co-founder and, until 1836, editor of the *New Sporting Magazine.* He published *The Horseman's Manual, Being a Treatise on Soundness, the Law of Warranty, and Generally on the Laws Relating to Horses* in 1831, and contributed to his own journal a serial, published in 1838 with twelve illustrations by Phiz — Hablot K. Browne (1815–82) — as *Jorrocks' Jaunts and Jollities, or the Hunting, Racing, Driving, Sailing, Eating, Eccentric and Extravagant Exploits of that Renowned Sporting Citizen, Mr John Jorrocks of St Botolph Lane and Great Coram Street.* Further adventures of Jorrocks, who is said to have given *Dickens the idea for *Pickwick Papers,* appeared in *Handley Cross, or Spa Hunt: a Sporting Tale* (1843), illustrated by John Leech (1817–64), and further novels in a similar didactic but predominantly satirical vein include *Hillingdon Hall, or the Cockney Squire: a Tale of Country Life* (1845), his best-constructed work, and *Mr Sponge's Sporting Tour* (1853). Surtees had a skilled novelist's perception of a situation and a character, and a feeling for enjoyable language. He was also the first to write about hunting and its social ethos. He was averse to seeing his name in print, and all his novels appeared anonymously. See Frederick Watson, *R. S. Surtees: a Critical Study,* 1933.

**Swift, Jonathan** (1667–1745), Irish prose writer, poet, and cleric, was born in Dublin of English parents (his father dying before he was born), and was educated at Kilkenny College and Trinity College, Dublin. After living with his mother in Leicester, he became in 1689 secretary to Sir William Temple, a retired statesman with whom the Swift family had connections, at Moor Park, Surrey. Here he met and was tutor to the eight-year-old Esther Johnson, whom he much later dubbed 'Stella'. He wrote poetry, including 'Ode to the Athenian Society', of a kind to which no doubt his cousin *Dryden was referring when telling him that he would never be a poet. In 1694 he took holy orders in the Anglican Church, spent two years in Ireland, and returned to Moor Park in 1696. Here he wrote his first two prose satires, *A Tale of a Tub,* a burlesque on the religious disagreements of the times with digressions into current philosophy and learning, and *An Account of a Battel Between Antient and Modern Books* ('The Battle of the Books'), a mock-heroic account of a literary controversy involving Temple—they were published together in 1704. On Temple's death in 1699 he returned to Ireland as chaplain to the Earl of Berkeley, and in 1701 became a prebendary of St Patrick's Cathedral, vicar of Laracor, Co. Meath, and received his DD. At his suggestion, Esther, with her close friend Rebecca Dingley as chaperon, moved to Dublin. They met constantly but never alone, and the suggestion that at some point they secretly married is as perplexing as the reason why they may never have married at all. From 1710 to 1714 he was mainly in London on political business for the Church, becoming a valued friend of and an active propagandist for the ruling Tory party, after abandoning his allegiance to the Whigs for their indifference to the interests of Anglicans in Ireland and to the Test Act. The letters he wrote to Esther during this period, partly in code and with excursions into baby talk, offer a fascinating, informal, and often indiscreet insight into London social and political life. They were first published in 1766–8, and from 1784 have been known as *Journal to Stella.*

Queen Anne opposed his preferment in England, but through the good offices of the Duke of Ormonde he became Dean of St Patrick's in 1713, and here he retired in 1714, to become an able church administrator and a thorn in the flesh of the English government. He also had a problem with another and younger girl-friend, Esther Vanhomrigh, whose attentions he had unsuccessfully tried to divert by his witty poem 'Cadenus and Vanessa'. She pursued him to Ireland and remained there, dying in 1723 from, it is said, shock at Swift's reaction to her letter asking point blank whether he and Stella were married. Under the pseudonym of M. B. Drapier, he published in 1724 *A Letter to the Whole People of Ireland,* inflaming the country to boycott a proposed new coinage. The Government imprisoned the printer and offered £300 for information about the author. Everyone knew it was Swift, but no one came forward with proof, or claimed the reward. The coinage was abandoned. He was acclaimed a national hero, and his return to Dublin from a visit to London in 1726 was greeted with bells and bonfires. The occasion for the visit had been the publication of *Travels into Several Remote Nations of the World by Lemuel Gulliver* ('Gulliver's Travels'). While it contains allusions to contemporary events and attitudes, it is of continued universal appeal for its satirical insight into the behaviour of man. In 1727 he made his last visit to England. He was deaf, an extension of the vertigo he had long suffered (now thought to have been Ménière's syndrome), but he continued to write. To these years belong his most notorious piece of satirical pamphleteering, *A Modest Proposal for Preventing the Children of Poor People from Being a Burthen* (1729) — his remedy was to eat them, for which he offered several recipes — and some occasional verse which is notable for its vigorous use of ordinary language. His brain began to fail in 1738, and in 1740 trustees took over his affairs. He was buried in St Patrick's next to his beloved Stella, who had died in 1728.

Apart from the driving *saeva indignatio* (fierce indignation) which he attributed to himself, and the playfulness with which he often exercised it, Swift's distinction is his prose, simple, controlled, and concrete. He inspired the love of literary and political friends (notably *Pope), as well as of women, not the least devoted of whom was Letitia Pilkington (1712–50), whose *Memoirs* (1748) are a valuable source of information about his personal habits. See *Selected Works*, ed. Angus Ross and David Woolley, 1984; *Complete Poems*, ed. Pat Rogers, 1983; David Nokes, *Jonathan Swift: a Hypocrite Reversed*, new edn 1987 (critical biography); Denis Donoghue, *Jonathan Swift; a Critical Introduction*, 1969.

**Swinburne, Algernon Charles** (1837–1909), poet, dramatist, and critic, was born in London, eldest child of Admiral and Lady Jane Swinburne, and educated at Eton, where he arrived clutching Bowdler's edition of *Shakespeare (a present from his mother when he was six), and at Balliol College, Oxford, from which he was rusticated in 1860, having that same year published two verse plays, *The Queen-Mother* and *Rosamond*. He was of ambiguous sexual inclinations, though an emotional romance with a cousin, broken off because of their consanguinity, inspired his fine lyrical poem, 'The Triumph of Time'. While at Oxford he became associated with the Pre-Raphaelites and he was for a time a member of D. G. *Rossetti's ménage. In 1862 he had poetry and essays published in the *Spectator*, including a defence of *Meredith's *Modern Love*, and the following year he completed *Chastelard* (1865), the first of three dramas about Mary, Queen of Scots, of which the two later ones became bogged down by historical fact. *Atalanta in Calydon* (1865) won the praise of the critics as a Greek drama and the applause of young men about town, who chanted to each other the melodic rhyming choruses, of which the most memorable is 'When the hounds of spring are on winter's traces...'. *Poems and Ballads* (1866) caused a sensation for what was seen as the expressions of 'the libidinous laureate of a pack of satyrs', a charge he rebutted in *Notes on Poems and Reviews* (1866). Renouncing for the moment freedom of speech in favour of the liberation of man, he followed his political poem, *A Song of Italy* (1867), with *Songs before Sunrise* (1871), in which he used his poetic talent and versatility to support Italian republicanism. *Poems and Ballads: Second Series* (1878) lacks some of the excitement of its predecessor, but contains some of his best poems, including 'A Forsaken Garden' and 'Ave Atque Vale'. He had by this time written most of 'Tristram of Lyonesse' (published in 1883), an uneven but thoughtful and sometimes powerful treatment of medieval romance (written as a counter-blast to *Tennyson), but his faculties were being destroyed by chronic bouts of alcoholism. In 1879 Theodore Watts (1832–1914), later Watts-Dunton, a solicitor turned literary critic and novelist, took official charge of him in his Putney house, where Swinburne lived on for 30 years, and continued to write, though in a subdued fashion. There is a vivid and sympathetic portrait of them both at home under the title 'No 2 The Pines' in *Beerbohm's *And Even Now* (1920).

Swinburne's poetry is notable for its emotional appeal, and almost shameless and florid glorying in language. His plays, however, lack the dramatist's art. His early study, *William Blake: a Critical Essay* (1868), is a significant contribution to the interpretation of *Blake's 'Prophetic Books', and modern critics generally confirm the underlying soundness of his judgments on other poets too. See *The Swinburne Letters*, ed. Cecil Y. Lang, 6 vols 1959–62; Jean Overton Fuller, *Swinburne: a Critical Biography*, 1968; Jerome J. McGann, *Swinburne: an Experiment in Criticism*, 1972.

**Synge, J(ohn) M(illington)** (1871–1909), Irish dramatist and poet, was born in Newtown Little, Dublin, youngest of five children of a barrister who died when he was one, and was educated privately and at Trinity College, Dublin, where he studied Irish and Hebrew. From an early age he took a great interest in natural history, and it was reading *Darwin at 14 which led him soon afterwards to renounce his religion. His first choice of career was to be a musician, for which he studied in Germany for two years. In 1895, however, he decided to become a writer, and for the next seven years spent each winter in Paris. Here he met *Yeats, who introduced him to Maud Gonne's Young Ireland Society (from which he soon resigned on political grounds), and who also suggested he should visit Aran to further his knowledge of Irish traditional life. He returned there time and again, recapturing its landscape and peasant society in his prose account, *The Aran Islands* (new edn with his own photographs, 1979). His personal experience of a romance blighted on religious grounds inspired his first, rejected, play, *When the Moon Has Set*, and much of his early poetry. Thereafter his plays are redolent of the lore and customs of the country people of Aran or of Wicklow, their language reflecting Gaelic syntax and incorporating in a natural way words, phrases, and speech rhythms which he had absorbed on his travels. *The Shadow of the Glen* (performed 1903) and *Riders to the Sea* (1904) are one-act tragedies based on folk tales. At about the same time as he was writing them, he embarked on *The Tinker's Wedding*, which was published, but not performed, in 1908. In 1904 he became a co-director with Yeats and Lady Gregory of the Abbey Theatre, which staged his *The Well of the Saints* (1905), in which the folklore has a supernatural element and the setting an equivalent remoteness.

*The Playboy of the Western World* (1907) opened to an unpredicted, if perhaps predictable, storm. The first-night audience erupted at the image of 'chosen females standing in their shifts', and on the second night the police had to be called in to calm rioters who saw the portrayal of the peasantry as an insult to Irish nationalism. This sparkling play goes at a great pace, moving effortlessly between tragedy, comedy, and farce to pathos at the end. Synge's relationship with the 19-year-old Abbey actress, Molly Allgood, is extolled in some of the poems he wrote at this time, such as 'Is it a month...' and 'The Meeting': so is the imminence of death, for he had Hodgkin's disease. When he died he was still revising *Deirdre of the Sorrows* (1909), an enduring and intricate excursion into Irish mythology. He was a meticulous craftsman, in whom an unusually high standard both of dramatic and poetic expression could be exercised simultaneously. See *Plays*, ed. Ann Saddlemyer, 1969; *Poems and Translations*, new edn 1972; *Autobiography*, ed. Alan Price, 1965; D. H. Greene and E. M. Stephens, *J. M. Synge 1871–1909*, 1959 (biography); Robin Skelton, *The Writings of J. M. Synge*, 1971.

**Taylor, Jeremy** (1613–67), prose writer and cleric, was born in Cambridge, son of a barber, and educated at the Perse School and Gonville and Caius College, Cambridge, becoming a Fellow and taking holy orders before he was 21. Archbishop Laud had him transferred to Oxford, where he became a Fellow of All Souls and in 1642 was made DD by royal mandate — he was a chaplain to Charles I. In 1645 he was captured and imprisoned by the Parliamentary army. On his release he was given protection by the Earl of Carbery, at whose seat, Golden Grove in Carmarthenshire, he spent much of the next ten years. After the Restoration he was appointed Bishop of Down and Connor, and Vice-Chancellor of Dublin University. A liberal churchman, it is for the baroque splendour of his exposition that he is remembered, and especially for his extended similes, often prefaced with, 'So have I seen...'. His style can be readily appreciated in *The Rule and Exercises of Holy*

*Living* (1650) and *The Rule and Exercises of Holy Dying* (1651), while his religious stance is best illustrated by *The Liberty of Prophesying* (1647). More unusual is *A Discourse of the Nature, Offices and Measures of Friendship, with Rules of Conducting It* (1657), addressed to Mrs Katherine Philips (1631–64), a minor poet and hostess who gave fanciful names to members of her circle — she was Orinda, and Taylor was Palaemon. See *The Golden Grove: Selected Passages*, ed. Logan Pearsall Smith, 1930; C. J. Stranks, *The Life and Writings of Jeremy Taylor*, 1952.

**Tennyson, Alfred** (1809–92), poet and dramatist, was born in Somersby, Lincolnshire, sixth of twelve children of an elder son who had been passed over in his wealthy father's will and had reluctantly entered the Church. The boy was educated at Louth Grammar School and by his father, and went to Trinity College, Cambridge, in 1827, about fifty of his poems having already been published in *Poems by Two Brothers* (1827). Of the brilliant young men he now met, he became especially close to Arthur Hallam, with whom he spent two idyllic holidays on the Continent, and who became engaged to Tennyson's sister, Emily. In 1829 he won the Chancellor's Gold Medal for poetry with a piece on the set subject of 'Timbuctoo', which encouraged him to publish *Poems, Chiefly Lyrical* (1830), whose main interest lies in the rhythmical and disturbing 'Mariana' and the impassioned 'The Ballad of Oriana'. In 1831 Mr Tennyson died, and the poet abandoned Cambridge to help look after the family. Though on the whole *Poems*, dated 1833 but published in December 1832, showed more promise than the earlier volume, it was coolly received, which is understandable in that memorable poems such as 'The Lady of Shalott', 'The Lotus Eaters', and 'Oenone' were not yet in their definitive versions. In September 1833 Hallam died suddenly in Vienna of a ruptured blood vessel. The shock to Emily was catastrophic: the effect on Tennyson was profound. On top of family and financial problems, he had lost not only someone closer than brother or mere friend, but the prop whose recognition of his artistic genius was essential at a time when his professional confidence was waning, as 'The Two Voices', written largely before the tragedy, demonstrates.

For two years he wrote little, and it was another seven before he published again, but in the meantime he had found his own voice. *Poems* (2 vols 1842) contains rewritten versions of 16 earlier poems, as well as the memorable blank-verse dramatic monologue, 'Ulysses'; 'Morte d'Arthur' and 'Sir Galahad', his first excursions into Arthurian legend; 'Locksley Hall', an attempt at social protest; and the classic lament, 'Break, Break, Break'. In 1845 he was granted a Civil List Pension of £200, which relieved his immediate financial worries and enabled him to travel. In 1847 he published 'The Princess: a Medley', an over-idyllic novella in verse supporting women's rights, punctuated with some of his finest lyrics, including 'Now sleeps the crimson petal...'. On 1 June 1850 he published anonymously *In Memoriam*, his tribute to Hallam in the form of a sequence of 131 poetic reminiscences, elegies, and reflections, which pronounced him not just the foremost poet of his age, but also a scientist and philosopher. On 13 June he married Emily Sellwood, whom he had known for 20 years — they had been engaged once before, but the match had been broken off because of his poor health and prospects. And in November he was appointed Poet Laureate in succession to *Wordsworth, a post he assumed with characteristic thoroughness, dignity and, occasionally, immortality, as with *Ode on the Death of the Duke of Wellington* (1852) and 'The Charge of the Light Brigade' (1854), written, according to him, 'in a few minutes'. This second period of poetic output closed with *Maud* (1855), a series of dramatic monologues (later called a 'monodrama') whose violent story-line incorporates some outspoken social criticism.

The *Idylls of the King* (1859), a series of Arthurian narratives, was the culmination of years of study, meditation, and practice. Expanded versions of the original four appeared at intervals, and further episodes were published in *The Holy Grail, and Other Poems* (1870) and as *Gareth and Lynette* (1872), with 'The Last Tournament'. The final order is that of the 1889 edition. The descriptive writing is fine and the poetry ripples along, but the characters are unconvincing on both an allegorical and realistic plane. The lack of a driving dramatic sense is evident, too, in the verse plays that he wrote between 1875 and 1892. There was no slackening in his output of occasional, lyrical, narrative, and meditative verse, and it is to his later years that 'The Revenge', 'Rizpah', 'The Voyage', and 'Crossing the Bar' belong. He was created a Baron in 1883, becoming Alfred Lord Tennyson. See *The Poems of Tennyson*, ed. Christopher Ricks, 3 vols, 2nd rev. edn 1987; Robert B. Martin, *Tennyson: the Unquiet Heart*, new edn 1983 (biography); Christopher Ricks, *Tennyson*, 2nd edn 1989 (critical biography); Roger Ebbatson, *Tennyson*, 1988 (introduction).

**Thackeray, William Makepeace** (1811–63), novelist and journalist, was born in Calcutta, son of the Collector of Alipore, and sent back to England after his father's death in 1816. He was educated at Charterhouse and Trinity College, Cambridge, from which he removed himself because he felt his studies would be of no practical use. In the expectation of a considerable legacy under his father's will, he travelled on the Continent and then studied law. When his inheritance did not materialise owing to the collapse of the Indian Bank, he became a journalist. In 1836 he married Isabella Shawe in Paris, where he was correspondent to the *Constitutional*. The paper failed six months later, and the couple returned to England, where he contributed regularly to *Fraser's Magazine*, as well as to other periodicals. A daughter, the novelist Anne Thackeray Ritchie, was born in 1837, but after the birth of a third child in 1840, Isabella had a mental breakdown from which she never recovered. In a variety of forms and under several pseudonyms (of which Fitzboodle and Titmarsh were the most famous), Thackeray now worked towards the novel of realism told with irony that became his hallmark, of which *The Luck of Barry Lyndon*, serialised in 1844, was the first. He also wrote *The Snobs of England* (1846–7) and a collection of parodies, *Punch's Prize Novelists* (1847). *Vanity Fair: a Novel without a Hero* (1847–8) was published in *Punch* in 20 monthly parts under his own name and with his own illustrations, and is especially notable for its time not only for its broad scope, but also for the depth and consistency of the characterisation, qualities which have enabled it to endure as much as any novel by his friend *Dickens, whose success he was so anxious to emulate. *The History of Pendennis* (1849–50) concentrates on a single character from feckless youth to maturity.

In 1850 Thackeray received a generous offer from Charlotte *Brontë's publisher for his next novel. *The History of Henry Esmond* (1852) is a dramatic historical study of a young man whose melancholy and misfortune were reflected in an unhappy incident in the author's own life, when in 1851 he was warned off the sympathetic and talented Jane Brookfield by her husband. *The English Humourists of the Eighteenth Century* (1852) and *The Four Georges* (1860) were based on lectures he gave in the USA in 1852–3 and 1855–6. Between visits he wrote *The Newcomes* (serialised 1853–5), a family saga. His last major novel, *The Virginians* (1857–9), is set in England and America. In 1860 he became the first editor of *Cornhill Magazine*, in which appeared his two further novels and a fragment of *Denis Duval*, left unfinished on his sudden death from a spasm. He imbued the English novel with a wider vision than it had had before, piecing together the action from the point of view of several characters. See Gordon N. Ray, *Thackeray: the Uses of Adversity*, 1955, and *Thackeray: the Age of Wisdom*, 1958 (biography); John Carey, *Thackeray: Prodigal Genius*, new edn 1980.

**Thomas, Dylan** (1914–53), Welsh poet and prose writer, was born in Swansea, only son of the English master at Swansea Grammar School, where he was educated. He was an undistinguished scholar, except in English, but he edited and contributed to the school magazine with some flair. For a year after leaving school in 1931 he worked as a reporter for the *South Wales Daily Post*. Then he became a professional poet. His first poem in the national press was published in 1933 by the *Sunday Referee*, which then awarded him its major literary prize and financed the publication of his first book, *18 Poems* (1934), in which the authentic voice of the frustrated teenager speaks out. In November 1934 he moved to London, returning periodically to Swansea, where he completed *Twenty-Five Poems* (1936), which are more derivative and on the whole more obscure, but 'This bread I break...' and the sequence of ten poems of which the first begins 'Altar-wise by owl-light...' express the Christian feeling which imbues much of his subsequent verse. In 1937 he married Caitlin, daughter of the Irish writer Francis MacNamara (1884–1916), and settled in Laugharne on the Carmarthenshire coast. He was unfit for service in World War II, which he spent in Wales, visiting London to see friends, publishers, and the BBC. *Portrait of the Artist as a Young Dog* (1940) is a series of humorous and compassionate autobiographical prose sketches. *Deaths and Entrances* (1946), his most considerable volume of poetry, contained several poems of a celebratory, nostalgic nature which were more accessible to the general reader than much of his earlier verse and of immediate popular appeal: such were 'Poem in October' ('It was my thirtieth year to heaven...'), 'Poem on His Birthday' ('In the mustardseed sun...'), 'Fern Hill' ('Now as I was young and easy under the apple boughs...'), and 'In the White Giant's Thigh' ('Through throats where many rivers meet, the curlews cry...').

After several nomadic post-war years, the family returned to Laugharne. He was now a much sought-after broadcaster, some of whose radio scripts are preserved in *Quite Early One Morning* (1955), the title-piece of which is the seed of *Under Milk Wood*. In 1950 he made the first of four lecture tours in the USA to earn money — as an earner he was improvident rather than unsuccessful. *Collected Poems* (1952) contained just 89 that he wished at that time to keep, including one of the last poems he wrote, 'Do Not Go Gentle into that Good Night', inspired by the tragic spectacle of his father's lingering death. *Under Milk Wood: a Play for Voices*, a topographical mood poem in prose with songs in verse, was first heard at the Young Men's Hebrew Association in New York in May 1953, with the poet reading First Voice and Rev. Eli Jenkins. He died of alcohol poisoning on a return visit later that year. The first broadcast of *Under Milk Wood* was made by the BBC on 25 January 1954. Though Thomas did not know the Welsh language, his poetic music and verbal extravagance are essentially Welsh, and at his best he is a poet of great feeling and originality. See *The Poems*, ed. Daniel Jones, new edn 1982; Paul Ferris, *Dylan Thomas: a Biography*, rev. edn 1985; Ralph N. Maud, *Entrances to Dylan Thomas's Poetry*, 1964.

**Thomas, Edward** (1878–1917), poet and prose writer, was born in Lambeth, London, and educated at St Paul's School and Lincoln College, Oxford. He married while still an undergraduate, and having no inclination towards a permanent job, and with a book *The Woodland Life* (1897) already written, he became a professional author. Between 1902 and 1915 he published 25 books, all prose — essays, travel and topography, literary criticism (including a study of *Swinburne), biography, myths and legends, and a novel, *The Happy-go-Lucky Morgans* (1913). Many are simply literary hack-work, but some, such as *The Heart of England* (1906) and *The Icknield Way* (1913), contain the germs and some of the main themes of his verse, which he did not begin to compose until he was 36, and then only at the express encouragement of the American poet Robert Frost (1874–1963). Even so, he chose to write poems under the pseudonym of Edward Eastway, and he only lived to see in print those privately published in *Six Poems* (1916). He was commissioned in the Artists' Rifles in World War I, and was killed in the battle of Arras. The war features only obliquely in his poems, which are particularly concerned with the English countryside and often have a wry, melancholic taste, with recurrent images of search and self-analysis. See *The Collected Poems of Edward Thomas*, ed. R. George Thomas, new edn 1981; R. George Thomas, *Edward Thomas: a Portrait*, new edn 1989; Andrew Motion, *The Poetry of Edward Thomas*, 1980.

**Thomas, R(onald) S(tuart)** (*b*.1913), Welsh poet and critic, was born in Cardiff and educated in Holyhead and at University College, Bangor, followed by a period of training for the ministry at St Michael's College, Llandaff. He was ordained in 1936 and served the Church of Wales as rector or vicar of country parishes until his retirement in 1978. He learned Welsh early on in his career in order to fulfil his vocation properly, and was impressed in the 1940s by the example of *MacDiarmid and others in attempting to recapture the true essence of Scottish poetry. The expression of Welsh literary nationalism in his first two (privately published) volumes of verse gave way in the 1950s to the themes of Welsh pastoral care of both flocks and souls, and latterly to poems about the nature of poetry itself, such as 'Poetry for Supper', in which he also employs one of his favourite motifs, the persona (often a peasant farmer) through whom he speaks to the reader or argues the opposite poles of a case. In spite of the graphic bleakness of his landscapes and the perfectly characterised indifference of so many of his parishoners, there are statements, and indeed whole poems, of redemption, compassion, and hope. He was awarded the Queen's Gold Medal for Poetry in 1964, and has edited *The Batsford Book of Country Verse* (1961), *The Penguin Book of Religious Verse* (1963), and selections of *Herbert, Edward *Thomas, and *Wordsworth. See *Selected Poems 1946–1968*, new edn 1986; *Later Poems 1972–1982*, new edn 1984; J. P. Ward, *The Poetry of R. S. Thomas*, 1987.

**Thompson, Francis** (1859–1907), poet and critic, was born in Preston, son of a doctor, brought up in the Catholic faith, and educated at Ushaw College and, at his father's wish, as a medical student at Owens College, Manchester. After failing his examinations several times, he left home in 1885 to try and earn a living in London as a writer — his mother's gift of *De Quincey's *Confessions of an English Opium Eater* may have influenced his decision and encouraged his addiction to opium. After two years living homeless in the streets, he was taken up by Wilfrid Meynell (1852–1948), to whose *Merry England* he had submitted two poems and an article on scraps of paper. Meynell and his wife cared for him, arranged his 'drying out' periods at a Welsh monastery, and organised his literary career. Three volumes of his poetry were published in his lifetime: *Poems* (1893), *Sister-Songs* (1895), *New Poems* (1897). In his mystical vision and symbolism, combined with ornate style and poetic diction, Thompson looks back to the Metaphysical poets. This is particularly true of his greatest poem, 'The Hound of Heaven', which represents the conflict between human and divine love in terms of Catholic dogma. He also wrote poems of lyrical simplicity, including 'Cheated Elsie', the sequence 'A Narrow Vessel', and 'At Lord's', the finest poem about cricket. His reviews are collected in *Literary Criticisms of Francis Thompson*, ed. T. L. Connolly, 1948. See Brigid M. Boardman, *'Between Heaven and Charing Cross': the Life of Francis Thompson*, 1948.

**Thomson, James** (1700–48), Scottish poet, was born in Ednam, Roxburghshire, son of a minister who died in 1716 while exorcising a ghost, and was educated in Jedburgh and at Edinburgh University, which he left for London after his prose exercises had been adversely criticised. He never returned to Scotland. His long, blank-verse poems, *Winter* (1726), *Summer* (1727), and *Spring* (1728), were collected with *Autumn* in *The Seasons* (1730), to which he added a Deistic 'Hymn on the Seasons' — he revised and enlarged them over the next 16 years. *The Seasons* is less a forerunner of the Romantics than a trendsetter in nature poetry, and Thomson's observation of and obvious delight in the minutiae of the natural world look back to earlier Scottish tradition. His other major work, *The Castle of Indolence: an Allegorical Poem. Written in Imitation of Spenser* (1748), contains more poetic invention than its sub-title would suggest. Among shorter pieces, 'Hymn on Solitude' and 'To the Memory of Sir Isaac Newton' are notable. He also wrote five moderate stage tragedies, and with David Malloch (*c*.1705–65) *The Masque of Alfred* (1740), in which is the poem, and the words of the song, 'Rule Britannia'. His literary activities earned him the sinecures of Secretary of Briefs in the Court of Chancery 1732–7 and Secretary-General of the Leeward Islands 1744–6, and a pension from the Prince of Wales. He died at his home in Richmond after catching a chill on the Thames. See Imogene B. Walker, *James Thomson: a Critical Study*, 1950.

**Tolkien, J(ohn) R(onald) R(euel)** (1892–1973), novelist, philologist, and literary scholar, was born in Bloemfontein, Orange Free State. He was then brought to England, but was orphaned when he was twelve and put in the care of a Catholic priest, and educated at King Edward's School, Birmingham, and Exeter College, Oxford. After serving in World War I, in which he contracted 'trench fever', he worked on the *New English Dictionary*, was Reader in English Language at Leeds University 1920–5, then Professor of Anglo-Saxon 1925–45 and of English Language and Literature 1945–59 at Oxford. From 1917 until his death he worked on a series of tales of 'Middle-Earth' through which he sought to express his theological and philosophical beliefs, posthumously collected into *The Silmarillion*, ed. Christopher Tolkien (1977). He drew on this imaginative storehouse for a children's fantasy, *The Hobbit* (1937). The 'sequel' for which the publisher then asked was not published for nearly twenty years, during which it had grown into the richly-original adventure saga of *The Lord of the Rings*, comprising *The Fellowship of the Ring* (1954), *The Two Towers* (1954), and *The Return of the King* (1955), for which he created a complete mythology. His contributions to literary scholarship are best illustrated by his essays on Beowulf, Gawain, and fairy stories in *The Monsters and the Critics, and Other Essays*, ed. Christopher Tolkien, 1983. He was made CBE in 1972. See Humphrey Carpenter, *J. R. R. Tolkien: a Biography*, 1977.

**Tourneur, Cyril** (*c*.1575–1626), poet and dramatist, was secretary to Sir Francis Vere, commander in the Netherlands in the Spanish wars, and may well have been the author of 'A Funerall Poeme Upon the Death of the Most Worthy and True Soldier Sir Francis Vere' (1609). He certainly wrote 'The Transformed Metamorphosis' (1600), a satirical allegory whose meaning is obscure, and *The Atheist's Tragedy* (printed 1611), a revenge drama with ghoulish goings-on in a graveyard and an unusual dénouement when D'Amville, the villain, acting the executioner, unwittingly brains himself with the axe. The authorship of *The Revenger's Tragedy* (1607) has never categorically been established, and because it is a better-constructed and more poetic play, it has been thought unlikely to be by the same hand as the apparently later *The Atheist's Tragedy*, though a number of critics have still assigned it to Tourneur. The chief character, Vindice, is concerned not just to avenge the poisoning of his fiancée by the Duke, but to eradicate the Duke's court and the corruption it stands for, and is himself finally punished for taking too far the practical expression of his moral passion. In 1625 Tourneur was secretary to Viscount Wimbledon's Council of War during the ill-fated expedition to seize Spanish treasure ships off Cadiz. The fleet turned back, and he was one of the sick men put ashore at Kinsale, Ireland, where he died. See *The Works of Cyril Tourneur*, ed. Allardyce Nicoll, 1930; and in T. S. Eliot, *Elizabethan Dramatists*, 1963.

**Traherne, Thomas** (1637–74), poet and prose writer, was born in Herefordshire, son of a shoemaker, brought up by his father's brother (who was twice mayor of Hereford), and educated at Brasenose College, Oxford. He was parish priest of Credenhill from 1661 to 1669, when he became chaplain to Sir Orlando Bridgeman, Keeper of the Seals. The only work published during his lifetime was *Roman Forgeries* (1673), a study of the authenticity of certain documents relating to Catholicism, though *Christian Ethicks* (1675) was probably ready for printing. His poems, many prepared for press by his brother Philip, did not come to light until 1896, when an unsigned manuscript book was discovered on a London bookstall. Subsequent research revealed an unfinished prose work, *Centuries of Meditations*, a series of spiritual guidelines which offer parallels with childhood. The innocence and experience of childhood runs through his verse, as in 'Wonder', 'My Spirit', 'Dreams', 'Poverty', and 'Shadows in the Water', which perfectly captures a child's fascination with and puzzlement at the 'other world' of the reflections. This recall of a child's-eye view of his surroundings and of God, as well as the variety of his stanza forms, give Traherne's verse an unusual charm which outweighs his limited range, often abstract vocabulary, and the inconclusive endings of so many of his poems. See *Centuries, Poems and Thanksgivings*, ed. H. M. Margoliouth, 1958; K. W. Salter, *Thomas Traherne, Mystic and Poet*, 1964.

**Treece, Henry** (1911–66), poet, historical novelist, children's writer, and critic, was born in Wednesbury, Staffordshire, and educated at Wednesbury High School and Birmingham University, where he was university boxing captain. Except for war service in the RAF, he was from 1938 until his death Senior English Teacher at Barton-on-Humber Grammar School. With the Scottish poet J. F. Hendry (1912–86) he founded in the 1930s the New Apocalypse, a literary movement concerned more with poetry which explored relationships with life and with the real world than it was with surrealism, but which also served as a fraternity of like-minded young poets, most of them living outside London, who welcomed this chance to meet and correspond with each other. Dylan *Thomas was drawn into this group, and Treece's *Dylan Thomas: Dog among the Fairies* (1949, rev edn 1956) was the first critical study of him. Treece published six volumes of his own verse, the last of which was *The Exiles* (1952). He now embarked on a new literary career as a historical novelist. His themes are the crossroads of history and the conflicts of cultures, and he is at his best when writing about the Dark Ages and more ancient times, as in *The Dark Island* (1952), *The Golden Strangers* (1956), and *Electra* (1963). He applied the same qualities and objectives to his books for children, by whom his Viking novels in particular are still widely read. See *How I See Apocalypse*, 1946; Margery Fisher, *Henry Treece*, 1969 (mainly on his children's books).

**Trollope, Anthony** (1815–82), novelist and short story writer, was born in London, son of an improvident and irascible barrister, and educated at Harrow, Winchester College, and then Harrow again when the family fortunes began to fail. His mother Frances, née Milton (1780–1863), returning from America after the collapse of one of her husband's madder financial schemes, determined to support the family by writing, and produced *Domestic Manners of the Americans* (1832) and many more novels and travel books. When her husband was declared bankrupt in 1834 she took the family to Belgium and got for the 19-year-old Trollope a position as clerk with the Post Office in London. After seven unhappy years he volunteered for a transfer to Ireland, where he became a good administrator, took up hunting, married an English girl, and began to write. *The MacDermots of Ballycloran* (1847) was followed by a second Irish novel, and then *La Vendée: an Historical Romance* (1850). All failed. From 1851 to 1853 he was charged with reorganising postal services in south-west England and the Channel Isles, in the course of which he invented the pillar-box, and in 1854 he was appointed Surveyor of Mail Coaches. He resigned in 1867, having made several foreign tours on business, and become a leading literary figure. He edited *St Paul's Magazine* 1867–70, and in 1868, as a Liberal, came bottom in the poll for the parliamentary constituency of Beverley, though the election was later declared invalid. According to his *Autobiography* (1883), by 1879 he had earned £68,959 17s 6d from his books. He settled in a Hampshire village in 1880, and died after a seizure which struck him while laughing at a book during a family dinner-party in London.

Trollope was a prolific but subtle writer. His fourth novel, *The Warden* (1855), was his first success and became the first of the 'Barsetshire' sequence, the others being *Barchester Towers* (1857), *Doctor Thorne* (1858), *Framley Parsonage* (1861), *The Small House at Allington* (1864), and *The Last Chronicle of Barset* (1867). Set in an imaginary county in the west country, they deal with the interplay between mainly ecclesiastical figures and with domestic events and issues. His strength is the delineation and development of character, which he employs with equal effect in the 'Palliser' series of novels of politicians and aristocrats, *Can You Forgive Her?* (1864–5), *Phineas Finn, the Irish Member* (1869), *The Eustace Diamonds* (1873), *Phineas Redux* (1874), *The Prime Minister* (1876), and *The Duke's Children* (1880). Of his many other novels, the love-tangled *The Claverings* (1867) and the satirical *The Way We Live Now* (1875) are of most interest today. He published five volumes of short stories, many of which are set in foreign parts, several books on his travels, and lives of *Thackeray (1879), Cicero (1880), and Lord Palmerston (1882). See James Pope-Hennessy, *Anthony Trollope*, new edn 1986 (biography); Richard Mullan, *Anthony Trollope: a Victorian Life*, 1989; Arthur Pollard, *Anthony Trollope*, 1978 (critical study).

**Vanbrugh,** (Sir) **John** (1664–1726), dramatist and architect, was born in London, son of a sugar-baker and grandson of Gillis Van Brugg, a refugee Flemish merchant, and was probably educated at Chester Grammar School. He had some architectural training in France between 1683 and 1685, when he was commissioned in the Earl of Huntingdon's regiment, served in France and was captured and imprisoned for two years, after which he resumed his military career. Two of his earliest plays, *The*

*Relapse: or Virtue in Danger* (1697) and *The Provok'd Wife* (1697), are also his most original, and though the former contains within two plots the standard devices of Restoration comedy — temptation, seduction, impersonation, and reconciliation — the latter is of one piece and has a genuinely, and at the end still unresolved, unhappy marriage motivating the plot. More than other writers of his time, he came to rely on the development of comic situations rather than dialogue or the expression of fanciful humours, as in *The Country House* (1704), adapted from a play by the French dramatist Florent Carton Dancourt (1661–1725). *The Provok'd Husband* was left unfinished and was completed by Colley Cibber (1671–1757). Vanbrugh was appointed Comptroller of the Royal Works in 1702, and was knighted in 1714. He designed Castle Howard and Blenheim Palace, the cost of which so appalled the Duchess of Marlborough that at one point she refused to pay the suppliers' bills. See Laurence Whistler, *Vanbrugh: Architect and Dramatist*, 1938.

**Vaughan, Henry** (1622–95), Welsh poet (he called himself a 'Silurist', i.e. man of South Wales), cousin of *Aubrey, was born in Llansaintfraed, Breconshire, and with his twin brother Thomas (*d.*1666) was educated by a local rector and at Jesus College, Oxford, after which he studied law and then possibly medicine. They both fought for the royalists in the Civil War, and were captured and imprisoned. Afterwards, Henry practised as a physician at Newton-by-Usk; Thomas studied and wrote treatises on magic and mysticism. Henry's first book, *Poems, with the Tenth Satyre of Juvenal Englished* (1646), is in the secular mode of the tavern poets, notably *Donne and *Jonson, and the form is repeated in *Olor Iscanus* [The Swan of Usk]: *Select Poems and Translations* (1651), which was published without his consent. For in the meantime, following the inspiration of *Herbert, he had turned to religious poetry, published in *Silex Scintillans* [The Sparks from the Flint]: *Sacred Poems and Private Ejaculations* (1650, enlarged edition 1655). The best of these poems, which include 'The Retreat', 'Peace' ('My Soul, there is a country...'), 'The World' ('I saw eternity the other night...'), and 'Man', sparkle with brilliant lines, and have a mystical depth and an understanding of the natural world. *The Mount of Olives: or Solitary Devotions* (1652) comprises meditations in prose. See *Complete Poems*, ed. Alan Rudrum, 1976; F. E. Hutchinson, *Henry Vaughan: a Life and an Interpretation*, 1947.

**Walpole, Horace** (or **Horatio**) (1717–97), novelist and prose writer, was born in London, youngest son by eleven years of Sir Robert Walpole (Prime Minister 1721–42) and his first wife, and was educated at Eton and King's College, Cambridge, and then toured Europe for two years with *Gray. He was a Member of Parliament 1741–67. In 1748 he bought a house on the Thames in Twickenham, which he refashioned inside and out into a Gothic castle and named Strawberry Hill. Here he established a private press, whose first product was Gray's *Odes* (1757), followed by Walpole's own gossipy compilation, *A Catalogue of the Royal and Noble Authors of England* (1758). He also printed his *Anecdotes of Painting in England* (1762–71), a pioneer among histories of English art. In 1764 he was moved by the lonely and romantic atmosphere of his house to write *The Castle of Otranto* (1765), initially published anonymously as a translation of an Italian book printed in 1529. This, the first Gothic novel, is full of terrible sights and sounds, with one or more tremendous climaxes in every chapter. Walpole's memoirs were at his request kept sealed for 20 years after his death, but it is his voluminous correspondence, largely written for publication, which best reveals him and his times. On the death of his nephew in 1791, he became 4th Earl of Orford. He never married. See *Letters*, ed. W. S. Lewis, 1951 (a selection: the full correspondence was published in 48 volumes, 1937–83); R. W. Ketton-Cremer, *Horace Walpole: a Biography*, 3rd edn 1964.

**Walton, Isaak** (1593–1683), prose writer and biographer, was born in Stafford and apprenticed to a London ironmonger, being made a freeman of the Ironmongers' Company in 1618. As a member of *Donne's congregation at St Dunstan's, he got to know the poet and, through him, Sir Henry Wotton (1568–1639), Provost of Eton and a poet in his own right. On Donne's death in 1631, Wotton undertook to write his biography, but he died without making much progress. Walton, who had acted as his researcher, was appalled at the thought of the great 1640 edition of Donne's sermons lacking a biographical introduction, and wrote it himself — it was also published separately in an enlarged version as *The Life and Death of Dr Donne* (1658). His simple piety and his lucid, unadorned prose made such an appeal that he was prevailed upon to write lives of Wotton (1651), *Hooker (1665), and *Herbert (1670). In the meantime, probably influenced by the defeat at Marston Moor of the royalists, to whom he was wholly sympathetic, he had in 1644 taken early retirement, to indulge in his hobby of coarse fishing. His best-known work, *The Compleat Angler, or the Contemplative Man's Recreation* (1653), a leisurely guide, as well as a literary experience, in the form of a dialogue interspersed with verse, anecdotes, and folklore, was reissued in 1676 as *The Universal Angler*, with a section on fly-fishing by his friend Charles Cotton (1630–87). See Margaret Bottral, *Izaak Walton*, 1968.

**Watkins, Vernon** (1906–67), Welsh poet, was born in Maesteg, of Welsh-speaking parents, and educated at Repton School and Magdalene College, Cambridge. Apart from the war years, when he served in the RAF, he worked as a bank clerk in Swansea from 1925 to 1965. The poetry of *Yeats was a guiding influence, as was the personal encouragement of Dylan *Thomas — see *Dylan Thomas: Letters to Vernon Watkins* (1957).

His first volume of verse, *Ballad of the Mari Lwyd and Other Poems* (1941), contained many simple evocations of Welsh childhood. In eight further significant collections, he developed his vision of the nature of time (images of the sea, fountains, and trees recur) and artistic inspiration (which he saw as a religious gift), particularly in the poems in which he uses the persona of the Welsh mythical bard Taliesin. Watkins called himself 'a Welsh poet writing in English', using what he regarded as the rich satisfaction of the language in a way that frequently resounds with musical rhythms and Welsh intonations, which are especially evident in his ballads. His translations, notably from the German of Heinrich Heine (1797–1856) and Friedrich Hölderlin (1770–1843), were for him a natural expression of his poetic craft, and were collected in *Selected Verse Translations, with an Essay on the Translation of Poetry*, ed. Ruth Pryor (1977). See *Collected Poems*, 1986; *Vernon Watkins 1906–67*, ed. Leslie Norris, 1970 (essays and tributes by various hands).

**Waugh, Evelyn** (1903–66), novelist, biographer, journalist, and travel writer, was born in Hampstead, London, younger brother of the novelist Alec Waugh (1898–1981), and educated at Lancing College and Hertford College, Oxford. He taught in three private schools in as many years before being employed as a journalist in 1927. His first book, *Rossetti: His Life and Works* (1928), in which he shows his intuitive sense for the dramatic moment, was followed by the novel *Decline and Fall* (1928), which draws on his experiences at Oxford and after, and was an immediate success for its ironic, often bitter, treatment of quite serious matters. In *Vile Bodies* (1930), he satirises the contemporary manners of young people in a recognisable but equally fantasised setting. A cruise in 1929 was the basis of *Labels: a Mediterranean Journal* (1930), while attendance at the coronation of Haile Selassie gave him the material for *Remote People* (1931) and the background of a further novel, *Black Mischief* (1932). Similarly, a tough safari produced *Ninety-Two Days: the Account of a Tropical Journey through British Guiana and Part of Brazil* (1934) and the tropical sequences for *A Handful of Dust* (1934); and an assignment to cover the Italian–Abyssinian war for the *Daily Mail* resulted in *Waugh in Abyssinia* (1936) and *Scoop: a Novel about Journalists* (1938). He had become a Catholic in 1930, and in 1937, his first marriage having been annulled, he married Laura Herbert. He saw active service in Dakar and Crete in 1940–1, and finished World War II as a member of the British Military Mission in Yugoslavia. *Brideshead Revisited: the Sacred and Profane Memories of Captain Charles Ryder* (1945) is both his most substantial novel and the first in which the characters are drawn as real people rather than figures of fun or pity. *The Loved One: an Anglo-American Tragedy* (1948) is an excursion into the macabre. *Men at Arms* (1952), *Officers and Gentlemen* (1955), and *Unconditional Surrender* (1961), republished together as *Sword of Honour* (1965), draw heavily on his wartime experiences as the background to dark military and social satire.

*The Ordeal of Gilbert Pinfold* (1957) is less a novel than a surrealist narrative, in which its disturbed hero, who bears an uncanny resemblance to the author, comes through self-revelatory hallucinations to comparative peace of mind. Even at his most disturbing, Waugh is essentially a comic writer, trying to come to terms with the contradictions he found in life. And throughout his novels the Catholic Church often appears symbolically as an oasis in prevailing chaos. Other biographies are *Edmund Campion: Jesuit and Martyr* (1935) and *Ronald Knox* (1959). *Evelyn Waugh: a Little Order* (1977), ed. Donat Gallagher, is a collection of his articles and essays. See *A Little Learning*, new edn 1983 (early autobiography); *The Diaries of Evelyn Waugh*, ed. Michael Davie, 1976; Christopher Sykes, *Evelyn Waugh: a Biography*, rev. edn 1977; Jacqueline McDonnell, *Evelyn Waugh*, 1988 (critical study).

**Webster, John** (*c.*1580–1638), dramatist, is said to have been by virtue of his birth a freeman of the Merchant Taylors' Company, but the first reference proper to him is in 1602, as a playwright for the Admiral's Men. After working with *Dekker, *Heywood, and others on some largely lost plays, he surfaces as Dekker's collaborator in two city comedies for the boy actors of St Paul's, *West-Ward Hoe* and *North-Ward Hoe* (both published 1607). *The White Devil — The White Divel, or the Tragedy of Paulo Giordano Ursini, Duke of Brachiano, with the Life, and Death, of Vittoria Corombona, the Famous Venetian Curtizan* (1612) — is based on events some thirty years earlier, and after an arresting opening moves through scenes of horror, gore, and ghostly appearances to its improbable end, enlivened by some splendid lines of poetry. *The Duchess of Malfi — published as *The Tragedy of the Dutchesse of Malfy* (1623) — was first performed in 1614, and is based on an English translation of a story of Matteo Bandello (*c.*1490–1561). Less well-constructed than *The White Devil*, and even more unlikely, it nevertheless has passages of profound theatre, notably the death of the Duchess which occupies Act IV, and lines whose effect is heightened by irregular metre, such as 'I am the Duchess of Malfi still' and 'Cover her face; mine eyes dazzle; she died young'. In his later plays he neither attempted nor achieved anything like this. See Clifford Leech, *Webster: a Critical Study*, new edn 1982.

**Wells, H(erbert) G(eorge)** (1866–1946), novelist and historian, was born in Bromley, Kent, son of a shopkeeper (and professional cricketer) and a lady's maid, and educated at Bromley Academy, which he left at 14 to become a draper's assistant, and later, at his own initiative, at the Normal School of Science of London University. He published two scientific textbooks in 1893, and in 1894 left his wife of three years and eloped with a student, whom he subsequently married. His first novel, *The Time*

*Machine: an Invention* (1895), is a fantasy of the future, whereas *The Island of Doctor Moreau* (1896), *The Invisible Man* (1897), and *The War of the Worlds* (1898) equate more to the modern genre of science fiction, with the addition of some implied social comment. At the same time he was writing short stories with a variety of themes and moods — see *The Short Stories* (1927) and *Selected Short Stories* (1958). The social milieu of his youth is reflected in the light novels *Love and Mr Lewisham* (1900), *Kipps: the Story of a Simple Soul* (1905), and *The History of Mr Polly* (1910). *Tono-Bungay* (1909) exposes the brittleness of society, exemplified also by the accusation of 'immorality' levelled at *Ann Veronica: a Modern Love Story* (1909), about an early twentieth-century feminist. Wells's vision and popular appeal are evident also in *The Outline of History: Being a Plain History of Life and Mankind* (1919–20). Among his many love affairs was one with the novelist, Rebecca West (1892–1983). See *Experiment in Autobiography*, 2 vols new edn 1984; Norman and Jeanne MacKenzie, *The Time Traveller: the Life of H. G. Wells*, rev. edn 1987.

**Wesker, Arnold** (*b.*1932), dramatist and short story writer, was born in London's East End of Jewish immigrant parents. After National Service in the RAF, he did many different jobs before having three linked plays performed in Coventry — *Chicken Soup with Barley* (1959), *Roots* (1959), and *I'm Talking about Jerusalem* (1960) — which were staged in London in 1960 as the Wesker Trilogy. There are political undertones in them as ordinary families face the realities of life in post-war Britain and gravitate between extremes of hope and despair. The main characters are from contrasting working-class backgrounds (metropolitan Jewish and rural Norfolk), and the dialogue captures exactly the appropriate accents and dialects. *The Kitchen* (1959), written originally for television, is a play of conflicts set in a restaurant kitchen which, to Wesker, also represents the world. In *Chips with Everything* (1962) confrontations between National Servicemen and regular RAF officers are used as a microcosm of what he saw as growing political control over freedom of thought. Later plays have won less recognition but include *The Merchant* (1977), in which *Shakespeare's *The Merchant of Venice* is re-presented as an exercise in racial integration. In 1960 Wesker's commitment saw the establishment of Centre 42, which aimed during its short life to exploit trades union support for the arts. Collections of short stories include *Love Letters on Blue Paper* (1974), the title story of which was published as a play in 1978. See Glenda Leeming, *Wesker the Playwright*, 1982.

**Wilde, Oscar** (1854–1900), Irish dramatist, novelist, critic, and poet, was born in Dublin, younger son of a surgeon, Sir William Wilde, and Jane, née Elgee (1826–96), who ran a literary salon and wrote revolutionary verse under the name of 'Speranza'. He was educated at Portora Royal

School, Trinity College, Dublin, and Magdalen College, Oxford, where he won the Newdigate Prize for poetry with *Ravenna* (1878), came under the artistic influence of *Ruskin and Walter Pater (1839–94), and got a first in Greats, having in the meantime toured Italy and Greece. He burst into London society, to which he preached the doctrine of aestheticism with wit and conversational skill. *Poems* (1881) is mainly derivative, but a few later poems stand out, for instance 'The Harlot's House', 'On the Sale by Auction of Keats' Love Letters', and 'Symphony in Yellow'. After a lecture-tour of the USA in 1882, he married Constance Lloyd, by whom he had two sons. He edited *Woman's World*, and wrote *The Happy Prince and Other Tales* (1888), a collection of witty and compassionate fairy stories for children (and their parents), and critical essays of which 'The Decay of Lying' (1889) and 'The Critic as Artist' (1890) are notable. More fiction followed in 1891, *Lord Arthur Savile's Crime and Other Stories* and *The Picture of Dorian Gray*, his only novel, a study of decadence and destruction. His early works for the theatre were sombre — *Vera, or the Nihilists* (produced in the USA 1882), a verse tragedy *The Duchess of Padua* (published 1891), and the uncomfortable *Salomé* (written in French in 1891, published 1893, performed in Paris 1896, but banned in England until 1905; English translation by Lord Alfred Douglas published 1894). Now came a string of successful social comedies. *Lady Windermere's Fan* (produced 1892, published 1893), *A Woman of No Importance* (1893/1894), and *An Ideal Husband* (1895/1899), are beneath their veneer of wit concerned with human nature and tinged with sentiment. *The Importance of Being Earnest* (1895/1899), however, continues to delight as a superb comedy of manners whose lightness of style, brilliant dialogue, and skilled construction carry along a series of absurd paradoxes.

In 1895 a libel action against the Marquis of Queensberry — father of Lord Alfred Douglas (1870–1945) — who had accused him of being a practising homosexual, failed. Wilde was then himself arrested, tried, and sentenced to two years' hard labour. In prison he wrote *De Profundis* (not published in full until 1949), a prose apologia for his conduct. His poetic reputation largely rests on *The Ballad of Reading Gaol* (1898), an understandably overwrought but moving account of prison experience. Shunned by society, he left England after his release, and lived wretchedly on the Continent as Sebastian Melmoth for three years until his death in Paris, having lost his ability to write. See *Complete Works*, 1983; Richard Ellmann, *Oscar Wilde*, new edn 1988 (biography); Christopher S. Nassaar, *Into the Demon Universe: a Literary Exploration of Oscar Wilde*, 1974.

**Wilson,** (Sir) **Angus** (*b.*1913), novelist, short story writer, and critic, was born in Bexhill, Sussex, and educated at Westminster School and Merton College, Oxford. He worked in the Foreign Office during World

War II, and was Deputy Superintendent of the Reading Room, British Museum 1949–55, and Professor of English Literature, University of East Anglia 1966–78. His first two books were *The Wrong Set and Other Stories* (1949) and *Such Darling Dodos and Other Stories* (1950), in which he often lets a realistic situation deliberately verge into farce or a bizarre act of violence. In that they are usually episodic, he carried over the short story technique to his novels, the first three of which, *Hemlock and After* (1952), *Anglo-Saxon Attitudes* (1956), and *The Middle Age of Mrs Eliot* (1958), are otherwise traditional in form. His analysis of character is deft and satirical, and done with a blend of cruelty and compassion, while he is often concerned with laying bare the private guilt behind the public appearance. In *The Old Men at the Zoo* (1961), he projects into the future the moral predicament of a public servant in a defeated society. *Late Call* (1964), *No Laughing Matter* (1967), and *Setting the World on Fire* (1980) are more concerned with family relationships and attitudes. His critical works include *Diversity and Depth in Fiction: Selected Critical Writings* (1983) and *The Wild Garden: or, Speaking of Writing* (1963), in which he describes the background to his fiction. He was knighted in 1980. See *Collected Stories*, new edn 1989; Jay Halio, *Angus Wilson,* 1964.

**Wodehouse,** (Sir) **P(elham) G(renville)** (1881–1975), novelist, short story writer, and dramatist, was born in Guildford, Surrey, and educated at Dulwich College. He spent two years in Hong Kong as a bank clerk, which he gave up for journalism, while at the same time writing boys' school stories and novels. He went to the USA in 1910 and settled there permanently after World War II, during which he was interned in Europe and while in German hands agreed to broadcast to America, causing much offence in Britain. He became an American citizen in 1955, his final rehabilitation in official British circles coming with his knighthood in 1975. While unfairly overshadowed by his ability to amuse and entertain, his skill at constructing plots, creating and sustaining characters (and a complete world in which to manipulate them), and producing visual and verbal effects with astonishing economy of language and delightful injections of literary and classical allusions, has never been in doubt. The accusation of repeating himself in his novels can be offset against the subtlety with which he varies the pace and the situations in his many short stories, and though his characters people a semi-mythical upper crust of society, the differences between the American and British ethos are lovingly recorded and satirised. The inane Bertie Wooster and the imperturbable Jeeves, and many of their dicta, have passed into English literary tradition. Only marginally less memorable, however, are Ukridge and Psmith, Aunt Agatha and Lord Emsworth, and the positive parade of rich characters who hack, bludgeon, finesse, or cleave, as the case may be, their way round the course in his inimitable golfing stories.

Wodehouse also wrote, on his own account and with others, over thirty plays and musical comedies. See *Over Seventy: an Autobiography with Digressions,* 1957; Joseph Connolly, *P. G. Wodehouse,* 1987 (critical biography); R. B. D. French, *P. G. Wodehouse,* 1966 (critical study).

**Woolf, Virginia** (1882–1941), novelist and critic, was born in London, third child of Sir Leslie Stephen (1832–1904), editor of the *Dictionary of National Biography,* and his second wife. She was educated at home by her parents and tutors. On her father's death (her mother had died in 1895), she, her elder sister Vanessa (Bell), and her two brothers, set up house in Gordon Square WC1, which became the centre of the Bloomsbury Group, an informal association of intellectuals wishing to free art and society from Victorian restrictions. In 1905 she began to contribute reviews and articles to *The Times Literary Supplement* and other journals, while teaching evening classes of working men and women at Morley College. She married Leonard Woolf (1880–1969), novelist and journalist, in 1912. They moved into Hogarth House, Richmond, in 1915, the year of her most violent recurrence of mental instability and of the publication of her first novel, *The Voyage Out,* conventional in pattern, which she had written between 1906 and 1913. In 1917 the couple bought a hand press on which they printed, as the first publication of the Hogarth Press, *Two Stories,* 'The Mark on the Wall' by Virginia and 'Three Jews' by Leonard. *Night and Day* (1919), written mainly as a recuperative exercise, was deliberately a less intense novel than her first. *Jacob's Room* (1922), in which she first demonstrated her distinctive impressionistic technique, was published by Hogarth Press, which had now become a commercial operation. In 1924 the firm and the Woolfs moved to Tavistock Square, Bloomsbury.

In her essays, 'Modern Fiction' (1919) and 'Mr Bennett and Mrs Brown' (1924) she propounded a new novelistic genre which became the literary element of Modernism and her own medium of expression. She first used the stream of consciousness technique in *Mrs Dalloway* (1925). In *To the Lighthouse* (1927), her exploration of various themes through psychological insight into the minds of her characters is at its most assured and poetic. With *The Waves* (1931), *The Years* (1937), and *Between the Acts* (1941) she took innovation and experiment even farther. Her slighter novels, *Orlando: a Biography* (1928) and *Flush: a Biography* (1933), were written in between times as a means of restoring her mental equilibrium. Shortly after finishing *Between the Acts,* originally called *Pointz Hall,* she drowned herself in the river by their country cottage, Monk's House, Sussex, fearful that her mental condition was irreversible. *A Room of One's Own* (1929) is a trenchant and witty plea for recognition of women writers. Two volumes of her enlightening literary criticism were published in her lifetime, *The Common Reader, First Series* (1925), *Second Series* (1932). See *Collected Essays,* ed. Leonard Woolf, 1966–7; *A*

*Writer's Diary,* ed. Leonard Woolf, new edn 1978; Quentin Bell, *Virginia Woolf: a Biography,* new edn 1987; Joan Bennett, *Virginia Woolf: Her Art as a Novelist,* rev. edn 1975; Hermione Lee, *The Novels of Virginia Woolf,* 1977.

**Wordsworth, William** (1770–1850), poet, was born in Cockermouth, Cumberland, second son of the business manager to the local magnate. After his mother's death in 1778 (his father died in 1783) he was sent to Hawkshead Grammar School, boarding with a family, where he indulged freely in the outdoor life and began to write poetry. In 1787 he went as a sizar to St John's College, Cambridge. His lack of enthusiasm for a career as an academic or in the Church gave him a detached attitude to his studies, and he was more interested in his walking tours in France, Switzerland, Germany, and Wales. After graduating as BA (without honours) in 1791, he spent several months absorbing the atmosphere of London before being attracted to a France which was in the throes of the Revolution. There he was converted to Republicanism and had a love affair with Annette Vallon, but had to return to London in December 1792 because his money had run out and his guardians would not advance him any more. A few days later his daughter Anne-Caroline was born in Orleans. In 1793 he published in separate volumes *An Evening Walk,* addressed to 'a Young Lady' — his sister Dorothy (1771–1855) — and *Descriptive Sketches Taken During a Tour in the Alps,* regarded by the critics as showing promise and by *Coleridge, who heard them read aloud at a literary club meeting, as the work of 'an original poetic genius'. For two years he moved uneasily about England, staying with friends, disturbed by his separation from France, by the excesses of the Revolution, and by the declaration of war between the two countries. His mental state and immediate future were saved by a legacy from a 21-year-old friend with the instructions that it should be used to further his poetic career. He and Dorothy were now offered a rent-free cottage in Racedown, Dorset; then in 1797 they rented Alfoxden House, near Stowey, to be near Coleridge, whom he had met in 1795. Free from worries, inspired by the proximity to nature, and encouraged by Coleridge, he was able both to think about poetry and to write it. In 1798 he and Coleridge published jointly, but anonymously, *Lyrical Ballads, with a Few Other Poems,* of which Wordsworth wrote in a short 'Advertisement' that 'the majority ... are to be regarded as experiments' in using conversational language in poetry — in the second, enlarged edition, published in January 1801, this had grown into a preface which sought to justify the new poetry in terms of normal literary criteria.

On their return in 1799 from a stay in Germany, the Wordsworths settled permanently in the Lake District parish of Grasmere. In 1802 they visited Annette and Anne-Caroline in Calais. Two months later Wordsworth married Mary Hutchinson, an old friend, who moved into the cottage with her new husband and sister-in-law — they had five children, of whom two died in 1812 and the poet's beloved eldest daughter, Dora, in 1847. *Poems in Two Volumes* (1807), the culmination of his poetic development and of five fruitful years of writing, included 'Ode on Intimations of Immortality', 'Resolution and Independence' (originally called 'The Leech-Gatherer'), 'Ode to Duty', 'Sonnets Dedicated to Liberty and Order', and some good poems inspired by a tour of Scotland in 1803 with Dorothy, on which they met *Scott.

In 1813 the family moved to Rydal Mount, and from then until 1842 he held the post of Distributor of Stamps for Westmorland, which involved the collection of Inland Revenue duties. He was appointed Poet Laureate in 1843. At his death, his creative and spiritual autobiography, the most sustained and original feat of poetry since *Milton's *Paradise Lost,* remained unpublished. The basis of *The Prelude,* which he wrote originally in two parts before the end of 1799, is an unfinished philosophical poem, 'The Recluse', whose central portion was published in 1814 as *The Excursion.* Between 1801 and 1805 he expanded it to 13 books, which he revised at intervals until 1839. The final version was published by his executors in 14 books, three months after his death. The title was given to it by his widow, who died in 1859 at the age of 89. Dorothy, who had lived with them throughout their marriage but whose mind had given way in 1835, survived her brother by five years. Her *Journals* are a valuable source of information about the poet's creative instincts and personality, as well as being literary records of social life, people, and places. See *Poetical Works,* ed. Thomas Hutchinson, rev. Ernest de Selincourt, new edn 1969; *The Prelude: a Parallel Text,* ed. J. C. Maxwell, 1971; Stephen Gill, *William Wordsworth: a Life,* 1989; John Purkis, *A Preface to Wordsworth,* 1986; Jonathan Wordsworth, *William Wordsworth: the Borders of Vision,* new edn 1984 (critical study).

**Wyatt,** (Sir) **Thomas** (1503–42), poet, was born at Allington Castle, Kent, son of a councillor of Henry VII, and educated at St John's College, Cambridge. He was appointed Clerk of the King's Jewels in 1529, and served Henry VIII in various capacities abroad. He was imprisoned three times: in 1534 for brawling, in 1536 on a charge of adultery with Anne Boleyn (he was knighted on his release in 1537), and in 1541 for treason, of which he was acquitted. He introduced into English from Italian, and passed on to *Surrey, the Petrarchan sonnet, which for all his irregularities of metre he often did better than his protégé (cf. 'The long love that in my thought doth harbour...' with Surrey's version, 'Love that doth reign and live within my thought...'). For all his travel abroad, his songs and lyrics are in the English tradition. His technique is best seen in 'My lute awake...', 'What rage is this...', 'Perdie, I said it not...', and 'In eternum...' and 'Blame not my lute...', in which he effectively uses a simple refrain at the end of each stanza gradually to build up to a final climax. The general tone of his verse, however, is gloomy and resentful. None of it was published in his lifetime, but a volume of translations of 'certayn psalmes chosen out of the psalter of David' was printed in 1549. Of the attributed poems in 'Tottel's Miscellany' (1557), 97 are by Wyatt, as against 40 by Surrey. See *Collected Poems*, ed. Kenneth Muir and Patricia Thomson, 1969; Patricia Thomson, *Sir Thomas Wyatt and His Background*, 1965.

**Wycherley, William** (1640–1716), dramatist and poet, was born in Clive, Shropshire, son of a country gentleman who educated him at home and when he was 15 sent him to France for five years. On his return he was briefly attached to The Queen's College, Oxford, which he left to study law in London. His poem *Hero and Leander in Burlesque* was published anonymously in 1669. The comedy *Love in a Wood, or, St James's Park* (performed in 1671, published 1672) was followed by *The Gentleman Dancing Master* (1673), *The Country Wife* (1675), and *The Plain-Dealer* (1677). His reputation and his position at Court were ruined after a disastrous marriage to the Dowager Countess of Drogheda — her will was disputed and he spent several years in prison for debt. Restored to favour if not funds, he published *Miscellany Poems* (1704), whose subsequent editions incorporated revisions made on the advice of the 16-year-old *Pope. He remarried in 1715, and died eleven days later, leaving his young widow £400 a year, which his nephew had to pay. His first three plays are in the Restoration format of rakes, fops, and amorous intrigues, though much better constructed and characterised, and more honestly vulgar than most, and with underlying hints of outrage. This satirical streak is more evident in *The Plain-Dealer,* whose hero (suitably named Manly) mistrusts mankind and is brought to his senses by a devoted female admirer. See *Plays,* ed. Peter Holland, 1981; Rose A. Zimbardo, *Wycherley's Drama: a Link in the Development of English Satire,* 1965.

**Yeats, W(illiam) B(utler)** (1865–1939), Irish poet, dramatist, and prose writer, was born in Sandymount, Dublin, eldest child of the artist John Butler Yeats (1839–1922) and brother of the artist Jack Butler Yeats (1871–1957). The family moved to London in 1867 but returned to Dublin in 1880, where he went to the High School, Harcourt Street, and then the School of Art. His first published poem appeared in the *Dublin University Review* in 1885. After the family once more settled in London, he made frequent visits to Ireland, and in 1888 edited an anthology of contemporary poetry, *Poems and Ballads of Young Ireland,* which contained four of his own poems. In 1889 he published in London *The Wanderings of Oisin and Other Poems,* whose title poem, based on elements he had found in translations of Gaelic mythology, marks the beginning of the Irish literary revival. He also met Maud Gonne (1866–1953), as beautiful as an actress as she was fervent as an Irish nationalist. He fell hopelessly in love with her and proposed unsuccessfully to her on many occasions. His first play, *The Countess Cathleen* (1892), which he composed in prose and then reworked in verse, was written for her, as was a group of poems under the heading of 'The Rose', published in *The Countess Kathleen and Various Legends and Lyrics* (1891) and subsequently in *Poems* (1895), a selection of what he wanted preserved. The rose, signifying eternal beauty, was one of the many symbols which he drew from Irish mythology and occult lore to illustrate his poetic themes. In the stories in *The Secret Rose* (1897), occultism is overlaid with Pre-Raphaelite detail, and poems reflecting his obsession with Maud occur also in *The Wind Among the Reeds* (1899), *In the Seven Woods* (1904), and *The Green Helmet and Other Poems* (1910).

In 1897 the second of his many visits to Coole Park, Co Galway, the home of Lady Gregory (1852–1932), dramatist, translator, and literary patron, led to the establishment of the Irish Literary Theatre, with *Moore, Edward Martyn (1859–1923), and Yeats as directors. It was replaced in 1902 by the Irish National Dramatic Society, with himself as President. An early production was his *Cathleen Ni Houlihan* (1902), a symbolic play about the struggle for Irish independence, in which Maud played an electrifying role. In 1905 he became a co-director with Lady Gregory and *Synge of the Abbey Theatre, where his *Deirdre,* a tragedy from the heroic sagas, was first performed in 1906. Later, he experimented with other dramatic forms: a series derived from the Japanese Noh plays was published as *Four Plays for Dancers* (1921).

In 1916 Maud's husband, whom she had shocked Yeats by marrying in 1903, was executed for his part in the Easter Rising. The next year, having been turned down yet again by Maud, and also several times by Iseult, Maud's illegitimate daughter by a Frenchman, he married Georgie Hyde Lees, whom he had known for some time and who had mediumistic powers. His wife's attempts to draw him out of his obvious unhappiness by automatic handwriting resulted, much to her surprise, in *A Vision* (1925), an exploration into the cyclical view of history and of human experience. It also revived his poetic impulse, leading to his collections *The Tower* (1928) and *The Winding Stair and Other Poems* (1933), in which a philosophical attitude to old age, wit, scorn, sensuality, and a sense of panic about the world's future predominate. Although he had often been ill, he was writing plays and fine poetry to the last. He died while wintering in the Riviera. He was interred in Roquebrune and re-buried in Sligo in 1948. Besides being an experimental dramatist in a variety of forms, he was a poet of many moods and skills whose work has had a dominant effect on much modern poetry. He was instrumental in founding an Irish national literary and, perhaps even more significantly, dramatic movement. His *Essays 1931–1936* was published in 1937, and he was editor of *The Oxford Book of Modern Verse 1892–1935* (1936). From 1922 to 1928 he was an active senator of the Irish Free State. He had refused a knighthood in 1915. He was awarded the Nobel Prize for Literature in 1923. See *Yeats's Poems,* ed. A. Norman Jeffares, 1989; *Collected Plays of W. B. Yeats,* 1952; *Autobiographies,* 2nd edn 1965; A. Norman Jeffares, *W. B. Yeats: a New Biography,* 1988; A. Norman Jeffares, *A New Commentary on the Poems of W. B. Yeats,* 1984; A. S. Knowland and A. Norman Jeffares, *A Commentary on the Collected Plays of W. B. Yeats,* 1975.

**Young, Andrew** (1885–1971), Scottish poet and naturalist, was born in Elgin and educated at the Royal High School of Edinburgh and Edinburgh University, being ordained in the United Free Church in 1912. In 1918 he became minister of the English Presbyterian Church in Hove, Sussex. During the 1930s he was converted to the Church of England, and was vicar of Stonegate in Sussex from 1941 until his retirement in 1959. He was made a canon of Chichester Cathedral in 1948. His first book of verse, *Songs of Night* (1910), was published privately, and it was only after the appearance of seven volumes in all that he reached a significant audience with a selection, *Winter Harvest* (1933). His themes were inspired by a minute observation and knowledge of nature and the landscape (as in 'The White Blackbird', 'Ploughing in Mist', 'Mountain View', 'The Snowdrop', 'Daisies', and the curious 'Hibernating Snails'), and profound religious meditation, and his poetry is notable for the precision with which it is crafted. His most sustained poem is *Out of the World and Back* (1958), the journey of a soul — the first part was published as *Into Hades* (1952). He also wrote a Mystery play in verse, *Nicodemus* (1937), and several botanical and topographical prose works, including *A Prospect of Flowers* (1945) and *The Poet and the Landscape* (1960). He was awarded the Queen's Gold Medal for Poetry in 1952. See *Poetical Works,* ed. Edward Lowbury and Alison Young, 1985; Leonard Clark (ed.), *Andrew Young: Prospect of a Poet,* 1957 (critical essays).

# The author of this Handbook

ANTONY KAMM was born in London and educated at Charterhouse and Worcester College, Oxford, where he read Classics and then English Language and Literature, and was President of the Oxford University English Club. He has held senior editorial positions with several leading publishers, most recently Oxford University Press. He was a Senior Education Officer, Commonwealth Secretariat, from 1972 to 1974, and he has on several occasions been a consultant to Unesco and other international organisations on the provision and production of books. He is now a freelance editor and writer, and part-time Lecturer in Publishing Studies at the University of Stirling. His publications include *The Story of Islam, Scotland,* and the York Notes on *The Long and the Short and the Tall* and *Journey's End.* He has compiled *The Scottish Collection of Verse to 1800* (with Eileen Dunlop), and *An Irish Childhood* and *A Jewish Childhood* (with A. Norman Jeffares).